The Best of *Inquiring Mind*

THE BEST OF
Inquiring Mind

TWENTY-FIVE YEARS OF DHARMA, DRAMA, & UNCOMMON INSIGHT

WISDOM PUBLICATIONS · BOSTON

Wisdom Publications
199 Elm Street
Somerville MA 02144 USA
www.wisdompubs.org

Library of Congress Cataloging-in-Publication Data
The best of Inquiring mind : twenty-five years of dharma, drama, & uncommon insight.
    p. cm.
A selection of articles from the journal Inquiring mind.
Includes bibliographical references.
ISBN 0-86171-551-9 (pbk. : alk. paper)
1. Religious life—Buddhism. 2. Buddhism—Doctrines. I. Inquring mind.
BQ4302.B47 2008
294.3—dc22

                      2008031761

12 11 10 09 08
5 4 3 2 1

Cover design by Pema Studios. Interior design by Margery Cantor. Layout by Jason Miranda. Set in Arno Pro 11/13.5.

Wisdom Publications' books are printed on acid-free paper and meet the guidelines for permanence and durability of the Production Guidelines for Book Longevity of the Council on Library Resources.

Printed in the United States of America.

♻ This book was produced with environmental mindfulness. We have elected to print this title on 30% PCW recycled paper. As a result, we have saved the following resources: 23 trees, 16 million BTUs of energy, 2,019 lbs. of greenhouse gases, 8,379 gallons of water, and 1,076 lbs. of solid waste. For more information, please visit our website, www.wisdompubs.org. This paper is also FSC certified. For more information, please visit www.fscus.org.

Contents

Preface

Twice a year for the last twenty-five years, the staff of *Inquiring Mind* has tried to create a beautiful, honest, provocative, and simply presented journal. From our very beginning as a twelve-page experiment in the fall of 1984, we have offered the *Mind* freely to our readers with no subscription fee. We have remained committed to keeping our means consistent with our message. We have no *Inquiring Mind* office or phone number, only a post office box, a locker to store back issues, and the desks, living rooms, and kitchen tables of our core staff, which now numbers six—all part time. We've depended on the generosity of our writers and artists in offering us their work without recompense. We've relied heavily on the work of volunteers for editorial assistance. We've resisted the temptation to go "glossy," continuing instead to choose recycled newsprint for our presentation. And most importantly, in what is certainly a rarity in the world of publishing, *Inquiring Mind* has managed to survive for a quarter century on the generosity of our community of readers.

Inspired by the Buddhist teachings on *dana* (in our case, the individual financial contributions of those who choose to donate), *Inquiring Mind* is mailed to anyone who sends us an address and is distributed freely at retreat centers around the world. Although many of our readers learn about the journal through vipassana centers in the U.S., such as the Insight Meditation Society or Spirit Rock Meditation Center, we are not officially affiliated with or subsidized by these or any other meditation centers or organizations.

We love publishing *Inquiring Mind* and feel a great deal of gratitude to those who have made our work possible, collaborating with us through contributions of articles and interviews, artwork, editorial skills, money, and enthusiastic responses to what we offer. This book is a testament to all of that energy—and to the teachings of the Dharma from which the journal has arisen.

To learn more about *Inquiring Mind*, visit www.inquiringmind.com, or write to us at P.O. Box 9999, Berkeley, CA, 94709.

—ALAN NOVIDOR,
PUBLISHER,
Inquiring Mind

Introduction

In the 2,500-year-old history of the teachings of the Buddha, the past several decades have been fertile as this ancient tradition has found a new home in the West. In just the past quarter century we have watched Buddhism take root in our soil, and in our minds and hearts, causing both a new flowering of the Buddha's teachings and, in turn, the addition of a new culture's wisdom and personality to the ongoing bloom of Dharma. As editors of *Inquiring Mind* we feel privileged to have participated in and chronicled the transmission.

Our journal serves what is commonly called the vipassana, or insight meditation, community, but the more accurate name for our root tradition is Theravada, which translates as the "path of the elders." The *Theravada* is a school of Buddhism that has flourished over the centuries in south Asia, primarily Burma, Thailand, India, Sri Lanka, Laos, and Cambodia. It encompasses hundreds of different meditation practices and rituals, as well as a way of life. In *Inquiring Mind*, we have primarily focused on the arrival of that tradition in the West through those trained in the teaching styles of Mahasi Sayadaw from Burma and the forest tradition of Thailand.

We have also welcomed voices from other streams of the Dharma flowing through our lives. In particular, we have followed various trends that have arisen in our own Buddhist spiritual circles over the years: the exploration of dzogchen with Tsoknyi Rinpoche and other Tibetan masters; the visits of Western Theravada teachers and students to the Hindu Advaita teacher Hari Lal Poonja; the appreciation of poetry, art, and teachings from the Zen communities of Suzuki Roshi, Thich Nhat Hanh, and Robet Aitken; the "engaged Buddhist" activities of groups such as the Buddhist Peace Fellowship and the Zen Hospice program; and the new-paradigm thinking of eco-Buddhist philosophers and activists. *Inquiring Mind* has tracked all these turnings of the Dharma wheel as it has rolled through.

We have been the fortunate contemporaries to extraordinary teachers of Dharma and honored to have conversed with them about our common human dilemmas. Among those who have been featured in *Inquiring Mind* are Asian masters with thousands of students worldwide as well as prominent Western teachers who are just now skillfully molding the Dharma into its new body here in the West. We have also called on the wisdom and creativity of Dharma-inspired artists and philosophers—Gary Snyder, Joanna Macy, Allen Ginsberg, Mayumi Oda, John Cage, and many others.

Twice a year we present a journal organized around one (or occasionally two) themes, sometimes to discuss the issues and personalities currently making "news" in our Buddhist world but more often to raise subjects that more generally delight, inspire, or challenge us in our practice and in our lives. We have included symposia on such topics as psychology and Buddhism, the meaning of *mindfulness*, and the Dharma and the environment. We've delved into tough issues such as our society's culture of "speed and greed" or our struggles over "money, power, and sex."

In this book you'll find a collection of some of the "best" of what we've published over the past twenty-five years. (Of course, we had to leave out many engaging pieces.) We open each of the eight sections of the book with art from one of the many artists whose drawings, paintings, sculptures, or photographs have been featured in the journal, not simply as illustrations but as independent pieces juxtaposed with the written work. In making our selections of articles, we have included a mix of genres—interviews, personal stories, philosophical essays, and poetry—and a mix of voices—women and men from various schools of Buddhism and from diverse racial backgrounds. Achieving this mix has been an ongoing challenge throughout the history of the journal. While diversity in gender and race has slowly continued to increase among Western Buddhists, there are still many more male than female meditation teachers and, with the exception of those in the Asian immigrant communities, there are few non-white Western Buddhist teachers and students. To some degree, this anthology reflects these imbalances.

We had a lot of fun rereading all our back issues, selecting favorite pieces, and playing with the conceptual framework for this book. We begin with a section called "Path of the Elders," featuring teachers who have played a key role in bringing the teachings of the East (primarily those of the Theravada) to the West. "Living and Dying in a Body" follows the cycle of the body through its vitality, aging, sickness, and death, and "Science of Mind" explores the interface of the sciences of the East and West as they come together to heal and develop the mind. "The Dharma and the Drama" presents personal stories, poignant and/or funny, about people grappling with the difficult predicament commonly known as life. "Complementary Paths" offers conversations contrasting different schools of Dharma and exploring how they can complement each other, while "Practices" offers a range of skillful means, from jhana to tantra. We end with "Artists and Jesters of the Dharma" expressing the Dharma in fiction, poetry, and humor, and "Tending to the World," discussions of compassionate action—from the endangered forests to the prison yard.

We hope you'll find *The Best of Inquiring Mind* to be rich in wisdom as well as a fascinating historical record of a new tradition of Buddhism, just now learning how to walk and talk in the West.

—BARBARA GATES *&* WES NISKER,
COEDITORS *&* COFOUNDERS,
Inquiring Mind

I

PATH OF THE ELDERS:
EAST MOVING WEST

Several streams of Theravada Buddhism arrived in the West in the 1960s and 70s, the main ones flowing from the monasteries and teaching schools of Burma, Thailand, and Sri Lanka. (Although Buddhism came westward earlier with Asian immigrant communities, it wasn't until the mid-twentieth century that it began to attract Western adherents in any significant numbers.) The Asian sources of the Theravada offered different flavors of Dharma, various styles and methods of exploration and realization. The lineages that had most impact in the West were those of Mahasi Sayadaw and Sayagyi U Ba Khin from Burma and the forest traditions of Ajahn Chah and Buddhadasa from Thailand. The journey begins here.

In the winter of 1970–71 in Bodhgaya, India, about forty people gathered for one of the first meditation retreats conducted by Satya Narayan Goenka, a student of U Ba Khin. In attendance were Joseph Goldstein, Sharon Salzberg, Daniel Goleman, and Ram Dass and his entourage, including Krishna Das, John Travis, and Wes Nisker, all of whom would eventually return to the West and bring the Dharma with them, becoming prominent meditation teachers and authors. Around the same time as the Goenka retreat, Jack Kornfield and the American monk Ajahn Sumedho (to be followed by many others, including the British monk Ajahn Amaro) were practicing Dharma in the monasteries of the Thai forest master Ajahn Chah. The westward movement of the "path of the elders" had begun in earnest.

In this section we chart this transmission by featuring interviews with seminal figures Joseph Goldstein and Sharon Salzberg (both of whom also studied with Anagarika Munindra and U Pandita of the Mahasi lineage), and an interview with S.N. Goenka, as well as remembrances of the beloved Indian teacher Dipa Ma. From the Thai Forest tradition we include an interview with

Ajahn Amaro. Addressing the increasingly broad and diverse dissemination of Dharma in the West, Jon Kabat-Zinn discusses secular adaptations of mindfulness practices, and "Dharma punk" Noah Levine describes taking the teachings to his own newer generation of Western seekers. Jack Kornfield concludes with his reflections on a meeting between Western Dharma teachers and His Holiness the Dalai Lama, which reveals how the traditions of Asia are being challenged and adapted by this new breed of Buddhists.

1 Conversation with a Spiritual Friend
An Interview with Joseph Goldstein

Joseph Goldstein has been teaching the Dharma and vipassana meditation for almost thirty-five years. He is the cofounder of the Insight Meditation Society and the Forest Refuge in Barre, Massachusetts, and he is the author of a number of books on Buddhism, including the classic The Experience of Insight *and most recently* A Heart Full of Peace. *The fact that many Western teachers of Theravadan Dharma consider themselves to be his students is evidence of the esteem in which he is held. Joseph Goldstein has been featured in many issues of* Inquiring Mind, *but we felt that our first interview with him, conducted in December of 1983, best captures both his wisdom and personality. Since this interview was the front-page article in the premier issue of our journal, it has sentimental value for us as well.*

INQUIRING MIND: Please describe how you see your role as a teacher.

JOSEPH GOLDSTEIN: In the Theravada tradition, teachers are known as "spiritual friends," which is quite different from the concept of *guru* either in the Hindu tradition or in some of the Mahayana schools of Buddhism. Within the Theravada tradition even the Buddha is spoken of as a spiritual friend in the sense that he only points out the way and that everybody has to do the work of purification themselves. I think that what happens between teacher and student is very complicated, and I don't yet have a full understanding of the relationship. Somebody recently said that what he got from me most as a teacher, aside from meditation instructions, was a quality of faith. I wouldn't conceptualize my function as being someone who inspires faith, but when he said that, it resonated. I do have unshakable faith in the

Dharma and that must be a source of strength when people are struggling in their own practice.

IM: You also have a very natural, unassuming way in which you present the practice. In spite of your height, you don't seem to place yourself in any way above the Sangha.

JG: I think part of that has to do with the feeling of still being very much on the path, without any illusions at all of having come to a place of completion. Every time I watch my mind, as with most people who watch their minds, I am reminded of the saying that self-knowledge is usually bad news. When one is sitting, in addition to the incredible purity of the Dharma field in which it's happening, what one sees so clearly and so explicitly and without compromise is the junk of the mind, all the defilements that are still there.

IM: When you are teaching, what questions do you get asked the most?

JG: Well, the preface to the question that's asked most is, "If there is no self, then…?" Fill in the blank. The idea of selflessness seems to be the hardest concept for people to understand.

IM: Do you think that difficulty is more characteristic of Westerners?

JG: It seems to be. In Buddhist cultures, the concept of selflessness is part of the cultural conditioning, whereas in the West it's almost the opposite— the classic example being Descartes' "I think, therefore I am," which revolves around positing a sense of self and then trying to figure out what it is. One of the most wonderful things in teaching retreats is to see people begin to open to that understanding of selflessness. It's tremendously liberating to begin to see that there's nothing to protect and nothing to solve and that rather than necessarily working out our problems, we can stop identifying with them.

IM: What about the problem of immediate survival? It seems that a lot of Sangha members are becoming involved in social action, especially around the issue of nuclear war. Do you have any thoughts about people putting their energy into saving the planet from destruction?

JG: There are a few considerations that come to my mind. One has to do with the context of our activity in the world. From the Buddhist perspective we see a much bigger picture than this planet Earth. If saving the planet is seen as being the end of one's endeavor, it seems very limiting to me. I think that if that activity were done within the framework of a larger context, for instance, the goal of alleviating suffering, then the cure would be deeper and the energy with which it was done would have a greater level of purity. Look at Gandhi. I think that a lot of his power came because he put the struggle in a much larger context. He wasn't simply a politician trying to liberate India. There was always a dedication to something much higher, a commitment to what was true, and he was always checking everything against that truth. So his politics were really an expression of a very high Dharma.

IM: If compassion is the motivation, then perhaps the actions are also purified or have a deeper meaning.

JG: I would agree, but I don't think there are any limitations to the manifestation of compassionate action. People often get stuck evaluating different kinds of action as being more or less compassionate. For example, going out and protesting against social injustice is often seen as being a more compassionate act than meditating in a cave in the Himalayas. From my perspective there isn't one form that is better than another. It depends totally on the level of compassion in the mind. It doesn't matter whether people sit in a cave or write poetry; they can be selling insurance, they can be protesting or doing anything. The state of mind and qualities of the heart are what truly count.

IM: Do you feel there is one type of economic or political system that is more compatible with the Dharma? Wouldn't a compassionate society manifest as some variation of socialism or communalism?

JG: If the people in the society are compassionate, I don't think the form would matter at all.

IM: But look at the current stage of corporate capitalism. Don't you think that it fosters greed and competition?

JG: I see it the other way around, that greed fosters the system. Social organization arises out of levels of consciousness, and there's no system that is going to work as long as there is greed and hatred in people's minds. So that seems to me the place to do the work.

IM: So it's about the "United States of Consciousness." Perhaps all of society could be taught metta (lovingkindness) meditation.

JG: Good idea. However metta meditation by itself will not lead to liberation because it's working on the level of relative truth in the sense of wishing all beings to be happy and free of suffering. The very concept of *beings* is a relative concept, so that's the level which that particular meditation plugs into, and it's wonderful because we live in that relative plane a lot. Lovingkindness meditation can make the mind very spacious and accepting and loving, but there's another kind of love that's a product of deep insight, and that is the kind of love you might feel for your hand. It's not articulated; you don't go around saying, "I love you, hand." It's simply a part of you, and so you relate to it in a very loving way.

IM: It's the Gaia hypothesis, the oneness of the new physics, the Hindu saying "Thou art That."

JG: Right. When we identify with being a small part of the whole, we create this very limited sense of self and imprison ourselves in that identification. When we let go of that identification, we become nothing—and being nothing, we become everything.

IM: And thereafter we love everything as ourselves. It sounds ecstatic.

JG: I have a sense that it's very ordinary in the same way we relate to our hand is ordinary; it's not ecstatic. Even appreciation of something is already an articulation. This state I'm talking about is a way of being that doesn't need any particular articulation.

IM: Are there any unique historical or cultural conditions that lead to Dharma practice or the spread of Buddhism? Why do you think it has taken hold in the West at this time?

JG: My sense is that a powerful source for Dharma practice is some level of discomfort in society, but it's not necessarily any particular kind of discomfort or suffering. For example, Soen Sa Nim, the Korean Zen master, has been going to Poland for the last few years, and he says that when he gives a talk thousands of people come. There's some kind of suffering there creating intense interest in the Dharma. Meanwhile, our American culture, so open to new ideas, has created a tremendously fertile ground for Dharma. But in America, we're experiencing another kind of suffering. I think one of the reasons that the Dharma is flourishing here is because we've experienced so much, and we have so much, yet we are still dissatisfied, still suffering. And that's what the Buddha taught—suffering and the end of suffering.

From Volume 1, Number 1 (Spring 1984).

2 **Master of the Dhamma**
An Interview with S.N. Goenka

During the third century B.C.E., *the teachings of the Buddha spread across the Indian subcontinent and into Southeast Asia under the auspices of the great Indian emperor Ashoka, also known as Dhammaraja, the King of Dhamma. According to legend, Ashoka's chief Dhamma teacher sent two monks to Burma to offer the triple gem to the people there, and as he sent them off he made this prediction: the Dhamma would one day disappear from India and the rest of the world but would be preserved in its pure form in Burma, the Golden Land. The teacher also predicted that 2,500 years after the Buddha, the Dhamma would be transported from Burma back to India and from there it would spread throughout the world.*

This prophecy is now being fulfilled to some degree through the work of S.N. Goenka, or Goenkaji, as he is affectionately known, one of the most influential Dhamma teachers in the world today. Goenka was born in 1923 into a wealthy Indian family living in Rangoon, Burma. As a young man he became very successful in business and at the same time began developing severe migraine headaches. Goenka traveled around the world searching in vain for treatments and cures until finally, back home in Rangoon, he began studying vipassana meditation with Saiyagi U Ba Khin. Eventually his headaches went away, but more than that, his life was transformed. Goenka became a devoted follower of the Buddha's path.

In 1969, Goenka moved to India, where he began teaching vipassana, helping to bring this age-old meditation practice back to the land of its origin. Since then he has taught thousands of people and has established meditation centers in India, America, Europe, and Australia.

A three-hour train ride from the urban chaos of Bombay on a hill overlooking the rural Indian town of Igatpuri, Goenka built Dhammagiri, which serves as his main meditation center. Established in 1976, Dhammagiri features a large Burmese-style pagoda, a spacious meditation hall, and over 300 individual meditation cells where students can practice in isolation. The grounds are planted with flowers and fruit trees, the living quarters are comfortable, and the food is clean and nourishing. Inside Dhammagiri the purity is tangible.

This interview grew out of several conversations with Wes Nisker in December 1986.

S.N. GOENKA: Purity is very important because what is going on at meditation retreats is nothing less than surgery on the mind. When you have surgery on your body, you go to the surgery theater, which is kept very pure. No contamination is allowed because a wound is being opened, and if some outside dirt gets in, it will cause infection. It is the same in this surgery of the mind.

INQUIRING MIND: The meditation retreats at Dhammagiri include people from many nations and from a variety of religious and economic backgrounds. You tell them that you are not teaching Buddhism but simply the laws of nature.

SNG: Buddha's pure teaching is nothing but the law of nature. The Buddha himself said that whether there is a Buddha in the world or no Buddha in the world, the law of nature remains. If you generate craving and aversion in the mind, you are bound to become miserable. If you want to come out of your misery, then get rid of craving and aversion. This is just the law of nature, and this law is applicable in every culture.

Even people who belong to sects that are totally opposed to Buddhism are now coming to take these vipassana meditation courses. For example, for twenty-five centuries in India the Jain community has been teaching that the Buddha's path is wrong. The same with the Hindu community. I was born in a conservative Hindu family, and from childhood we were taught that even if you are going down a very narrow lane and a wild elephant is coming at you about to crush you, and you see an open door of a Buddhist temple on your right and an open door of a Jain temple on your left, it is better to get crushed by the elephant than to escape through those doors. But now there are a great many of these Hindus and Jains coming to the meditation courses. Once the practice is established, it is all just the law of nature. The law of nature does not give preference to a Christian or to a Hindu. If you place your hand on the fire, your hand will burn. It is so simple. This is the Dhamma. I have no belief in Buddhism. I believe only in Dhamma. For me Hinduism and Buddhism are both madness.

IM: When you are teaching the Dhamma, do you find that the Indian students are different from Westerners? And do you ever alter your teaching to accommodate people of different cultures?

SNG: The basic teaching remains the same and the meditation technique remains the same. But there are some differences. The Indians have more trouble with their philosophical beliefs, especially concerning the "soul." One community believes that the soul is the size of the thumb. Another believes that it is the size of a persimmon seed. And there are so many different gods here in India, gods with two hands or four hands, gods of this shape or that color. So I tell the Indians that it is all right to believe in this kind of soul or that kind of soul, or this god or that god, but you still have to purify your mind. Otherwise you will remain miserable.

On the other hand, when I am teaching Indians, I don't need to place so much emphasis on sila (morality). It is not that the people in India are full of sila, but at least they understand sila and it is very important to them. So I don't need to talk too much against free sex or drugs. But in the West, I have to give more emphasis to those issues.

IM: Many spiritual teachers who have come to the West in the past few decades have been discredited or somehow mixed up in scandal involving sex, drugs, and money. Why do you think this is occurring so frequently?

SNG: Well, if some teacher goes to the West with the ambition to acquire material wealth, then this person has nothing to do with Dhamma. The meditation techniques can be kept pure, the Dhamma can be kept pure only if the teacher expects nothing in return, not even any fame or status. If there is any such craving in the mind of a teacher, then this person is not worthy of becoming a teacher. If a teacher is a monk, then he must beg for his food, and if the teacher is a householder, then he or she must have another means of livelihood. The teaching of Dhamma cannot be a means of livelihood.

Another problem for many teachers in the West is the great freedom of sex that exists there. But how can any vipassana teacher even think of passion toward his own students of the opposite sex? For vipassana teachers all female students are their daughters and all male students are their sons.

Everyone who received the Dhamma from the Buddha was his child. If you are teaching Dhamma, that means you are giving people a new life, a new birth, and those people then become your children. If a teacher has sexual relations with a student, you will not have pure Dhamma.

IM: Do you feel that Westerners are more attached to the concept of *self* than the Indians?

SNG: If by *self* you mean a soul, then the Indians have a harder time with it. But when you talk of *self* as *ego*, then it is the same everywhere. In Burma, India, or America, people are mad with their ego. That is why the meditation technique is most important. The technique is to dissolve the ego.

IM: However it is undoubtedly more difficult for Westerners to accept some of the traditional Buddhist beliefs, such as the idea of rebirth. How does this affect their meditation practice?

SNG: A belief in rebirth is not important, but as you develop in vipassana, it will become clear to you by your own understanding. Anyway, to me this present life is much more important than a future life. Why worry about a future life? If you do something to better your present life, then your future life will automatically become better. But if you are doing something for a future life and it doesn't help you in your present life, then to me it is useless.

IM: You teach a meditation practice that involves moving the mind through the body and focusing on physical sensations. This technique has become widely known as the "body scan," and sometimes is called "sweeping." What is the origin of this technique?

SNG: Buddha is the origin! (Laughs) Nobody else can be the origin. In the *Satipatthana Sutta* there are the words, "*Sabbakaya-patisamvedi assasissamiti sikkhati...passasissamiti sikkhati.*" (Feeling the whole body I shall breathe in... feeling the whole body I shall breathe out.) One should learn how to feel the entire body in one breath, breathing in and breathing out. Perhaps I am responsible for calling it "sweeping," but this is the Buddha's teaching.

The whole technique of the Buddha is to move you from the gross level of reality to the subtle. The apparent truths are always gross and solidified, full of illusions and delusions. The purpose of vipassana meditation is to penetrate the gross and go to the ultimate truth. The ultimate truth of mind and body is nothing but vibration, and that is what you are observing when you practice this technique.

IM: In this meditation practice, you do not give much emphasis to *cittanupassana* (observation of mind) or *dhammanupassana* (observation of mental contents). Is there a reason for this?

SNG: Observing thoughts is never taught by the Buddha. In the *Satipatthana Sutta* in the section on *cittanupassana*, the Buddha says, "Here a *bhikkhu* understands properly mind with craving as mind with craving." Craving for what is not important. If you observe the thought, then you start rolling in its contents. So instead you simply observe that craving has started in the mind, and at the same time you feel the arising and passing away of sensations in the body. If you are equanimous with the sensations, then you are also equanimous with the craving, and in this way, layer after layer of that particular sankhara (reaction) in your mind will be erased automatically.

IM: It sounds like you are dealing here with a very deep, subconscious level of the mind.

SNG: Yes, and that is why this technique was developed by the Buddha. First he had tried eight jhanas (levels of absorption), which had purified his mind, but not to the depth. Deep inside there was what the Buddha called "sleeping impurities," meaning that the roots of the impurities were still there. He realized that these could be taken out only through the practice of vipassana, through awareness of sensations.

Buddha understood that the unconscious mind is constantly in contact with the body sensations. So if we are going to purify the unconscious mind, we have to work with these sensations. If you forget the sensations of the body, then you are dealing only with the surface of the mind. The surface of your mind will become purified and you will benefit from that also, but those complexities lying deep below, the deep conditioning of the past, will remain unchanged.

IM: So you are training the mind not to react in a habitual way to any sensations that may arise.

SNG: Yes, exactly. Whatever external event happens will generate sensations in the body, and you will have trained your mind to be equanimous with those sensations. So you are at the roots. If the roots are healthy, then the tree will automatically be healthy. You need not worry. This is how it works.

⋮ From Volume 4, Number 1 (Summer 1987).

3 Stories of Dipa Ma

Someone once asked Dipa Ma, "What is it like in your mind?" She closed her eyes for a moment and answered, "In my mind there are three things: concentration, lovingkindness, and peace." "That's all?" "Yes," she answered, "that's all."

Dipa Ma Barua (1911–89) grew up the oldest daughter in a Buddhist family in Bangladesh. She was married at age twelve to her husband, age twenty-five, arranged marriage being the norm. It wasn't until she was thirty-two that she gave birth to her first child, a daughter who died three months later. When she was thirty-six, she gave birth to her daughter Dipa, who survived. At thirty-seven, she was giving birth to a son, but he also died. Soon thereafter, her husband, who had been quite healthy, died without warning. The grief over so much loss was overwhelming, and Dipa Ma became sick and bedridden for a long time. A doctor finally told her that she had to get her mind together or she too would probably die. Because she still had her daughter, Dipa, to care for, Dipa Ma realized that she had to do something. Finally she decided to go to a monastery in northern Burma to practice vipassana meditation.

The first day of her practice, while doing walking meditation, she suddenly realized she couldn't walk. She noticed painful sensations and that her leg was heavy. When she looked down, she saw a dog with its teeth sunk deep in her leg. She had been so concentrated that she hadn't been aware of the pain. Dipa Ma went very deep, very quickly. When she learned meditation from Mahasi Sayadaw at Mahasi's monastery in Rangoon, within one week she experienced some of the deepest stages of insight and awakening within the vipassana practice.

Dipa Ma later trained in concentration practice with Munindra-ji. She had extraordinary concentration and developed many psychic powers. She said she was able to go back in time to listen to the Buddha's sermons. When asked how she could accomplish such a thing, she smiled and said, "I went back mind-moment by mind-moment, but you don't have to do that!"

The Mahasi monastery asked Dipa Ma to stay and teach at the center. However, Dipa Ma wanted Dipa to remain in contact with her Bengali roots, so the two moved to Calcutta, where they lived for twenty-eight years. Dipa Ma taught retreats around India and came to teach in America in 1980 and 1984. Mostly people came to see her in her tiny room in Calcutta. There they received tea, food, teachings, and wonderful blessings.

—MICHELE MCDONALD

We would walk to Dipa-Ma's apartment through the streets of Calcutta—which were a mass of people, buses, taxis, rickshaws, bicycles, ox carts, and small herds of goats, cows, and dogs—through an intensity of noise and dust and smells, down a narrow alley and up flights of darkened stairs to a couple of small and very special rooms. These rooms were special because of Dipa Ma's amazing presence, because of the stillness she created in the midst of one of the noisiest, most crowded cities in the world.

Often, just watching Dipa Ma do the ordinary things of her life was the greatest teaching. One particularly vivid image is of her in the meditation hall at IMS in Barre, Massachusetts, bowing to the Buddha. It was the first time I really understood the meaning of a bow: respect, devotion, love, and deep, deep selflessness. It was the Dhamma bowing to the Dhamma.

Dipa Ma could also be a demanding teacher, pushing us past self-imposed limits. Just a few months before she died, we were with her in Bodh Gaya, and she suggested I sit for two days—not a two-day retreat, but a two-day nonstop sitting. At first I laughed; it seemed like such an impossibility. She simply said, "Don't be lazy." She was a very little lady with a heart and mind of great power.

—JOSEPH GOLDSTEIN

When I first met Dipa Ma, I went to her little apartment in Calcutta. It was awkward because I had been a monk for a while, and I was used to bowing to all these teachers sitting up there in front with the big Buddhas. You would put a little incense in front and get down on the floor. I started to bow to Dipa Ma, but she picked me up off the floor and gave me this great big bear hug. She wasn't a monk; she was a householder. None of this bowing stuff. "I'm not this big teacher that we have to make a big deal about."

I remember going to see her once after I had been studying and training in India. I had been through a lot of difficulty in my life at that time. I forget what the difficulty was, but it was something like money or women or ego—an identity crisis. I went to Calcutta to pay my respects to Dipa Ma on my way back to teach the next three-month retreat in Barre, Massachusetts. She and I spent some time talking, and when I was about to leave, she gave me her usual big bear hug and then she said a blessing.

To receive her blessing, you got down on your knees; that would put you on the level of her hands. She would gently stroke your head and your whole body, blow on you, and say Buddhist prayers at the same time. This was a very long blessing. It was probably five minutes, but it seemed like it was forever. At first it felt nice, and then, as she kept doing it, if felt better and better. Gradually, I started to smile. By the time she was done, I was grinning nonstop; everything was lit up and open. She said, "Go and teach a good retreat for all of those people. Go with my blessings." It was like a grandmother sending you off: "May you be blessed."

I left her place to go to Dum Dum Airport. It was summer, and let me tell you, there is heavy traffic in Calcutta in the summer. It took about two hours in a taxi with the driver leaning on the horn the whole way and dodging between rickshaws, with traffic jams, fumes, pollution, and incredible heat, humidity, and poverty. Finally I arrived at the airport, got through Indian customs, which was another hour of standing in line, people stamping your things and grilling you. Then I got on the airplane, took the flight from Calcutta to Bangkok, and again stood on long lines and went through customs. I got in a taxi, drove an hour and a half through Bangkok traffic to my hotel. I did not stop grinning the entire way—in the taxis, sitting on the plane, standing in lines, going through customs, and through all the traffic jams. I just kept smiling; it wouldn't wear off. "May you be blessed."

—JACK KORNFIELD

I last saw Dipa Ma in Bodh Gaya in February 1989. I was in poor health at the time. At one point she called me to her to give advice and a blessing. I cherish the memory because so many seemingly contradictory aspects of her nature shone forth. The clear and uncompromising teacher told me to make my peace with my death and the limitations of disease, and then ignore them and get on with my life. The metta-filled, gentle, and compassionate grandmother spent many minutes blessing me through touch, voice, blowing on me; I felt her love radiate through me. Then the strong and practical woman of the world advised me to do exercises. To demonstrate, she leapt up and went through several vigorous exercises, including jogging in place. She quite tired herself out and sat down puffing. This from a woman with a heart condition, who looked to be only four feet tall!

—CAROL WILSON

I did almost all of my research on meditation in Dipa Ma's room in Calcutta. We'd spend the day interviewing or testing, usually one person per day. Afterward, her small room would begin to slowly fill up with people who would wander in to see her, usually students of hers, other middle-aged and older women like herself for the most part. She said she had quite a few men students as well, and that they would have been good subjects too, but that they were usually working during the day, and so I was seeing mostly the women. I had a feeling, though, that most of her students were women, and that they had a special bond with her as a wife and mother like themselves, and a woman who commanded respect in a society that was even more male dominated than ours.

One day, it happened, I was not interviewing or testing. Munindra-ji was visiting Calcutta, and she had invited him over to meet with some of her students. I picked him up at the Mahabodhi Temple and brought him over to Ma's. When we arrived, she knelt down and *pranam-ed* him, kissing his feet as she usually did. She always venerated him as her teacher, even though I think they both knew and accepted the fact that she had attained more deeply. He had taught her all the jhanas and psychic powers at an earlier stage of her training, over which she had attained an unusual degree of mastery.

We were all sitting on the floor of Ma's room. It was very crowded. And very hot. Munindra-ji was sitting on a chair in the corner talking to Ma's students about Dharma and about their practice. Munindra-ji and I were the only men in the room. While Munindra-ji talked, Ma, who hadn't been well, was sitting on her wooden bed, leaning back against the wall with her eyes closed. It looked like she had dozed off. The conversation was about rebirth. Somehow it got on to the rebirths of the Buddha. Obviously not thinking much about it since it was part of the tradition, Munindra happened to mention that only men could take birth as Buddhas. Suddenly, Ma bolted upright, eyes wide open, and said in a tone of spontaneous and utter conviction, "I can do anything a man can do!" Everyone's reaction was immediate. We all laughed—Munindraji included—I think because we all knew it was absolutely true.

—JACK ENGLER

From Volume 6, Number 2 (Spring 1990).

4 The Happy Monk
An Interview with Ajahn Amaro

After spending time with the Western monk Ajahn Amaro, one is left with the unique feeling of having been in the presence of a truly happy man, and one whose happiness is born of wisdom. He has spent his entire adult life in the monastery. He was ordained in Thailand in 1979 by the late Ajahn Chah and then lived for many years at Amaravati Monastery in England. He is now abbot of Abhayagiri Monastery in California and one of a definite minority of Western Dharma teachers-gone-East to remain in robes.

The following interview was conducted by Wes Nisker and Terry Vandiver in March 1995 in Sonoma County, California.

INQUIRING MIND: How would you assess the study of Buddhadharma and the practice of meditation now being taught in the West?

AJAHN AMARO: In the West people tend to separate their meditation practice from their lives. Ajahn Chah emphasized that "if you have time to breathe, you have time to meditate." You breathe when you walk. You breathe when you stand. You breathe when you lie down.

I think part of the problem in the West is the emphasis on retreats. If you do a lot of intensive retreats, you will develop strong concentration. Many of the people I meet in America have been doing retreats for fifteen to twenty years or so, and they are really quite accomplished concentrators. But I'm afraid they have not found much freedom.

Notice how the word *sitting* has become synonymous with meditation or with practicing Dharma. *Sitting* is the operative word, meaning "I am here on my cushion, my eyes are closed, the world has dissolved into emptiness." We have learned how to concentrate our minds and then to push out our worldly irritations and responsibilities. We create this great space inside and become very good at getting rid of thoughts and feelings. Meditation can thus become rather like being in a shooting gallery with the little ducks. You can become a great marksman or markswoman, shooting down the thought ducks and the feeling ducks.

IM: Is this emphasis on intensive meditation retreats unique to the West? Or is it imported from Asian traditions?

AA: One reason for the retreat emphasis, at least in vipassana circles, is due to the Asian systems that have fostered many of our teachers and styles of practice. Goenka-ji and Mahasi Sayadaw's disciples emphasize a very controlled retreat situation as the primary path. Retreat, retreat, retreat. Those teachers have had enormous influence and have helped tens of thousands of people, but I think that their style has led to this imbalance, the unhealthy separation between life and retreat.

Of course, if you go on retreats for twenty years, you can create tremendous inner space. But it can become almost like a police state. You just clear the streets of all the unruly inhabitants of your mind. And while you may get them off the streets, the guerillas will still be active underground. So when you leave the retreat, you begin to experience your ordinary life as difficult and turbulent. Then you can't wait to get to the next retreat. I am speaking very generally here, and maybe exaggerating a bit, but I think I am describing a pattern that many of your readers will recognize.

IM: In contrast, Ajahn Chah and teachers in the Thai forest tradition did not emphasize retreats so much and placed equal importance on community and daily life.

AA: Ajahn Chah would have us do periods of intensive practice, but we would still go out on alms round in the morning, and there would always be work to do around the monastery. So even the times of intensive, formal practice were not so separated from life or so completely free of stimulus.

I have recently been addressing this issue through the story of the Buddha's enlightenment. During the course of the night, as the story goes, the Buddha-to-be made his vow not to get up from his seat until he was completely enlightened. The Lord of Illusion, Mara, tried to disturb his meditation with fearful and sensual images but was unsuccessful. By the end of the night, the Buddha's realization into truth was complete, but although he was fully awakened, the armies of Mara were still around him.

Then Mara asked him, "What right do you think you have to claim enlightenment?" The Buddha reached down and touched the earth, invoking the Earth Mother, who appeared and said, "This is my true son, and he has done everything necessary to claim complete and full enlightenment. He is the supremely awakened one." Then from her hair she produced a great flood of water, which washed away the armies of Mara, who eventually returned carrying flowers and other offerings.

I think the story is saying that if our liberation is simply a subjective, mental, interior experience, then we are only half-cooked. Wisdom has to reach out into the world. Even the Buddha has to make that gesture of humility and ask the Earth for her blessing. In order for the armies of Mara to really be dispelled, we have to open our eyes and step out of that blissful interior space. For liberation to be finalized we have to touch the Earth.

IM: What prompted you to become a Buddhist monk?

AA: When I first visited Ajahn Chah's monastery in Thailand, I found a group of Westerners like myself, with very similar backgrounds, who were living in the forest doing Buddhist meditation practice. And they all seemed remarkably cheerful.

When they explained their way of life and the basis of their practice, it made perfect sense to me. Previously I had assumed that freedom came from having no rules and no boundaries. I'd never really questioned that premise, even though trying to live that way had been painful and difficult. These monks suggested that I look for freedom where it could actually be found. They pointed out that the material world is filled with limits, and you don't look for that which is boundless in the place where you find limitation. They explained that by living a life that is disciplined, simple, and harmless one could discover the true freedom that lies within us. Upon hearing their words, my immediate reaction was, "How could I have been so stupid?" I felt simultaneously embarrassed and relieved.

IM: Did the monk's life live up to your initial expectations?

AA: Absolutely. Even though the last thing I would have planned for myself was a lifetime of celibacy and renunciation, what I discovered was a new delight in simplicity and the deep satisfaction that comes from not actively seeking satisfaction. It is a strange but sweet irony that in the monastery I find the very delight that I was so rabidly searching for outside the monastery. It just looks like I've given up everything, but actually the inner experience is one of great delight. In fact, this monk's life is a feast! When I was first ordained I used to think, "I don't deserve this," or "I'm not going to get away with this for very long."

IM: Are there any particular difficulties that you encounter as a Buddhist monk in the West? How do you feel walking around in robes in this culture?

AA: For me it has always seemed like the most normal thing in the world. I think, to a degree, we all feel like outsiders in life. We all feel slightly different from other people in one way or another, and being dressed as a Buddhist monk in the West is just another form of being different.

Besides, even though we are Buddhist monks and nuns, we are only alien when we are outside of the monastery. Inside the monastery it is normal to have a shaved head and wear brown robes. The women have shaved heads and the men wear skirts. (Laughs)

Living as part of a Buddhist monastic community makes all the difference, whether you are in the West or the East. Ajahn Chah always emphasized the Sangha, the community, as a method of practice in and of itself. It wasn't a matter of living with a bunch of other people just in order to do meditation practice. The life of the community of monks and nuns was itself a method of practice and a method of liberation. Although Ajahn Chah did teach individual meditation techniques, over and over again he stressed the importance of community. I think that is one of the reasons why our monasteries have succeeded in the West.

Also, when you live in a community, then the monastic traditions make a lot of sense. They work, and they work well. We aren't just trying to sustain some archaic Asian system as a curio or a formality. The life of renunciation—living on alms, wearing the same robes as everyone else—and all of the rules are methods whereby we train ourselves. Through those forms, the heart can be liberated.

IM: Most Westerners don't seem to be very attracted to community as a path. Perhaps one reason is because that path clashes with our cultural belief in the primacy of the individual, the importance of going it alone.

AA: I would agree. Community life is about setting aside my own desires for the sake of the group. It's self-sacrifice. To the individualist, that sounds like death. But the training in communality is, for many Westerners, a blessed shift in perspective. Because what makes us suffer most of all in life is having "me" at the center of it all. Our society supports and validates that attitude, which has led to deep feelings of alienation and insecurity.

When we learn how to surrender our own urges and biases, we are not inherently giving up our freedom or denigrating our individuality. Being able to listen and to yield to other people is a way of recognizing our relationship with them and our interdependence with all the life of the planet. As we let go of our selfish demands we begin to recognize the vastness of our true nature. That dynamic is extremely important in the full development of spiritual life.

IM: Do you feel there are significant differences between being a monk in Europe or America and being a monk in Asia?

AA: One of the great blessings of Buddhist monasticism in the West is that it becomes free of the formalism, ritualism, and cultural accretions of Asia. In many ways, it is much easier for Westerners to get to the essence of the teachings. Even our Asian teachers have remarked on this. They say, "You are really lucky. We have all this cultural baggage that we have to work through with our students." Westerners don't know anything about the "ism" of Buddhism before we start our studying and training.

IM: On the other hand, Western monks and nuns don't get as much support from the lay population as their Asian brothers and sisters.

AA: Yes, and that respect and support is very sweet. When I go to Thailand, I get treated like a visiting dignitary. In the West we still have to earn our respect. I've had people say to me, "What do you do for a living? What do you contribute to the Gross National Product?"

IM: You should just tell them you are working on the Subtle National Product.

AA: I respond by asking them what makes a nation healthy? Does it depend on how many sacks of wheat it exports or how many tons of steel it sells? Or does the health of a nation include the well-being of individuals, and furthermore, is that well-being only dependent on their physical health and comfort, or does it also involve their peace of mind? I try to expand the definition of national well-being.

IM: What are the hardest monastic rules to keep when you are living in Western culture?

AA: It is different for different people, I think, but for many of us the hardest rules are those around celibacy, maintaining a kind of evenness in our relationships with other people. And it's not just about refraining from sexual intercourse. Ordinary human affection and friendliness can easily lead to a flow of emotion that suggests something more intimate. While there is nothing wrong with that flow between human beings, when you have taken vows of celibacy, then that suggestiveness or flirtation is in violation of your commitment.

IM: What about entertainments? Do you miss listening to music?

AA: Not much, although I used to be a big music fan and listened to it all the time. Now that I don't deliberately listen to it, I find that when I do happen to hear music, it's as if I'm hearing it for the first time. Music used to be such a constant presence in my life that it had lost its power. If I hear it now, it has an astonishing quality of freshness. I am with every note, every phrase.

When we adopt the renunciate life we aren't condemning the world of the senses per se, because that leads to aversion and negativity. Instead we are learning to accept whatever is offered to us with full appreciation. Whatever arrives is received and cherished, but we don't try to add anything. I think many people listen to music because they love the place that the music takes them to, which is the present moment. You are not thinking about anything else; you are experiencing the harmony, balance, and rhythm that the music suggests. But all of those qualities are present in a meditative mind. If we need music in order to get us there, then when there isn't music (or delicious food or beautiful surroundings or whatever it might be), we are likely to feel bereft. We immediately start to look for another experience that will take us to that place of beauty.

What the precepts do is to shut the door on all our habitual sources of satisfaction so that our entire attention is directed inward. That is where we discover a beauty, clarity, and vastness of being that is unshakable, independent of circumstances and conditions. Then when we hear a piece of music or see a beautiful blue sky or the fine shape of a tree, that's an extra.

Believe it or not, I became a monk because I am a hedonist at heart. The fun began when I became a monk. I am not trying to be flip by saying this. For me at least, being a monk is the way I can most enjoy my life, and I do mean "en-joy." My life is en-joyed, filled with joy as an ongoing experience.

IM: Everybody is going to want to ordain after they read this interview!

AA: That's fine. But remember that the joy only comes after the self-surrender and sacrifice. I think that as a culture we are afraid of sacrifice. We feel we must own and accumulate things in order to be complete, and not just material objects but people and relationships as well. It is hard for us to understand that letting go is not a loss, not a bereavement. Of course, when we lose something that is beautiful or dear to us, there is a shadow that crosses the heart. But we enlighten that shadow with the understanding that the feeling of loss is just the karmic result of assuming we owned anything in the first place. The renunciate life is based on the realization that we can never really possess anything.

From Volume 12, Number 1 (Fall 1995).

5 The Timeless Teachings
An Interview with Sharon Salzberg

Sharon Salzberg began her spiritual quest when she was only eighteen years old. In 1970 she left the University of Buffalo and went to India, where she studied with a number of Buddhist teachers, including S.N. Goenka, Anagarika Munindra, and Dipa Ma from the Theravadan tradition and Kalu Rinpoche from the Tibetan. When she returned to the United States, Salzberg began teaching with Joseph Goldstein. In 1975, along with Goldstein and Jack Kornfield, she helped establish the Insight Meditation Society in Barre, Massachusetts. A number of years later, the Burmese master U Pandita Sayadaw became her primary teacher, and she made several extended trips to Burma to study with him. U Pandita inspired in her a deep devotion to the classical Buddhist teachings; after studying with him, Salzberg's approach, both as a yogi and as a teacher took a new direction.

The following interview was conducted by Barbara Gates, Wes Nisker, Joseph Goldstein, and Mudita Nisker in January 1998 at the home of Mudita Nisker in Oakland, California.

INQUIRING MIND: When you sat your first retreat with Goenka in 1970, did you see this teaching as the truth?

SHARON SALZBERG: Yes. I felt complete faith. But it was really hard for me to bring the teaching into practice. I had a lot of physical pain, a lot of mental torment. I couldn't sit for five minutes; I was sweating and crying. And yet, even though my moment-to-moment experiences were often painful and I wasn't sure I could be a good yogi, if somebody said to me, "Liberation is a possibility," I knew that's what I had to work for.

My major asset as a yogi was that I had no preconceptions; I was very young and very obedient. When somebody said, "Do this," I'd say, "Okay." I surrendered completely without even thinking about it. While this could have had its dangers, it enabled me to commit myself wholeheartedly.

IM: How would you describe Goenka as a teacher?

SS: Goenka is an inspirational person. As a teacher, he was very technique-oriented. The burden of understanding was really on the student. People would ask him about manifestations of the Dhamma in their lives, and he would say, "Go back and sit," or "Just sit every day," without elaboration about a cosmology or world view. When I was with Goenka I didn't read any Dhamma books. At that time, he did not encourage people to read or study, but rather to have a pure experience without anything to judge it by, or a standard to live up to. That was very strong for me; I had to rely on myself, on my own experience in practice.

Then, when I studied with Munindra I began to understand the breadth of knowledge that was possible through acquaintance with the Buddha's teaching. For example, when I was sitting with Goenka, I didn't realize that in the act of moving my mind through my body I was developing the seven factors of enlightenment. Once I began to study more under Munindra, I had a much broader appreciation for what was going on.

IM: In more recent years you became a student of U Pandita Sayadaw of the Mahasi Sayadaw tradition. Where did his teaching take you?

SS: Working with U Pandita over the years has been like a magic show. He has an amazing understanding. Over and over again the level of his knowledge has awed me. Without his inspiration I don't think I could have done the kind of meticulous practice I do now. I would not have been motivated enough. It's so easy to kind of "mosey along" in your practice.

I met the Sayadaw when he came to teach his first meditation course in the United States. The connection was strong and immediate. I watched myself rising to his demands. I might come into an interview walking very mindfully, observing every single thing I was doing. I'd sit down and bow in the same way, with delicacy and precision. Then the hair would fall in my face and I would whisk my head back. He might have been reading a magazine, but as soon as I whisked back my hair, he would look up and say, "Did you note that?" I would say, "No." He would say, "Do you believe in what the

Buddha taught, that uninterrupted mindfulness can really bring you to enlightenment?" I'd say, "Yes." And he'd say, "Don't you think it might be better to actually realize it rather than just believe in it?" I'd say, "Yes."

IM: U Pandita is in the Mahasi lineage. How would you describe the Mahasi school's methodology?

SS: In the model used by the Mahasi school, the path is a progression of deepening insight into *anicca* (impermanence), *dukkha* (suffering), and *anatta* (selflessness), not necessarily in that order, but ever deepening understandings and intuitive openings into the three characteristics of existence.

Often people follow the progression of that model, but they lack understanding of their experiences. I've seen this in my own practice while studying with U Pandita and with students since. A person might mistake the opening into the truth of suffering as her own personal pain. She'll experience the dukkha of life as regret about her past actions or doubt about her love relationship.

It's truer to see the pain one experiences not only as one's personal suffering but as an insight into the nature of existence. The Mahasi school method teaches us to move from the particular to the universal, or to use the particular to reveal the universal. The particular serves as the conduit for the other levels held implicit within it.

IM: So there is very little emphasis placed on the psychological or content level of the mind.

SS: I don't think it's possible to avoid the content level altogether, but I think there are times in this system—not in the beginning when the content is all important—when a student who has a decent foundation in the practice can see the content as an expression of something else.

For example, sometimes people experience great loneliness in their practice and feel it quite personally as a yearning for home, for a job, or for people they left behind when they came on retreat. Yet this loneliness may be an expression of a more universal feeling: the fundamental loneliness of the samsaric world where everything is changing and there is no place or person one can rely on, a longing for our one true home—the unconditioned, or nibbana.

Also, the Mahasi model leads to perception on a moment-by-moment level and the insights which arise out of those perceptions. When I was sitting with U Pandita in Barre, Massachusetts, I went through a period when I was feeling really dizzy. When I walked I held on to the walls because everything was swimming around. I thought to myself, Oh, God, I need some protein fast or I'm going to die. Couldn't someone send me a hard-boiled egg? When I went to my interview, I was incredibly dizzy. I bowed and looked up, but then I had to look down again because the whole room was spinning. The first day I reported, "I'm really dizzy." The second day I said, "I'm really dizzy; there's something wrong here." Then the third day I was just saying, "I've got to stop. I've got to go to bed. This is horrible."

U Pandita finally relented and said, "What happens in real life if you're watching something move around and around really fast?" I said, "Well, I get dizzy." He said, "That's what's happening. You're seeing impermanence on a very fast level. Your perception is at that level, but your conscious understanding is not at that level yet. You don't know that's what you're seeing, and that's why you're getting so dizzy."

I thought to myself, "If my perception is picking up this rapidity of change, I should know it. I should be having insights, like 'Oh, now that things are changing so fast you can't hold on to anything.'" I wasn't having those insights, so I didn't believe him. However in a day or two, when my conscious understanding caught up to the perception, I could see he was right.

In general, working with U Pandita has given me a great deal more confidence in myself. The Burmese teaching methods include a lot of challenges to the student. For instance, a teacher might ask a question in such a way that he implies that the wrong answer is correct. The student has to look within herself and proclaim what she knows for herself as true, without pretending just to please the teacher. It's like the lion's roar the Buddha described, a declaration of truth, deeply and personally known. But it is hard to be so honest as to say, "My experience seems to be the opposite of what you're implying is desirable. Too bad; that's my actual experience."

Here's an example. When I was doing intensive metta meditation under Sayadaw's guidance, I had directed metta toward different categories of beings—myself, a benefactor, a beloved friend, someone I hardly knew, and someone with whom I had difficulty. At the end of this time, U Pandita said to me, "Imagine you are in a forest along with your benefactor, a friend, a neutral person, and a difficult person. A bandit comes up and demands that you choose one person to be sacrificed. Which one will you choose?"

I looked deep into my heart and couldn't feel any distinction among all those people, including myself. Finally I looked at U Pandita and said, "I couldn't choose; they seem all the same to me." Then he asked, "You wouldn't sacrifice your enemy?" I said, "No, I couldn't." Then came the clincher. He said, "Don't you think you should be able to sacrifice yourself to save the others?" He asked it as if more than anything else in the world he wanted me to say, "Yes, I'd sacrifice myself." A lot of conditioning rose up in me—an urge to please him, to be "right" and to win approval—but there was no way I could honestly say yes, so I said, "No, I just can't see any difference between myself and any of these others." He just nodded and I left. Later, I looked this up in the Visuddhi Magga and found that the answer I had given had been the appropriate one for doing intensive metta. In ways like this, I am continually forced to recognize what I know to be true and to assert it no matter what.

IM: Some Westerners aren't comfortable with aspects of traditional Buddhism and suggest making adaptations. What are your thoughts about that? For instance, what do you think of the adaptations of Buddhism to address the concerns of women?

SS: Every single one of us probably has our own ways we would like to change the teachings. Some would like them to be more austere, some more comfortable; some would like them to be more expressive of our conception of the feminine. So we each develop our own relationship to the Dhamma, take from it what we find relevant, and leave the rest. It would be a tragedy to abet that process in my teaching. For instance, I can't imagine teaching the mind control aspect of the practice without the moral basis. And yet that's what happens in a lot of programs that are trying to introduce people to a form of stress reduction or relaxation. The Dhamma can be lost in the translation.

It's crucial to remember that the Dhamma contains within it the path to the complete end of suffering, to the realization of the highest happiness. For me, this is the Dhamma as it has been passed down from the Buddha. It is important not to confuse a timeless teaching with a temporary social balancing that feels essential today but which we may let go of later.

IM: As a teacher, what do you hope to leave as your legacy?

SS: When teachers of Buddhism begin to adapt the Dhamma to fit their preferences, the main thing I fear is that something essential will get left out. Believe me, it's easy to leave things out. Sometimes you think your students won't like you or they'll be angry at you because you've said something they don't like. You become afraid you're going to lose them. Yet the very teachings you are tempted to change may be necessary to maintain the integrity of the system. I would hate to think that I, or my generation, were the ones who lost the idea of enlightenment because it raises a lot of uncomfortable questions, has a possible negative interpretation, or because people seeking enlightenment might become really goal-oriented and forget the present moment. The result would be that we'd have lost the heart of what the Buddha taught.

From Volume 4, Number 2 (Spring 1988).

6 Bringing Mindfulness into Mainstream America
An Interview with Jon Kabat-Zinn

Jon Kabat-Zinn got more than fifteen minutes of fame. He and his work were featured for almost an hour on the Bill Moyers PBS special "Healing and the Mind" in 1993, and Dr. Kabat-Zinn has been very busy ever since. He deserves the attention. For over twenty-eight years, Kabat-Zinn, a long-time Zen and vipassana meditator who is closely associated with the Insight Meditation Society, Spirit Rock Meditation Center, and the Cambridge Insight Meditation Center, has been exploring the healing power of Buddhist meditative practices within the mainstream of Western medicine and health care. His Dharma vehicle is the Stress Reduction Clinic within the Center for Mindfulness in Medicine, Health Care, and Society at the University of Massachusetts Medical Center, both of which he founded, where he and his colleagues offer a series of eight-week courses based originally on his own training in Buddhist mindfulness meditation. The approach, now known as Mindfulness-Based Stress Reduction (MBSR), has spread to hospitals, clinics, and medical centers around the world and continues to be the subject of a great deal of high-level research.

The following interview was conducted by Barbara Gates and Wes Nisker in May 1993 and updated in December 2007.

INQUIRING MIND: When you founded the Stress Reduction Clinic, what were your goals?

JON KABAT-ZINN: When I set out to do this work, it was with the intention of bringing the Dharma into the mainstream world of medicine and health care. I wanted to try to create one little nucleus of a model that might demonstrate in a coherent way that, through rigorous and systematic training in mind-

fulness, people could build on strengths that they already had and do something for themselves that would improve their own health and well-being.

IM: You've had remarkable results for a program in which people meditate
for at most an hour a day over eight weeks. How do you account for this?

JKZ: The motive for coming to the class in the first place is profound.
Remember, people are not coming to learn meditation. They are not coming because they have concerns about "where I fit in the world" or about
interconnectedness or meaning. They are coming because they have cancer
or heart disease or chronic pain. They are coming to relieve their suffering
or to gain control in a new way. They have experienced the limits of medicine. Here we are suggesting that maybe there is something you can do for
yourself that no doctor or anybody else can do for you. What they are facing is pressing and immediate, like something's on fire. This, of course, is
wonderful motivation to come to meditation practice.

The first thing that we observe over the course of eight weeks are major
improvements in people's symptoms, independent of what kind of medical
problem they have. This includes not only physical symptoms such as pain,
heart palpitations, headaches, and blood pressure, but also psychological
symptoms such as anxiety, depression, anger, and hostility. Over this period
of time there are dramatic changes in the majority of participants—at least
in their symptoms or surface manifestations of their conditions.

But there are also deeper things going on that we've started to look at,
such as how you hold the notion of "self," issues of being a person in relationship to the world. There's a lot of evidence that how you view the world
and how you operate in it, based on your belief system, is an indicator of your
risk for various kinds of illnesses further down the road. There's evidence that
mind states are, in fact, connected over a lifetime with physical disease.
Particularly, people in our culture who tend to have high levels of hostility
are much more susceptible to death from all causes, including cancer and
heart disease. Even high use of the personal pronouns in speech has been
associated with increased risk of various chronic diseases—a very interesting observation from a Dharmic point of view.

What we are finding in the Stress Reduction Clinic is that people who are
exposed to relatively intensive mindfulness practice will, after a short period
of time, not only show positive changes in symptoms like anger and hostility but changes in other things that aren't supposed to change when you are
an adult, such as the personality measures known as a sense of coherence and

stress hardiness. These are ways of measuring how you view yourself in relationship to the world. Our patients change in the direction of a greater expansiveness, a greater sense of meaningfulness, and of seeing the world as a challenge and as comprehensible. People who have been through the program often begin to make more of a commitment to the nitty-gritty aspects of daily life and become more comfortable with change.

IM: Do you think there is a difference between teaching mindfulness as you do and teaching Dharma?

JKZ: I believe that on the deepest level we are teaching Dharma. But obviously we don't frame it that way. We try to stay as far away from all of the trappings of Buddhism as possible. Because in our setting it's not effective to deliver meditation in that way. Not that we attempt to hide the source. What we're really trying to do is to create an American Dharma, an American Zen.

IM: Since he first taught courses in this country, Thich Nhat Hanh has been urging American Dharma students to discover an American Buddhism. Maybe your work is part of that new vehicle.

JKZ: Well, my Zen training was certainly helpful to me in that regard. I felt a certain irreverent emphasis in Zen that gave me permission to break out of constraining and possibly unskillful forms. Koans like "If you meet the Buddha in the road, kill him" suggest that the essence of the practice has to be lived, has to be continually regenerated and recreated. Yesterday's answer, or last moment's answer, won't suffice for this moment.

IM: So give us an example of how you translate the fundamental Buddhist teachings to people who aren't particularly interested in Buddhism. Clearly, you talk about the first noble truth of suffering. How do you talk about it?

JKZ: When I use the phrase "the full catastrophe" to describe what many people are facing in their lives, that's one way of formulating the theme of dukkha. Dukkha almost completely transposes with our word *stress*. In fact, in his writings Ajahn Maha Boowa of Thailand uses the word *stress* directly for *dukkha*. One of the interesting things about stress is that it is nonspecific. Everything is stressful; "bad" things are stressful and "good" things are stressful too. Getting married is stressful; getting divorced is stressful. We call what we do at the hospital "stress reduction" simply because it's a gigantic umbrella under which you can hold all of human experience, the human condition itself, and begin to approach it, work with it systematically—through the cultivation of mindfulness.

IM: How do you talk to people about stress?

JKZ: We emphasize that it's not the stress per se that is the problem. What is important is how you hold it, how you position yourself in relationship to it, how you *respond* to it. Like dukkha, it is a perceivable fact if you look deeply into experience. But then the question is, "Now what? How do I handle it?" The other noble truths go on to assert that there is a way to understand this dukkha and to work it, and that way will take you through it and out beyond it. And that's what we are basically offering people in MBSR— the invitation to experiment with the possibility that there may be things you can do for yourself, that no one else can do for you, which can free you from some of the biggest prisons you create for yourself or that your body can lock you into. That doesn't mean you are going to meditate your tumor away, or that you will live forever, or that you won't yell at your teenager. But it means you will hold your experience in a way that will be somehow wiser and freer.

Now, I want you to know that I don't really see what we are doing as just stress reduction or stress management. We just call it that. I really see it as Dharma, as I said before. I am completely open to the possibility that this might be a major delusion. Maybe we're watering down the true Dharma and trying to justify that to ourselves. I actually ask myself that every day, and I don't believe that's the case. Nor do my colleagues near and far.

IM: Do you attempt to talk to the people in your program about the Buddhist concept of "no self"?

JKZ: No, I don't go anywhere near the traditional Buddhist formulation of it, because people just don't understand it, and it can actually generate an enormous amount of unnecessary fear. But when people say, "I really can't stand this pain," I say, "Who is it that's saying that?" Or I'll say, "When you say I, how many different I's are in there?" Then I might jokingly say, "Well, maybe there's a whole platoon in there! One I may want to go to the movies, but another I doesn't want to go to the movies. One I feels one way about something, but then another I doesn't feel that way at all." In this way we try to get at the notion that, in fact, none of us has all the answers about who we are. It can be a very liberating experience for people to get to a point where they actually see for themselves—by watching their thoughts—that I am not my thoughts, that I is just another thought. Approaching no-self in that way doesn't smack of Buddhism at all. It doesn't have anything to do with any ideology or philosophy. It's just an observable fact.

IM: Are you suggesting that sacred context of the practice is not necessary?

JKZ: Not at all. It is more a matter of what is skillful means and also how big you are willing to let the sacred get without getting attached to particular forms. For me, all moments of silence are sacred space. The breath is sacred, the body is sacred. And the Hippocratic relationship in medicine is universally held as sacred, at least in principle, if not always in practice.

As for Buddhism itself, I'd say we wouldn't even be having this conversation if a sacred context didn't exist. The more traditional spiritual framework of Buddhism is what got many of us interested back in the mid-sixties and beyond. Many of us, including Allen Ginsberg, Gary Snyder, you and I, and a lot more people we know and love, became engaged in meditation and in Dharma because it spoke directly to our experience and our aspiration in profound ways.

IM: But I think we entered it with more of a desire for a romantic or mystical experience...

JKZ: Exactly. Seeking enlightenment of some kind or other.

IM: So what you do attracts people in a different way to a path that just might lead them in the same direction.

JKZ: Absolutely. That is my conviction, anyway, and the whole point of our work. There are many different ways to connect up to what is deepest in oneself, but ultimately they all come down to mindfulness. My feeling is that there is a way to take perhaps 80 percent of what might be valuable in the traditional Buddhist teachings and articulate it in such a way that people won't be repelled by it. Why not then use it? There are things that I've learned on the cushion, that I think anybody could use—my parents, for instance, and my children. But they're not necessarily going to go out looking for enlightenment. I really believe that mindfulness practice is universal. We need to develop new ways to allow it to express itself, and then to trust that. If it's as powerful as we all believe it to be, and perhaps have tasted it to be in some small way, then the power of it is not coming from us in the first place. So that power will express itself through anyone walking on the face of the Earth, given the right conditions. And we can sometimes influence those conditions favorably.

IM: Have you been pleased by the results of the publicity you've been getting or has it created difficulties for your ongoing work?

JKZ: The biggest danger in all the publicity is that people will make meditation into just one more concept and prescription to do something to improve themselves and miss the essence of it completely. And in the process of making it into some kind of trip, they'll actually denature it or turn it into a recipe of some kind. In our professional training retreats we emphasize that health professionals need to deeply develop their own mindfulness practice before they can use it to benefit others. A lot of people want to rush in and start teaching mindfulness out of enthusiasm, or now as a smart career move because it has become so popular and widespread. But they don't realize at first that it cannot be done unless it comes from the depth of their own inner being and practice.

IM: What gets lost?

JKZ: Just everything. The wisdom, the compassion, the appreciation for silence and stillness and nondoing get lost in the energy, the agitation, and the excitement of something "new." Americans would love it, of course, if we could just give it out in a pill form: Hey, I don't want to meditate for forty-five minutes a day. Just give me a pill I can take once a day. A mindfulness pill.

IM: What a challenge to distill Buddhist practice and bring it to a broad public—without losing the essence!

JKZ: In 1990 when I was with the Dalai Lama for the Mind and Life III conference in Dharamsala, one of the participants attacked what he was calling "the secularization of the Dharma" through the kind of work that I do. He was basically saying that we were taking some half-baked, reduced version of Buddhism and putting it out there as the total thing. He argued that such occurrences contribute to the decline of religion by secularizing it so that its sacred power is lost. I thought to myself, If that were true, I would quit tomorrow.

At one point, the question got put directly to His Holiness, "Is it wrong action to teach Buddhism without the Buddhism, so to speak? In places like hospitals and schools and prisons where it's obvious that people don't want to become Buddhists and equally obvious that people are suffering tremendously?"

His Holiness responded that there are four billion people on the planet, and only one billion of them are Buddhists. He queried, does that mean that we should ignore the suffering of the other three billion? To me he was saying that if we know anything, what we know has to be universal enough to embrace everybody on the planet. In the ensuing years, His Holiness has emphasized more and more the importance of a secular, non-Buddhist approach to contemplative practice that might draw deeply from Buddhism's experience but would be profoundly universal.

IM: Among other venues, you have branched out into the inner city health centers and the prisons, where there is indeed incredible suffering.

JKZ: I believe in my heart that, if you have a mind and you have a body, meditation is relevant. For the most part, we've found in our prison and inner city programs that—when under the right umbrella, framed in the right way, and integrated into the community in the right way—people take to mindfulness practice like ducks to water.

IM: Do you have a good story from your prison class?

JKZ: Sometimes in meditation practice, I like to give a Zen shout in the middle of a sitting. To wake people up. It intuitively comes up when the time is right to do it. But I didn't feel that you should shout in prison without warning, because you might have guards with guns come down on you in no time. I was in the classroom alone with the inmates, although there were TV monitors. So I told the class, "Sometime during the next half hour of this sitting, I'm going to shout." Ten minutes later, I went around correcting people's posture. I hadn't shouted yet. One African American inmate who had put out some serious resistance to the class since the beginning was sitting there shaking. I whispered to him, asking what was going on. He whispered back, "I can't take this. I'm a nervous wreck." I said, "Why?" He said, "I'm just waitin' for the shout." I said, "Listen, don't worry about the shout. You just stay with your breathing. Whenever the shout comes, the shout comes."

I did shout, finally, and later it opened up a very rich conversation. All these big guys who had done heavy-duty things to wind up in prison were saying things like, "People have been shouting at me my entire life. I can't stand it." Many talked about how traumatic their arrest experiences were, and how violent. I never thought all that would come out of one shout. The shout was just to give them the sense that if you jump, it's because you're not really right there in the moment. But these guys were jumping a half hour before I even gave the shout. It turned out to be a wonderful way to tap into the underlying feelings that these men carry all the time, emotions that have never been appreciated, never even been heard by themselves or others. It was beautiful.

Teaching in prison is great training for meditation teachers. You can't go in there and bullshit. If you do, you are dead. Maybe not literally, but the word goes out in the yard so fast that you just can't operate. It doesn't work to be a tough guy either. No dissimulation is possible. Sometimes I used to joke, "So you want to teach meditation? OK, we'll just put you in a prison setting; and if you come out alive, maybe you will be ready to teach in the hospital."

IM: So after the hospitals, the inner city, and the prisons, where do you go from here? What is your vision for where mindfulness might be taught next?

JKZ: I can tell you one story about taking mindfulness to the public schools. A year ago at a workshop in Salt Lake City, a fifth-grade public school teacher named Cherry Hamrick came up to me and said, "I really want to bring this into the classroom." And I said, "I don't think that's such a wise idea. This is Mormon country. People have strong misconceptions about what meditation is. If they hear you are doing meditation with their children in a public school, it could create a lot of problems."

But she didn't listen to me. She went ahead and did it under the umbrella of stress reduction and mindfulness. She asked the kids to write about "what mindfulness and stress reduction have done for me." The kids wrote things like: "Now when kids tease me I realize that just because their mind is waving, my mind doesn't have to wave," or "Now I find I'm coming more from my heart than from my head," or "I'm less sarcastic." The kids weren't just writing down things the teacher had written on the blackboard. What they wrote was heartfelt, not just one or two sentences, but several pages. I read all thirty of them. She selected the five "best," and those kids got to attend a two-day meditation retreat I was leading. There were 500 adults and five eleven-year-olds and their teacher. They sat in the front row. And they really sat...for two days. It was amazing! Hamrick's passion, her energy for it, figured out a way to make this happen.

IM: Somebody with that kind of passion could take the Dharma into any of life's arenas.

JKZ: That's right. We're basically saying to people who have been sitting for years and want to bring their Dharma practice more into the mainstream world: Trust more in yourself, take a few more risks, and see what your intuition says about how mindfulness and this kind of approach might make a difference in your world, wherever you find yourself and a profound need.

From Volume 10, Number 1 (Fall 1993).

Note from Jon Kabat-Zinn: In 2007 a paper came out in the criminal justice literature describing our prison program and the results we obtained. See Samuelson, M., Carmody, J., Kabat-Zinn, J., and Bratt, M. A., "Mindfulness-Based Stress Reduction in Massachusetts Correctional Facilities," *The Prison Journal* (2007) 87: 254–68.

Cherry Hamrick brought mindfulness into her fourth- and fifth-grade classrooms for over ten years. In that time, other teachers in earlier and later grades were inspired to do so as well, following her imaginative lead and teachings. Cherry died tragically in February 2006 of a heart attack while in her early forties. A task force associated with the Mind and Life Institute is currently looking into conducting a long-term follow-up on her students to see whether there were any lasting impacts from being exposed to mindfulness training at such an early age. A chapter entitled "Mindfulness in the Classroom" in the book *Everyday Blessings: The Inner Work of Mindful Parenting*, by Myla and Jon Kabat-Zinn, describes aspects of Hamrick's work.

7 Talkin' 'bout Our G-G-Generations
Noah Levine in Conversation with Wes Nisker

Noah Levine loves punk rock and loves the Dharma. He teaches meditation and Buddhism to a new generation of American rebels. He tells his story in his books Dharma Punx *and* Against the Stream—*and in the following conversation with baby boomer Wes Nisker in the fall of 2003.*

WES NISKER: Even though you and I are of different generations, I feel as though we have a lot in common as students of the Dharma, and also as rebels against mainstream American culture. Your generation's rebellion has its own fashions, and you may have been taking different drugs than we did, but we are in the same lineage.

NOAH LEVINE: I think both generations were rebelling against their parents and the styles of the previous generation. The boomers were trying to break out of the uptight, straight world of their parents, who came out of the Great Depression and World War II. Many of my generation were also rebelling against our parents, and some of them had been hippies. We were questioning the boomers who had held a pseudo-revolution, taken acid and dropped out, and in the end hadn't achieved very much social change at all. Your attempts to create a world of peace and love led to Ronald Reagan, George Bush, and the nasty current world situation.

WN: We stand accused! Most of our attempts at revolution do seem to have failed, except perhaps in the spiritual realm. But the idealistic flavor of my generation's rebellion seems so different from the dark anarchy of your generation's rebellion. The hippies were dressed in clothes of many colors, and we were celebrating life, having be-ins, optimistic about creating a new world, a new consciousness. If only everybody took acid...

NL: I think some of the punk ethic of my generation came out of our contempt for this oversimplified hippie LSD view that life was all about peace and love. Just put flowers in your hair and into the rifle barrels of the military and everything will be all right. My generation saw the first noble truth: that life was full of violence, oppression, suffering. And we saw that taking acid wasn't going to solve anything. Our attitude was that you've got to fight against the system. It was all expressed by the rock and roll coming out of England in the late '70s, by kids who were feeling the failure of capitalism and imperialism in that country and seeing the poverty and hopelessness.

WN: It's interesting to note that both of our countercultural movements used rock and roll music as a primary means of expression. As a further parallel, the Beatles from England were instrumental in defining the hippie sensibility, and in *Dharma Punx* you say that the Sex Pistols, also from England, really set the tone for the punks.

NL: Right, the Sex Pistols toured America in 1978, and their attitude on and off stage was: "We're not here to entertain you. We're playing this music because this is how we feel, and if you feel this way too then jump up and down." Johnny Rotten of the Sex Pistols once famously said, "Do you ever feel like you're being cheated?" And the answer from a lot of young people in this country was, "Hell, yes!"

WN: I saw the Sex Pistols when they performed at Winterland, and I could not believe my eyes or ears. The buzz-saw guitars were blasting out these three-chord songs with that intense, unvarying four-four drum beat, and the singer was snarling and sneering. The audience was throwing bottles and shoes at the band, and people were smashing into each other on the floor. It was all so violent and edgy. As an old hippie, I was shocked. Actually, I was appalled.

NL: (Laughs) I guess the Pistols were successful in their expression. This was not our parents' rock and roll.

WN: The punk ethos, at least as expressed in the music, seemed to be saying, "Screw it all! To hell with the system!" It didn't seem so much about fighting for social change.

NL: Maybe you never heard one of my favorite bands, called Crucifix, which played at my book release party. They have a song on their first recording, which I bought when I was fourteen years old, that begins with a poem: "From dehumanization to arms production, for the benefit of the nation or its destruction, power is power, it's the law of the land. Those who live for death will die by their own hand. Life is no ordeal if you can come to terms and reject the system which dictates the norm. It's your choice. Peace or annihilation." That's a song with a strong social message.

More importantly, just as with your psychedelic rock, the punk rock music was a focus of our community. There's an old English punk rock song by Sham 69 that says: "I look out for my friend 'cause I know my happiness depends on his and he knows his happiness depends on me." Another song by the hardcore band H2O says: "My friends look out for me like family 'cause my mom's been struggling since I was three." Our parents don't understand us, but we understand each other. The music was saying that we are a community.

WN: Those sentiments sure sound familiar to me. As we used to say back in the late '60s, "They can't bust our music." I guess I really didn't know the content of punk rock because I could never understand the lyrics.

NL: Of course, a lot of the punk attitude was purely anarchistic. We saw what the world was like, we were really angry, and we decided to express that anger and disgust. We weren't going to buy into the capitalist dream that happiness comes from having a lot of money, and we rejected the hippie solution of dancing joyously in the sun. Instead, we got into this attitude of anarchy, a kind of rough, defiant nihilism fed by hopelessness. And for many of my generation this attitude led to suicide and overdoses—the fates of Sid Vicious, Darby Crash, and many others.

WN: As you say in your book, a lot of your friends have already died, many from overdoses.

NL: Out of a group of six close friends who were in the punk scene with me in Santa Cruz, four of them are dead. Looking back at our larger group of fifty punks, probably fifteen of them are dead.

WN: And you could easily have been among them. In fact, in your book you describe a failed attempt to kill yourself and reveal that what saved you in the end was the simple act of paying attention to your breath.

NL: I was on the phone from jail with my father, Stephen, and he told me to just be present with my breathing. I must have heard that a million times from him and others, but at that particularly difficult moment it made sense. That was the turning point. Remember, I had grown up around the spiritual scene and had rejected it. Spirituality was associated with my parents and hippies, and if that wasn't enough to condemn it, my own rebellious attitude and outlook just didn't include that aspect of life. But after a horrible struggle with addiction, lawlessness, and incarceration, I had reached a depth of hopelessness that led to an attempted suicide. It was at that moment, when all other options had been exhausted, that I heard what was necessary for me. I didn't come to spiritual practice because it sounded like a good idea. I came because I felt like there was nowhere else to turn.

WN: I'm interested in what it was like for you to sit in meditation, coming as you did from a punk milieu, with all of its stark, violent iconography. That world seems so antithetical to the ambiance and flavor of Buddhism.

NL: Well, remember that the Buddha was once into mortification of the body. He realized that it wasn't the right path, but during his period as a sadhu his earlobes got stretched way down from his piercings.

WN: I thought he was born with the long earlobes. But who knows, maybe there was a punk period in the Buddha's life as well.

NL: He did spend seven years on the street, so to speak. (Laughs) But just the fact that the Buddha finally rejected all extremes and found a middle path, a balance between denial and indulgence, was very inspiring. I had just spent seven years on the street and had also been mortifying my body, so his lesson spoke directly to me.

WN: But it must have been strange for you to go to retreats and sit there with all us ex-hippies and yuppies.

NL: For sure. I was the only person in his early twenties, and the only person with tattoos and spiked hair. So I felt very separate. At first it didn't matter much, because I had been lost at sea, and the life raft that came along was full of hippies. I was either going to get in that raft and save my life or drown waiting for a lifeboat full of punks. So in the beginning I was just happy to have been picked up. But after several years of sitting with you old-timers, I started wondering if I had to hang out with you guys the rest of my life.

WN: Are you saying that you'd rather not hang out with us?

NL: Well, it really isn't my cultural world, and even though the retreats gave me sustenance, I felt somewhat alienated. There was even a period where I began to question my punk identity, thinking that being spiritual was somehow separate from being punk. Then in the late '80s and early '90s, I began to feel supported in my spiritual life when parts of the punk scene turned toward Hindu consciousness. There was a trend toward nonviolence and becoming vegetarian, and rock bands like Shelter and 108, which got its name from the Hindu-Buddhist mala with 108 beads. They played hard metal punk rock with spiritual lyrics, mostly in praise of Krishna and in defiance of the material world. At that time if you went to the Hare Krishna Temple in Berkeley, you would find quite a number of punks living there.

WN: Well, the punks' already had bald heads, so all they had to do was grow the little topknot.

NL: That's right. Do Bonzai on the mohawk. (Laughs) But eventually that scene died out, and around the same time I realized that Buddhist practice was what resonated most deeply with me.

WN: In the early days of my practice, my mind used to insist on singing to me while I was meditating. Many people have commented on this phenomenon, which I call "jukebox karma." I remember a few of the songs that ran through my head over and over again—"Proud Mary" by Creedence Clearwater Revival and "Strawberry Fields" by the Beatles. You know, "Rollin' on a river" and "Nothing to get hung about." When you sit in meditation, do you get punk rock songs playing in your head?

NL: Sure, especially on retreats. On a recent three-month retreat, a Black Flag song stuck in my head for a week, with the lyrics: "I'm about to have a nervous breakdown. My head really hurts. If I don't find a way out of here, I'm gonna go berserk 'cause I'm crazy and I'm hurt. Head on my shoulders, it's going…berserk!" I also got to hear my favorite childhood band from Santa Cruz, called Blast, which had a song that went, "It's in my blood, it's in my blood, it's in my blood to try to make things change. I look out at this world and I can't believe what I see. It's in my blood, it's in my blood to try to make things change." And then as the lyric comes up, the memory of a show appears, and slam dancing, and maybe getting drunk that night. That's what's known in Dharma language as papañca (proliferation).

During the three-month course, I kind of went through a life review, and a Social Distortion song kept coming up, called "Story of My Life." The lyrics go: "High school seemed like such a blur. I didn't have much interest in sports or school elections. And in class I dreamed all day about a rock 'n' roll weekend and the girl in the front of the room, so close yet so far. Y'know, she never seemed to notice that this silly school-boy crush wasn't just pretend." That was the story of my life, and during the retreat the song played whenever the appropriate mind-state was unfolding.

WN: Now that you're into Buddhadharma, do you still look forward to the rock and roll weekend?

NL: Sure, but without the same intention to become unconscious, and without the same attachment to the event. I still enjoy the music and the community.

WN: Aside from teaching in correctional facilities and at Spirit Rock Meditation Center, you have also begun to create your own spiritual community—people of your generation who are practicing Buddhadharma. That must feel very gratifying for you.

NL: For sure. I organized a sitting group in San Francisco that attracts fifty or more people every week. My role is simply to make the practice accessible and applicable for my generation, who can't hear about it from your generation. And maybe even "my generation" isn't the right term, because the people I'm talking about are really members of the counterculture of my generation. They're punks or skinheads or surfers or skaters, the ones who aren't in the American mainstream. One of the most important messages I can relay is that spiritual practice isn't just for hippies anymore. I want to open the gates of Buddhadharma to the next generation.

WN: Perhaps your life experience and your identity as a punk is saying to people in your counterculture that spirituality and practicing meditation are not about selling out.

NL: What I'm trying to say is that spiritual practice is the ultimate defiance: refusing to be a slave to the dictates of your own mind; defiance of the greed, hatred, and delusion within the self. I am asking people to defy the internal system of oppression, as well as the external. The Buddha said that his teaching went against the stream, and I'm saying that it's the highest form of rebellion, even more rebellious than being a street punk. (Laughs)

WN: Are your counterculture friends going to meditation retreats, or interested in going?

NL: Yes, but they can't afford them. We're going to have to find some way to create our own retreats. If you had to pay the prices you are now charging at your retreat centers back when you were starting to practice, you couldn't have afforded them either.

WN: Perhaps as more people of your generation get involved in Dharma practice you'll create not only your own retreat centers but also your own Buddhist symbols and special Buddha statues.

NL: We already have a ceramic Buddha statue with a Mohawk haircut, and some friends of mine painted tattoos on him. That's just spiritual materialism: unnecessary but fun. I also created "Dharma Punx" as a name for our movement, partly because it's a play on Kerouac's "Dharma Bums" and reveals that we are all in the same lineage of spiritual American rebels. But I think the name also relieves some of the pressure of being perfect, or even of being a Buddhist. The name Dharma Punx says, I love what I love, and I still get angry and have lust and all that stuff, and I dress funny and have funny hair and lots of tattoos, and I am intentionally offensive in punk ways—and beneath this disguise, this uniform, I'm deeply committed to personal growth and spiritual awakening and service to others.

From Volume 20, Number 1 (Fall 2003).

8 Advice from the Dalai Lama

By Jack Kornfield

From March 16–19, 1993, the first in a series of international Buddhist teacher meetings was held in Dharamsala, India, between His Holiness the 14th Dalai Lama and a group of twenty-two Western Dharma teachers from the major Buddhist traditions. These Westerners were the first generation of authorized European and North American Buddhist meditation teachers, and all had practiced for at least a dozen years each in the schools of Japanese and Korean Zen; the four major Tibetan schools; Thai and Sri Lankan Theravada; and the Friends of the Western Buddhist Order, an entirely Western school based in Great Britain. These were laypeople, monks and nuns, psychologists, scholars, essayists, translators; some had meditated in caves, while others had Western doctorates. Most were actively teaching Buddhist meditation, not only in the West but in Asia, Russia, South Africa, and Brazil. The aim of the meeting was to discuss openly a wide range of issues concerning the transmission of the Buddhadharma to Western lands.

The following report on this meeting was adapted from a talk by Jack Kornfield, who moderated the meeting.

In the last great teachings of the Buddha before he died, he spoke about how important it is for those who follow the path of the Dharma to gather together regularly; that they gather in harmony, meet in concord, and disperse in concord; that they honor the great traditions of the elders; that they speak truthfully with one another; and that they preserve the practices of awakening and encourage one another to live with peace and harmony in the world. I felt that the Buddhist teacher meetings we had with the Dalai Lama were held in exactly that spirit.

We gathered in Dharamsala, a little town in the far north of India, perched on the wall of the Himalayan mountains. It is the site of the Tibetan government in exile, and the meetings were held in the Dalai Lama's residence. The Western teachers sat in a circle facing the Dalai Lama, who was flanked by six other respected Tibetan lamas. He would come in, smile, and go around and shake everybody's hand. When the Dalai Lama shakes your hand, he looks at you to make sure that you're really there, and then the handshake lingers for a minute. He gives it that extra couple of seconds to make sure that you really make contact.

At the opening of our meeting, vipassana and Zen teacher and historian Stephen Batchelor gave a lecture on the 2,500-year-old dialogue between the Buddha and the West. He began with the Greek teacher Menander, who had some knowledge of the Buddha's teaching, and also referenced sutras in which the Buddha mentioned the Greeks. Even at the time of the Buddha, the East and West were talking to each other!

From the beginning of the gathering, the Dalai Lama emphasized that what truly matters is the spirit of compassion, actions that benefit beings in every form, in every realm on this Earth. Speaking to us as fellow Dharma teachers, he said, "Don't think about how I can spread Buddhism. It doesn't matter if there is even one or two more Buddhists. The only thing that matters is the well-being of each person and the well-being of the Earth that we live on. The rest is really secondary."

So we began to talk about our concerns. One of the first discussions we had was about who is a genuine teacher, the transmission from teacher to student, the authorization of teachers. "Strictly speaking," the Dalai Lama said, "no one can create a teacher; no one can authorize a teacher. Only the students of a teacher can do it. If a teacher brings benefit to the hearts of those students, brings awakening to the lives of those students, then you can say, 'Yes, that is a true teacher.'"

The Dalai Lama paused for a minute. Then he continued, "You should remember that nirvana has a beautiful scent like flowers. You can tell when you are around people who are connected with nirvana; you can tell when you are in a place where there's a fragrance of peace, a fragrance of well-being, a fragrance of liberation. So you should look for that, smell that, listen for that."

The Dalai Lama told us, "You must go back and caution these Western students not to take teachers so quickly. They should spy on their teachers for many years. You must be convinced that a teacher is authentically awakened in some way that will be of benefit in your life. Only then should you follow them."

Our discussion with the Dalai Lama shifted to the role of the Dharma teacher and how isolating it can be, how one needs time to rest. Someone said that as a teacher it was important to be "off duty" sometimes. The Dalai Lama was puzzled by this expression and asked, "What does this mean 'off duty'?" We tried to explain what we meant, and finally he figured it out. "Oh," he said, "Off duty." He sat silently for a few minutes and looked at us Western teachers, his gaze traveling around the room. Finally he said, "Bodhisattva off duty? Buddha off duty? Very strange concept!" After our laughter died down, the Dalai Lama continued, "You might not be teaching all the time, but your responsibility is to your practice. Every place you are must be your practice, no exceptions."

We talked about what to do when we have a conflict with our own teachers. For example, what if we find that our teacher is doing something unethical, and yet we have taken these great vows that bind our spirit to that teacher? For people who have that experience it can be agony, because they love their teachers and yet have discovered these disturbing things were going on.

The Dalai Lama told us, "You know, it was the same for me. When I was younger, in Tibet, I had two regents who were supposed to care for Tibet until I came of age. These regents, who were also my teachers, were power hungry and began to fight among themselves. They even got the Tibetan army involved, and it was terrible for our country. At one point I even had to call in the Chinese army, which was a very terrible thing, because the consequence of that was further loss of Tibetan freedom. I had to publicly denounce my own regents and teachers to all of Tibet and say, 'This is wrong, this is not following the Dharma.' You must always let people know when things are wrong. Put it in the newspapers if you must do so. Tell people there is no price that is worth paying to cover up that which is wrong. We must let people know."

Talking about corruption in high places inevitably led to the subject of sexual misconduct. Someone brought up tantric practices, which teach the marriage of masculine and feminine energies and make use of a symbolic wedding and sexual union. These practices are depicted in paintings of men and women joined together, and there are stories of teachers who engage their students in such exercises. The Dalai Lama was asked if such stories were true.

His Holiness replied that there were stories about gurus such as the great Tibetan teacher Tilopa who had sex with various students who were subsequently enlightened. Then he said that he didn't know how to do this practice. He said, "People have asked me to do this practice with them, but I'm a monk, so it is never appropriate. Truthfully, you can only do such practice if there is no sexual desire whatsoever. The kind of realization that is required is like this: If someone gives you a goblet of wine and a glass of urine, or a plate of wonderful food and a plate of excrement, you must be in such a state that you can eat and drink from all four and it makes no difference to you what they are. Then maybe you can do this practice."

Then somebody in the back of the room joked, "If we want to make sure someone is ready to do this practice, at least we now have a taste test." After the laughter died down, someone else asked, "How many lamas or teachers can do this?" The Dalai Lama replied, "Very few." One intrepid woman pursued this further, "Well, who?" And he thought for a while and then he looked up and said, "Zero. Nobody that I can think of."

There were a series of presentations about Dharma psychology, one by Edie Irwin, who works with Akong Rinpoche in Scotland helping develop a five-year Dharma/therapy program, which includes three years of work with the emotional and physical body as part of the preparation for deep meditation. The Dalai Lama's questions about psychology were simple: is it of benefit to students; does it help their practice; is it in accord with the Dharma? He suggested that, just as they have counselors in the big monasteries in Tibet, perhaps we need counselors in our centers as well as meditation teachers.

One of the most interesting discussions we had with the Dalai Lama concerned the issue of women in Buddhism, and particularly how women have or have not fit into the patriarchal structure of Buddhism in Asian cultures. One of the women at the meeting was Sylvia Wetzel, who is both a vipassana and Tibetan teacher in Germany. She began by addressing the Tibetans: "Your Holiness, rinpoches, lamas, I would like to teach you a new meditation, a visualization that you have not practiced before." All the Tibetans suddenly perked up. Then she said, "I would like you to begin to meditate. Imagine that you enter this hall, a wonderful room with a big golden Buddha at one end. When you look closely, you see this big golden Buddha is a female Buddha, a Tara. Then you look around, and all the great paintings (there were dozens of beautiful paintings on the walls) are of women bodhisattvas, all female. They are choosing to be female because it is the most beautiful and best way to express the teachings of enlightenment in the world. Then you look in front of you, and sitting there in the center is the 14th Dakini Dalai Lama, who has always come back as a woman because it is the deepest expression of compassion to incarnate in the world in a female form. Next to her are all of the other great women teachers of the lineage. Then they begin to teach the great sutras, in which the Buddha says this and she says that. Of course, when we use the word *she* we mean to include you men as well in that word. We welcome you. There's a place for you in the back. You can sit with us, but do not speak too much. In our great monasteries we teach about the benefit of being born in a female body and how, yes, it's possible to be enlightened in a male body, although it has some difficulties, but we will assist you the best we can. If you want to, you can visit our monasteries. We have some little cottages on the side for you, if you don't mind helping with the cooking and cleaning."

You should have seen the faces of the assembled teachers as she offered this visualization! In all likelihood, none of us had been presented with this issue in such a powerful and imaginative manner.

Sylvia was followed by Ani Tenzin Palmo, a Western Tibetan nun with thirty years of practice. She had spent six years in a monastery in Ladakh, then twelve years in a cave in Lahul Valley on the border of Tibet. She approached the Dalai Lama and said, "Your Holiness, I would like to speak about what happens to women as nuns. The Buddha invited the sons and daughters of good families to go forth, to take ordination, as you have, Your Holiness, and to live a life of simplicity, kindness, and contentment, totally devoted to truth and compassion. And it is these people, the monks and nuns, who for over 2,500 years have gone off to become a shining example for the world. Their joy demonstrates that one can live independent of mate-rialism, of grasping, of all the things that entangle and bring so much pain to this Earth. The Buddha asks the monks and nuns to go forth and be this kind of example."

The Dalai Lama loves monks and nuns, and Ani Tenzin Palmo spoke so eloquently that I was ready to be a monk again by the time she had finished her introduction. Then she said, "Now, let me tell you, Your Holiness, how it actually is for us as nuns. We ordain out of this great faith and wonderful inspiration, and we're given our robes, but then a few days later our teacher leaves. We're not told how to wear our robes; we're not given teachings on the vows that we've taken; we're not given systematic teachings at all because the women have such a low rank in the monasteries. Often we're not given places to stay; we have to fend for ourselves and find our own food. The great lamas are too busy teaching at big centers and traveling in the West, trying to spread the Dharma, and nuns are the last of their priorities. Sometimes we're sent to help as secretaries, or to cook, or to support others. I've seen so many women, Your Holiness, come and ordain with a desire to live the holy life, the sacred life that you offer, and they end up so incredibly disheartened and discouraged. They try to practice, as I did in a cave in India, with so little support that in the end they leave, and it's not because of lack of sincerity, but because no one even knew that they were there doing it."

She spoke in such an eloquent way that by the time she was finished, the Dalai Lama put his head in his hands and began weeping. Everybody in the room cried. The Dalai Lama finally looked up at her and said, "This is outrageous. I didn't know it was that difficult. What can I do?"

His question was answered by Ani Thubten Chödrön, a nun from Seattle, who said, "Well, Your Holiness, we have a list. First of all, we would like there to be a slow selection process to guide who should actually be ordained, with Western nuns and monks as well as Tibetan lamas involved in the process. We would also like there to be a nunnery that is built to train and support women teachers." The Dalai Lama said, "Done. We will do that."

Then she said, "We would also like there to be a council to look at the inequities between men and women and to figure out ways to change these things, especially as Tibetan Buddhism comes to the West."

The Dalai Lama told the women that he would call a council. They asked him when he would call it. He replied that he would do it soon. They asked him how soon. He finally said, "Okay, six months. I will do it in six months."

A couple of Tibetan monks from Europe also spoke in a very candid way with the Dalai Lama. They told him they wanted a special teacher training for Tibetan lamas who are coming to the West, so that they can learn about the emotional and psychological problems of students they'll encounter, the ethical issues that have beset teachers, and the ways they can support Western teachers and students. The Dalai Lama told the monks that he would set up such a training. As the Western nuns and monks presented their concerns, the Dalai Lama listened and began dealing with them immediately.

At our gathering we also spoke about engaged Buddhism, which is very dear to the Dalai Lama's heart. We discussed the issues of poverty, injustice, and the arms race. When someone brought up the issue of overpopulation, the Dalai Lama said that he practiced a very gentle form of birth control. Then he looked at another monk, Ajahn Amaro, from Amaravati in England, and asked, "You, monk, what do you think of birth control?" Ajahn Amaro replied, "I think it's a very good idea, but actually I think we Buddhists also practice rebirth control." The Dalai Lama cracked up; he thought that was one of the funniest things he had ever heard.

When we were talking about engaged Buddhism, the Dalai Lama said that he has a personal crusade to stop arms sales throughout the world. He said, "If people get angry and they have weapons, they can do horrible damage. If they're angry and they don't have weapons, maybe they hit each other with their fists, but that's not so bad. We must speak out about this terrible spreading of weapons. We must make a change."

The spirit of our meeting with the Dalai Lama was very empowering. At one point he said, "Drop the titles. You don't need to call yourselves lamas or roshis. Drop the costumes. Change the teachings to fit your own culture. Even I am not sure about some of our teachings about heaven and hell realms. So maybe the Dalai Lama is a heretic too, except that I am the Dalai Lama and they will not kick me out. But you must see what is true for yourself and what is true for your culture. You must be the judge of that. We have to make these changes even if some of our Asian teachers don't understand."

Finally, together as a group we drafted a letter that spoke of the issues we had discussed. We went over this letter with the Dalai Lama, and it was wonderful to watch him listen to all the points of the letter, because his mind was so lucid, compassionate, and diplomatic. He would stop us and ask, "Is that the best word? Maybe people will feel that is judging or condescending. It doesn't honor them. Let's change the language a little bit." It was like being with Thomas Jefferson.

At the close of the last meeting, we all gave prayer shawls and scarfs to the Dalai Lama, and he gave gifts and blessings back. Then he looked around and said to us, "You know, when we began, you were all so serious and so respectful, and you had so many problems. As the week went on I saw everyone smiling more and more. Today everyone is smiling and very happy. I think that means we had a very good meeting."

From Volume 8, Number 2 (Spring 1992).

Author's Note: Fifteen years later in 2007 there have been some positive developments on the issues we discussed. There have been nunneries built and councils held for the support and empowerment of Buddhist women and nuns, and the Dalai Lama has participated in this. But the process is still in the early stages. There is also better understanding among many Asian Buddhist teachers about what is needed to support Western Dharma students for the long term and more attention given to teacher-student ethics. Unfortunately, the Dalai Lama's and the meeting participants' call to end the spread of weapons sales worldwide has thus far gone unheeded.

II

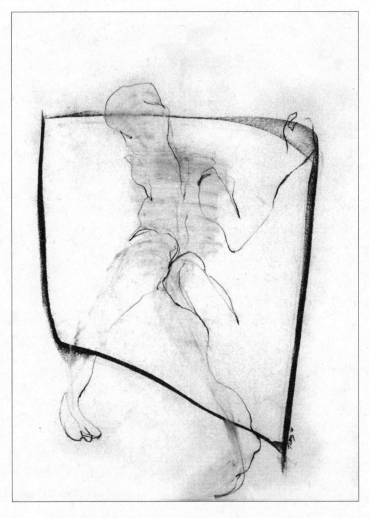

LIVING & DYING IN A BODY

W alking the path requires a body, accompanied by its nervous system, primal instincts, emotions, and the overrated and desperately insistent ego. In this section we explore the flesh and its attendant joys and conflicts. As a novice nun, Diana Winston finds unexpected wisdom through her menstrual cycle. Celebrating her fiftieth birthday and struggling with aging, Terry Vandiver tries to seduce the Buddha with a belly dance. Meditation teacher Caitriona Reed tells us that he is a she. Author Kate Wheeler liberates us from attachment to the body by contemplating the "loathsome." Frank Ostaseski of the Zen Hospice tells us inspirational stories of "lives lived and now ending." Writer Rick Fields introduces a teenage boy to the Medicine Buddha when they are both dying of cancer. And Ronna Kabatznik gets a powerful lesson in the aftermath of the recent tsunami in Thailand as she holds the hands of family members searching through bodies for their loved ones. As the Buddha said, "Within this fathom-long body the entire universe may be known."

1 Mr. Lucky

By Rick Kohn

"Of all the gin joints in all the world, you have to walk into this one."

A billion cold rocks, scarred and pitted,
Hurtle through space. Given the odds,

Aren't we lucky, so unfathomably, incomprehensibly lucky,
Just to be alive.

A stray beam of light careens from one of these rocks.
Hits something. Bounces to something else
In a thing called my eye.
Behold—a magnolia in full bloom—
hanging like an apparition above the San Francisco Bay—
a lotus field from a Buddhist paradise.

How can I say I am not lucky? When a billion years of intergalactic
accidents have conspired to bring me this gift.

Indecision. Right? Left? Right? Left? I walk through a door
and there is the love of my life.

How lucky, how unfathomably, uncharacteristically lucky, that I just
didn't blow it.

Her face reddens and strains. She screams. Another minute surely she shall die. Or I will. Then the baby's head emerged, tiny tired perfection, weary as an old man, radiant as an angel.

How can I say that I'm not lucky? Just to be alive.

A doctor walks in. She need say nothing. The answer is etched in her eyes. Those shadows on your liver are cancer, metastatic cancer.

But how can I say that I'm not lucky?
Just to be alive.
Like you.

⋄
⋄   From Volume 17, Number 1 (Fall 2000).
⋄

2   Getting It? Or How I Learned to Let Go

By Diana Winston

The night before I left for Burma to ordain as a Buddhist nun, I held a good-bye gathering with a group of my friends in San Francisco. Moving around the room, I asked everyone in the circle to offer me blessings for my trip. The replies ran a loving but predictable gamut from wishes for health and adventure to a safe return. When I got to my friend Maura, she paused for a moment and then said, "My blessing for you is menstruation." Huh? The room was stilled by a confused silence. "Well," she continued, "when you are there, if you lose touch with yourself, if you become overwhelmed by an ascetic, male-dominated tradition, when you bleed you can remember your connection to the Earth and yourself as a woman."

At fourteen I had been one of the only girls in my class not yet to have gotten her period. This was a tremendous source of pain and embarrassment to me. My father attributed it to my mother's insistence on a vegetarian diet for me since the age of seven. Whatever the reason, as a fourteen-year-old I had a short, scrawny ten-year-old's body without the slightest hint of the woman to come. So while the pretty girls with developed breasts and pubic hair dated, I studied. I was way ahead academically but a million years behind socially. And so was my blood, which at some unforeseen moment (please, oh please, soon) would flow from between my legs and mark my entry into true womanhood.

The wait was excruciating. I pleaded, prayed, and bargained with God: "If it comes soon, I promise never to hit my brother again." I wondered, like a woman fearing an unwanted pregnancy, how it could be induced. I endlessly compared myself to all my friends who talked with secret smirks about pads and cramps and the trauma of buying the necessary paraphernalia at the local drugstore. I covered my face with my long red hair and tried to pretend I wasn't different.

It did come of course. One day I went to the toilet and found brown stains on my underpants. The mixture of sheer relief together with a feeling of revulsion brought stinging tears to my eyes. I was normal. I, too, now had my badge. And in that tender state of exultation, I also became aware on a deeper level of a truth about my life. You can't make things happen; they will come in their own time. My job was simply to be patient and to stop the mental flurry of anxiety and worry. It may have been my first lesson in trusting things as they are.

Seventeen years later, on the day I ordained as a nun, my period stopped. I jokingly attributed its absence to "having given myself to God" (and its re-emergence a few months later to an unstoppable biological process that wouldn't take no for an answer). Was my ordination an act deliberately to defeminize myself? Unquestionably. For a year I was choosing to enter the ranks of the thousands of women who had come before me, the nuns who had followed the Buddha's injunction to abandon their lives as wives and mothers, to become celibate, committed only to Dharma. By shaving my head, taking the eight precepts, donning the salmon-colored robes (I wouldn't be caught dead in pink, the other alternative), I was saying good-bye both to my possessions and to my identity as a woman.

As I first had my head shaved with a new Schick Injector razor, waves of fear and excitement coursed through my body. Thirty years of pride, sexuality, and personal history fell off in clumps, landing in my yellow plastic bucket. My new robes covered up my curves, their four layers preventing anyone from seeing what was underneath. I chose to look in the mirror only on the days of my weekly head-shaving (an event that rapidly grew easier until, after seven months, I could, all by myself, reach a smooth skull in twenty minutes flat).

I put my female self on hold. For a year. As a nun I chose to observe the workings of my mind around my identity as a woman. It was an experiment I willingly undertook, not out of some internalized puritanism, misogyny, or hatred of my body, but as a deliberate attempt to see what else might arise when I looked beyond how I had always defined myself. It was much like my decision to watch my mind around food cravings, having also committed myself to no longer eating after noon.

After the first few months of nunhood, despite the occasional faux pas such as "scandalously" (and unintentionally) revealing my underskirt, or allowing the stubble on my scalp to reach the "indecent" length of half an inch, I was mostly able to adjust. Through these acts of renunciation, I gradually stopped focusing on myself as a woman. With that, I could then turn my attention to what becoming a nun was really all about: Getting Enlightened.

After six months of intensive monastic practice—and on the heels of years of ongoing meditation, study, and devotion—I presumed it was finally time I reached nibbana. My practice was good, or so I thought. Everybody else had "gotten it," or so it seemed. I had worked hard, I was ready, and I deserved it. I fantasized about a mind free from egoic grasping, a mind that was pure and wise. I wanted enlightenment, and I was here in Burma in hopes of inducing it.

But when it didn't seem to be happening for me, I began to pray, to plead, to cry. I started the bargaining process: If it comes soon, I promise to use my wisdom only for the benefit of all beings. I strategized, If I sit for just one more hour… Then I began the ghastly game of comparing myself with everyone I saw: That monk is easily a stream-enterer, and he's younger than I am! And what about all those people at the time of the Buddha? Just one word from him and they were liberated on the spot. It's not fair, why wasn't I born then? What about me? It was nonstop self-hatred, comparing mind, anxiety, the works.

This leaning-forward created a tremendous cycle of suffering for me. Each moment of anything other than enlightenment (which seemed to be every moment) was a huge disappointment. I would stuff the disappointment deeper inside me and longingly view a future that the sayadaws so readily assured me was at my fingertips. I was convinced that at some point my mind would open to the moment when delusion would be uprooted forever. I was on a mission and would not settle for anything less. Any beautiful mindstate; any peace or equanimity or joy; any insight into anicca, dukkha, or anatta were nothing compared to what was undoubtedly to come (please, oh please, soon): my nibbana.

As the craving for enlightenment grew more intense, my "strong" and "competent" practice began to spiral downward. My mindfulness grew murky, imprecise. I started having crying fits. I began to doubt myself more and more. As deeper and deeper levels of self-hatred pounded me like crashing waves, I dutifully tried to "note" them away. This went on for many weeks, and the pain became unbearable. I finally announced to the sayadaws that I hated everything, and I threatened to leave. There would be nothing they could do to stop me.

In the agonizing days that followed, my mind alternated between an overwhelming sense of failure and elaborate fantasies of escaping to the beaches of southern Thailand. Then one morning while attending to my menstrual ablutions, I looked down at the blood on my fingertips. Suddenly the memory of being a teenager resurfaced. All this wanting, I realized, was just like my fourteen-year-old self trying to speed up a process that's natural and has a logic of its own. It can't be sped up. My approach to reaching enlightenment was strangely aligned with my fourteen-year-old experience of reaching womanhood.

The memory sank into me. How ironic. I laughed and cried. I had been applying little-girl logic to a process that may take eons. I told myself to relax, to stop trying. I realized that I had to learn to sit with the suffering of wanting things to be different—a challenge, if nothing else, I had no choice but to rise to. All the leaning forward of my mind had clearly been preventing me from accepting whatever was present. Subtle and not so subtle craving for things to be different seemed a hallmark of my practice.

This realization was the beginning of my letting go of enlightenment as a goal. I saw that planning for my liberation had been underlying my practice for nearly ten years. At its core lay the belief that in some future moment I would be cured of all my dreadful imperfections—my anger and rudeness, my sometimes cruel and hurtful sarcasm, my lust and uncaringness. Not only would my personality be transformed so that I'd never hurt another being, but I would undergo such a life-transforming experience that when I came out the other side I would have the sage-like wisdom to know exactly how to help this suffering planet in its time of crisis. Just plain Diana, as I was, simply was not good enough. I had never wanted to be me.

Taking a deep breath, I decided to stay on at the monastery. My practice began to shift from being about something specific to being about nothing in particular. In that shift was a different kind of freedom that I had never before experienced. The following months were ripe with a joy and brilliance that I can barely begin to describe. Enlightenment for me came to rest squarely on freedom in the moment. At the same time, I recognized the enormous mystery of enlightenment's unfolding, involving many moments of freedom both large and small. From that point in my practice, I could no longer view it as a goal outside of myself. That craving had caused me too much pain and suffering. No matter what I got or didn't get, I had to simply continue practicing.

Later in the year, many more months into my retreat, a German woman about my age stopped me on the path by the lake. A fellow practitioner, she looked at me cautiously and asked, "Would you like to have tea in my room?" My look of surprise told her she had trespassed a bit, but in a welcome way. It was the first contact I'd had with a Westerner in months.

I gratefully followed her, and for the next three hours we sipped too-sweet Nescafe from packets and talked nonstop, eyes glowing, about the snakes and scorpions at the center, future plans (she was leaving Burma in a week), and monastery politics. We laughed about the time I had gotten in trouble for complaining about the size of the lunch table. We discussed which translator was best, whether Burmese Pali pronunciation was even remotely accurate, and whether we'd ever have children.

Even though we had never talked until that day, at the end of the morning we were hard and fast friends, bonded in that way that comes only from months of silent practice together and a mutual love of the Dharma. As I got up to go she suddenly said, "Wait. My mom sent me hundreds of tampons, and I want to offer them to you as dana. I can get plenty in Europe. Could you use some?"

I had read that nuns at the time of the Buddha were allowed only four worldly possessions. Like monks, they had two sets of robes, a bowl, and a razor. Unlike monks, nuns were given a string to tie on old rags for menstruation. "Well, of course," I smiled in reply. "What girl couldn't?" I was running low on tampons, having originally planned for only six months at the monastery.

There it was. A female-to-female transmission. You take care of me. I take care of the Dharma. The Dharma takes care of the world. Amid the confines of the ascetic and male-dominated monastic system, our feminine hygiene exchange felt intimate and delightfully subversive. My friend Maura's words of blessing echoed in my head as I mindfully almost-skipped back to my kuti.

From Volume 16, Number 1 (Fall 1999).

3 Mara's Daughter Turns Fifty
Belly Dancing for the Buddha

By Terry Vandiver

I swished my blue feather boa at the Buddha and tried to entice him with undulating belly rolls and hip circles full of promise, but the Buddha wasn't impressed. Maybe it was because of my aging body or maybe it was because I hadn't belly danced for fifteen years. Or maybe it was because he was the Buddha.

Whatever the reason, I had been flattered and amused when asked to play Mara's daughter in a children's production about the life of the Buddha. In this play, Mara, the embodiment of greed, hatred, and ignorance, is dressed as a sleazy playboy, with cigar, dark glasses, and smoking jacket. As the Bodhisattva sits under the bodhi tree on the eve of his enlightenment, Mara sends his luscious belly-dancing daughter (me) to distract him.

I may have failed to entice the Buddha, but the dance sparked an ember that still smoldered in my aging loins. I remembered how good it felt to flirt and dance seductively, and so, wanting more, I decided to do a really hot belly dance to celebrate my fiftieth birthday.

Isabel Allende published a sexy cookbook in her fiftieth year. She wrote, "The fiftieth year of our life is like the last hour of dusk, when the sun has set and one turns naturally toward reflection. In my case, however, dusk incites me to sin." As for myself, dusk incited me to belly dance, and when the opportunity arose to perform at a big millennial New Year's party, I seized the moment. I wanted this dance to be my celebration of life, the feminine, the body—an expression of universal creativity. It would also be my one last fling as the seductive belly dancer, and then I would take seriously the Buddha's teachings about the pain of attachment to beauty and youth and slip gracefully into freedom.

I had thought fifty was going to be just another birthday, but as I approached the dusk of life and my big performance, I began to reflect on my future options and my fading physical assets. Most of my life I had enjoyed the attention I got for being pretty and having a nice soprano voice. One of my most fulfilling moments had been when I starred as Maria in a high school production of *West Side Story*. I glowed as I danced in front of the mirror and sang, "I feel pretty, oh so pretty." I thought being pretty was the most important thing a girl could be.

In my twenties I discovered that I could use my petite body to attract men. A love affair with my Greek folk-dance teacher, who showed me how to translate the passion of Greek music into my body, led to belly dance classes and eventually my first dancing job at a Greek nightclub, a fling with a bouzouki player, and then on to the Casbah, an Arab nightclub in San Francisco.

I was small-breasted and skinny-legged, but I had learned the power of a well-timed hip drop, the allure of a graceful hand delicately poised at the brow, head tilted, smoky eyes aimed at someone in the audience. I let my hand slide smoothly down over a shoulder to perch lightly on a hip, as I inscribed a perfect figure eight with my body. I enjoyed moving seductively and feeling men's eyes on me.

But at some point what began as a glamorous adventure and a love of the art of Middle Eastern dance began to feel degrading. Entertaining men in a hot, smoky bar just wasn't fun anymore. Finally, one night at 3 A.M., fully made-up and bejeweled, I climbed into the old, beat-up Dodge truck I used for my daytime job as a gardener and said good-bye to Arab men and tourists sticking moist bills into my bra.

After I quit the Casbah I didn't belly dance again for fifteen years. I devoted myself to my gardens and studied yoga and Buddhist meditation. As I began to awaken to my own conditioning, I saw how attached I was to looking good. For instance, I continued to wear eye makeup on silent retreats, where eye contact was discouraged. Sometimes on retreat, I even caught myself walking slightly swishy if I imagined that someone was watching. Eventually, on a two-month intensive, I gave myself the practice of not looking in the mirror, which brought me a taste of the relief that can come from not identifying with the features of one's body and face.

Still, at forty-nine, I was committed—and looking forward—to dancing at the millennial party. In order to prepare, I started taking Middle Eastern dance classes at Suhaila Salimpour's School of Dance. At that time, the teacher, Suhaila, was eight-months pregnant, and I marveled at how she could move with such energy and control. I joined the group of young women that snaked around her mirrored studio, buoyed by the compelling rhythms of the drums. I could still move pretty well myself, and I didn't care if I was the oldest woman in the class. Besides, I told myself, this was strictly about fun and exercise.

Suhaila's classes weren't like the belly dance classes that I had taken in the past. We didn't swish chiffon veils, and we didn't bounce, thrust, or shake wildly. In the interests of creating a unique and artistic American belly dance form, Suhaila had us practice control. We learned how to isolate our "glutes," quickly squeezing and releasing one buttock and then the other to facilitate precise hip movements. Our upper body undulations were distinct from our lower body undulations. We practiced "layering," fast hip shimmies with smooth rib-cage circles on top. I loved the challenge and the restrained passion, the circle of hip or torso exuding possibility.

I became so drawn to these dance classes that I left a ten-day meditation retreat where I was teaching yoga to enter Suhaila's hot, humid inferno where beautiful young women in tights and work-out bras gyrated to the beat of a Lebanese techno-rock band.

Yet even though the dancing made me feel young and sexy, sometimes after class I would become sad or agitated. I realized that I was having fantasies about dancing in a nightclub again, but then, suddenly, I would remember that I had undependable knees, frequent backaches, and wrinkles in my cheeks. Perhaps I would be better off putting my energy into some other pursuit.

Meanwhile, the New Year's party was fast approaching. I was wavering about belly dancing in front of my friends but didn't want to back out of my commitment. Finally, the day arrived. As I stood in front of the dressing room mirror, I pinched the flesh on my exposed belly and heard myself say aloud, "Cellulite! Oh well." I applied a final bit of hair spray to guarantee that my short hair looked rumpled and sexy, like I had just gotten out of bed. I was wearing a leopard print see-through T-shirt which revealed a black padded push-up bra underneath. Twenty-inch black fringe swished over a silver skirt carefully slit to reveal bare legs.

I heard the emcee announce, "And here she is." I evoked hoots and hollers as I entered the crowded room. I had prepared well but still suffered the pre-performance pain of hope and fear. Will the audience see the greatness of the dance? The greatness of the body? My greatness? I longed for perfection.

The music started and stopped as the DJ fiddled with the sound. I started again. I had painstakingly choreographed this introduction but now became rattled. My first turns were tentative as I felt my high heels slip on the hardwood floor. I hadn't worn heels for fifteen years.

But then the music picked up and everyone cheered. In an instant I was back, gone, in the "zone," Mara's daughter in her fullness. A man rose from the front row and came to me. He tried to tuck a bill into my sequined hip wrap. I remembered that this was something I knew how to do. Playfully I wove my shimmying hip, moving so that it was challenging for him to complete the tuck. He managed, and I beamed at him and took off. I began to abandon all choreography, improvising with the different currents of the music, punctuating with a hip drop, a quick undulation of the spine, a subtle toss of the head. Hips responded freely to the underlying beat while the upper body was expressive, mirroring the fluid melody. Spine rippled up to down, down to up. Interior hip circles created intrigue. Where would it go next?

After the performance I soaked up the compliments from both men and women. Several women thanked me for "honoring the feminine." I felt affirmed when one said that the dance immediately made people feel happy. The highest honor came from a young woman who described my dance as "awesome."

I felt light and happy. Until later, when I watched the video of the performance. The dance seemed to lack pizzazz: the music called for faster shimmies and more fiery turns. Forgotten were years of work trying to "correct" rounded shoulders and sunken chest. I saw life's difficulties reflected in the carriage of the little dancer on the screen. As I continued to watch the moving black-and-white image of myself, embarrassment and disappointment finally began to soften into compassion. I saw fearful eyes peering from behind the mask of an aging woman, and waves of acceptance for being human brought relief.

Now that the party is over, what stays with me are the few perfect moments in the dance, but even more so the moments of letting go as I watched the video. These days I am much more aware of the mind clutching as I look into the mirror and pour over lines and gray hairs. Sometimes the mind lets go, and sometimes it doesn't. Now and then Mara, dressed as a slick traveling salesman, knocks on my door and thrusts the latest wrinkle cream in my face. Sometimes I buy, and sometimes I politely say to him, "I'm not interested."

From Volume 17, Number (Fall 2000).

4 Coming Out Whole

By Caitriona Reed

This past April I gave up hiding. The energy I had been using to maintain a life of secrecy was exhausted. I could no longer bear to live with the fear and shame that had haunted me. I let it be known that I am a transgendered person, a transsexual. I came out of the closet!

For about sixteen years I have taught Buddhism and Buddhist meditation. For the last eight years or so it has been my main occupation, my job description. Although I have been "out" among certain friends for about twenty years, to truly come out of the closet has always meant coming out within my community of students and fellow teachers. Only now do I realize how incomplete I have been because I have not had the courage to do that. The whole process of my transition, whatever that might turn out to be, has been on hold.

I, like all of us, have been afraid. Fear makes us lie. It cripples us, even though we may get comfortable enough to move around within the confines of our deceptions. Then we end up inhabiting them, and they become an invisible shell that we drag around with us. I wandered, lost in obsession and fantasy, not knowing where my secret would lead me. I couldn't imagine it would lead anywhere but to more shame and to rejection by the people I cared for. I started to come out once, over ten years ago, and began to make a transition. My fear quickly drove me back into the closet.

I assumed that an apparently intelligent male person, a literate person, a spiritual person (a Buddhist teacher, for goodness sake!) could hardly be taken seriously in a dress. After all, wasn't I supposed to have smoothed out all the rough edges and transcended desires altogether? Perhaps if there were some demon desires still lingering, I should simply go away and meditate some more!

The assumptions we have about our gender are reinforced on a daily basis. We have layers of social, cultural, and emotional conditioning supporting our ideas of what it means to be masculine or feminine. For most of us, our designated gender is at the very core of who we think we are and goes largely unquestioned. We would question our race, cultural or economic station, religion, politics, and just about everything else before questioning our assumed gender.

The common assumption is that what you have between your legs is your gender, but there is a constellation of other factors—hormonal and behavioral—that make us masculine or feminine. What you have between your legs is sex (male or female). Gender (masculine or feminine) is between your ears; it is the whole of your life, your emotional and mental makeup, the way you present yourself in society, the way you interact with others, your imagination, the theater of your being.

Sex is the American obsession, so it's not surprising that almost everything gets sexualized. The first thing people wonder about a transgendered person is how they have sex and who they have it with; but being transgendered may have as much to do with sex as riding a bike or baking cookies. Some of us are born male and feel we are women; some of us are born female and feel we are men. Some of us are gay, some straight, some asexual, some bisexual. We should avoid generalizations.

In recent years, the term *transgendered* has allowed a community—which includes cross-dressers, drag queens, and transsexuals—to describe ourselves and to unite to gain recognition and civil rights. There is an increasing movement away from stereotyping, and there is also an increasing demand that we be demedicalized. The society that has confused gender identity with reproductive organs has little tolerance for variation. It's hardly surprising that someone not fitting the stereotypes is rejected as a freak. Personally, I would like to question the paradigm that insists I must be unmistakably either a man or a woman.

My earliest memories have to do with understanding myself to be a girl rather than, or perhaps as well as, a boy. I still have a scar from the brick that was thrown at me in kindergarten because I always played with the girls. It was, of course, the boys who objected and came to get me, bricks and sticks in hand.

Boarding school was a strange ordeal. Looking back at the ways I managed to compensate, I am amazed and saddened. For me, to be a man was to be afraid, angry, and alone. I once wrote a poem titled "I'd Rather Be a

Woman Than Have to Be Right." There's something about the burden of the stereotypical masculine role that always remained extremely uncomfortable, a barrier between myself and the world.

The Dharma, the practice of Buddhism, has been my refuge. For a while it was a way to be safe behind my wall. More recently, though, despite my best efforts, it became the means to break down the wall. I never meant it to happen that way, but now my life, my heart, insist that I be honest. As the barriers disintegrate, I step out from behind them, just as I am. Of course, I have always been aware of the puritanism, homophobia, and intolerance that lurk within Buddhism and within institutionalized spirituality in general, especially in America. The pomposity and posturing, the reluctance to come clean and be simple, honest, and human is astonishing and utterly sad; and it still frightens me. Buddhism is not always the Dharma; just as the Church is not always Christian. Despite that—because of that—I step out anyway.

I still don't know where this road will lead. I have now resumed the use of hormones under medical supervision after erratic self-medication for a number of years. If I end up undergoing sex reassignment surgery, it is not so much to cure the malady of Gender Identity Disorder as it is to continue the celebration of life.

I am in a monogamous relationship with a woman, with whom I teach and to whom I am married. Michele and I are best friends. She has known who I am since we first came together seventeen years ago. I feel blessed that Michele and I have something much more akin to a partnership, in which we are strengthened by a mutual and ongoing determination to question all stereotypes.

Four months have gone by since my April coming out. I could never have guessed the response I would get from friends in our community and now also from strangers as I teach around the world. "Thank you for coming out. I feel I now have permission to be who I am," was a response I received from more than one person. "Thanks for challenging our expectations. That is your job, isn't it?" said one of my students. "This means we'll all have to come out," said my friend and teacher Joanna Macy, with whom I had shared my secret years ago but who had tears in her voice when I spoke to her on the phone about my coming out. She was expecting the birth of her grandchild within the next day or two. She said, "Now I can celebrate two births." When I saw my teacher Thich Nhat Hanh, he simply asked, "Do we call you 'Caitriona' now?"

Where does this leave me? I've spoken the words, declaring myself to be a transgendered person. I have painted my nails and painted my face. Every day I move a little further into this newfound freedom. I am undergoing intensive electrolysis to eliminate my beard. When I go out for the evening, it feels fine to put on my face and dress up. It doesn't feel like it's such a big deal anymore. So, what do I do now? Is my life doomed to become no more than a series of fashion statements? A little experiment in performance art? The first Buddhist teacher in America (that I know of) to be a transsexual? I don't pass as a woman—many transsexuals don't—but that is not the issue. Passing may mean going back into another closet, that same closet of unquestioned stereotypical identity. Even so, I am delighted to be called "ma'am"—especially when I'm not even trying to pass.

A part of my motivation in coming out was to stand up and be counted. Knowing what it's like to hide, I hope to make it a little easier, by my example, for others to reveal themselves. Moreover, I wish to challenge the rigidity of gender stereotypes, which makes hiding necessary for the transgendered person in the first place, often for reasons of physical safety. If by not passing, by sticking out like a sore thumb even, I have helped to save the life of one transgendered suicidal teenager who thought he was alone. Or if one genderphobic, homophobic thug is stopped in his tracks (because, after all, I am six foot two); or if one stranger, put at ease because I am at ease, catches my eye, and we smile and all fear is dissolved, for an instant, for both of us, then my life is being well spent.

There is still fear. Perhaps I will ultimately find myself lonely and despised. Perhaps this is proof, after all, that my "spiritual" life has no validity, nor any real meaning. Perhaps, if I had attained successful insight into the nature of self, I would know that all this business about male and female, masculine and feminine, is just a dance of shadows.

Well, perhaps this is precisely what I do know, having devoted most of my life to exploring such things. Perhaps it is because this is what I know best, know in my bones, that I have the strength to come out. Perhaps it is because I have come to an appreciation of impermanence and the breathtaking interconnectedness of things that I have come to value the precious particularity of every detail of my being. I may lose a lot, I may even lose you as my friend, but I have reclaimed my life. Arrogant as it may sound, that is my gift for both of us.

How strange that organized religion has always aspired to express a certain androgyny of spirit yet insists on absolute physiological gender differentiation. To realize androgyny in our bodies is to challenge the status quo to its core. It is called the work of the Devil—or of Mara (a Buddhist counterpart). Why is desire considered so dangerous? Why is the body despised? Why do we give up the authenticity of our life to realize an invented God or a contrived Enlightenment? Is the fear of death so great that we must bargain away our natural wisdom, our sensuality and passion, our celebration and joy?

Is what I am doing skillful? Is it harmful? Am I a fool to imagine anyone will take me seriously anymore? I am beyond caring. The soft echo of this moment is enough; the softness I feel in my body, the sweetness and energy inside me. Thanks to my teachers, thanks to life, thanks to my friends, thanks to the silver light of afternoon on the delicate leaves of the trees of the chaparral forest behind our house.

Life is given to us for free. How can we repay such a gift except with the fullness of our own life? What could be better than to return life entirely to itself? I can't hesitate any longer, nor delay my own freedom. I have chosen to be whole.

From Volume 14, Number 2 (Spring 1998).

5   Meat Puppets

By Kate Lila Wheeler

Pus, boogers, peepee, poopoo. Would you believe that there is a meditation practice based on contemplating these items? It isn't for two-year-olds; it's for adults. And it is intended to lead to peace of mind, not agitation, amusement, and disgust. It's one of the classic meditation practices of the Theravadan tradition, an orderly contemplation of the thirty-two parts of the body, starting with hair of the head and ending with urine.

If this sounds gruesome, consider that life is gruesome: no one survives. Our opinions and beliefs about life and death won't offer us any special privileges. Worse yet, it's the nature of all bodies not only to die but to rot, crumble, shiver, itch, and to display various forms of ugliness. Yet the extra pain that all of us give ourselves over this entire situation seems, on reflection, unnecessary.

Buddhism offers a number of practices designed specifically to cut through our delusions about the body—charnel ground meditations, contemplations of death and loathsomeness. They are meant to undermine our normal relationship with our bodies. They ease the moment of death and the moments before death. They don't aim to ruin our happiness; instead, they expand the scope of love. If taken to heart, they exhaust the source of our greatest terrors.

The sheer volume of thoughts we devote to the body is dismaying. If we look closely at our moment-to-moment experiences, our thoughts, our wishes, and feelings, we will see that we constantly strain for more pleasure and beauty. We feel that we should be immersed in a constant orgasm of satisfaction and attractiveness.

Meanwhile, our elderly and uncompromising tradition asks us to recognize the pain involved in carting our body around, to look directly at what goes into keeping the body together. As long as we're healthy adults, we ignore it as much as we can, denying the amount of work it takes to keep it clean, fed, and exercised; submitting without a second thought to the pressures to create for ourselves a super-bionic, pleasure-giving, pleasure-attracting, never-sick body. Then we're trying to lift a heavy box and suddenly—Spang!— there's a muscle spasm in the lower back and we fall to the floor wondering if we'll ever walk again. Or, trying on jeans in the ugly light of the changing room, we see ten pounds of clabber hanging off the backs of our thighs. Any unexpected physical event can open the gates to terror; seeing a lump in our lower belly that wasn't there before, the chill of death can bolt us to our seats.

And that dauntless, unstoppable little commentator that lies inside us utters a peep of shock. This fear that is so overwhelming: where was it stored? Up to a second ago we thought we knew all the cozy rooms of our body's mansion; now we suddenly find ourselves alone and frightened, as if we were stranded on a high crag in a thunderstorm. Indeed, we may be passing into the dreaded kingdom of the ill, where we are no longer the persons we wanted to be, no longer able to become what we wanted to become, do what we wanted to do. We will be ruled by unwanted problems: pain and exhaustion, obsession and fear. We may feel that we have failed—failed to eat properly, failed to be tranquil enough—as if a life properly lived would never end.

The source of our terror is attachment: the feeling that our bodies are the most precious possessions we have. It is within this attachment and all of its associated assumptions that we live most unquestioningly. The body: what is it really? Do we actually possess it? Is it really precious and beautiful?

The good news is that even the bodies of movie stars—our gods and goddesses—are transitory. Besides, they require eight-hour workouts on top of genetic endowment. After meditating even a little on the thirty-two parts of the body, we have a different feeling about seeing anybody's bone structure—we see bones, not a cultural value.

In contemplations of the loathsome, we are asked to examine carefully all parts of the body, their actual qualities, and to ask ourselves whether we should value it the way we do. What is a human face? It is a piece of skin full of holes, "like an insect's nest," the Visuddhimagga says. The brain "is the lumps of marrow bound inside the skull. [I]t is the color of the flesh of a toadstool;...the color of turned milk." All of the body parts are visualized specifically, in detail. The twenty nail plates. The skeleton, with many bones. Imagine, as you walk along, the movements of your tiny toe bones inside your shoes; take a few minutes to remember the skull behind every face.

Do you feel horror, or a kind of relieved and interested recognition, or both? If it's horror, does it weigh the same as your denial? As the meditation progresses, with a clear picture of the body parts in mind, the instruction for entering jhanic absorption is to say suddenly to oneself, "Repulsive! Repulsive!" Acknowledging the truth is an immediate, delightful relief—the mind flips over into letting go.

It's crucial to the success of foulness practices not to get sidetracked by psychological defense systems. Remember that the small mind pursues an ostrich strategy, as if not thinking about bad things would cause them to disappear. Death and decay are the worst things, so all resources will be deployed to forget about them. One defense can be humor. You might feel highly amused by the solemnity of the creepy language in the classic meditation texts, imagining them being read in the voice of Lon Chaney. "Just as duckweed and green scum on the surface of the water divided when a stick...is dropped into the water and then spread together again, so too, at the time of eating and drinking, etc., when the food, drink, etc., fall into the stomach, the phlegm divides and then spreads together again." UUUG-GHH!!! you say. Those guys could really dish it out!!!

The mind defends itself, too, by fascination and curiosity. A friend who went to the morgue in Bangkok reported that she could feel her mind developing a sense of fascination to cover up her fear. Eventually, however, nausea overtook her and she tried to escape through the back door—only to find a courtyard full of rotting body parts and pools of blood swarming with flies.

Yet another defense can be pride in what we see as our spiritual progress through contemplating the repulsive. During one three-month course at the Insight Meditation Society, yogis were passing around photographs of three corpses. "Wow," we said, peering at the bloated face of a young woman who had drowned. It was kind of scary, kind of fun, like a game at a slumber party. Most of all, we felt we had in our hands a special means to meditational success—not an image of what we would surely, one day, become.

It's easy to dismiss and denigrate these loathsomeness practices. With yet one more line of defense we protest: Why not deny the truth as long as we can? Why dwell on the horrible side of life when, after all, we can put the same amount of energy into distracting ourselves and pursuing pleasure? Do we want to become inhuman beings who don't care whether we live or die?

But we might just as well ask if the result of loathsomeness practice might be a profound and subtle, wild and fearless joy. Perhaps, through this practice, we will come to really love life without holding back from any part of it, including the infirmities and decay of sickness and old age. Perhaps we will even be able to develop a mind that laughs at death. Why not begin to free ourselves from attachment to the body, which is disappearing anyway? What would it feel like no longer to be identified with these meat puppets we think we drag around?

From Volume 11, Number 1 (Fall 1994).

6 Stories of Lives Lived and Now Ending

By Frank Ostaseski

Inspired by a 2,500-year-old spiritual tradition, Zen Hospice Project encourages and supports a mutually beneficial relationship among volunteer caregivers and individuals facing death. Started in 1987, the project established the Guest House, a home-like residence providing twenty-four-hour care, and a twenty-eight-bed hospice unit at Laguna Honda Hospital, the nation's largest public long-term care facility. Each caregiver cultivates the "listening mind" through regular meditation or spiritual practice. This helps to develop the awareness, compassion, and balance to respond to the unique needs of the dying and to hear their stories.

The following article is adapted from an interview with the program's founding director, Frank Ostaseski, by Barbara Gates and Wes Nisker. Names have been changed to protect the confidentiality of clients.

Adele was a no-nonsense eighty-six-year-old Russian Jewish woman staying with us at the hospice. I got the call that she was dying and came to her room to find her curled over in bed, gasping for a breath. Her eyes were wide open with fear. An attendant tried to reassure her, "You don't have to be frightened. I'm right here with you." Adele replied through her gasps, "Honey, believe me, if this was happening to you, you'd be frightened." The attendant began stroking her while she continued to heave. "You're awfully cold," the attendant said. And Adele, again through her gasps, shot back, "Of course I'm cold. I'm almost dead!"

As I sat there I noticed that first Adele wanted complete honesty. She didn't want dogma or to process her dying or to talk about moving into the light. She wanted the truth and someone who could listen to her and move with her changing reality moment to moment. Secondly, there was struggle.

There is often struggle—there is a labor to dying like giving birth. Even with the appropriate pain medications there can still be suffering. For Adele it was manifesting in the breath. While she was gasping for the air, she was suffering. While she was pushing out the air, she was suffering. Every inhale, struggle. Every exhale, struggle.

Now Adele didn't meditate, and she didn't care beans about Buddhism. But she was highly motivated to be free of suffering. I simply said, "I noticed a place right there at the end of your exhale where you could rest. Can you feel it?" Gradually she was able to bring her attention to that place, the in-between place. For an instant, she rested there. Her eyes softened and the fear drained from her face. She took four or five more breaths and she died quite peacefully.

I have a precept that guides my hospice work: "Find a place of rest right in the middle of things." This place of rest is always there for us. Adele found it in the midst of chaos. The conditions of her life remained the same—her breathing hadn't changed, she was still dying—and yet she found this place of rest. "Can you find it?" That was all I said. And she did everything else. She was honest and straightforward in her process all the way.

At Zen Hospice Project, we act with minimal intervention and attempt to meet whatever is arising in front of us. Sitting on the cushion we watch the mind do its myriad activities. Hopefully we are attending to it with some degree of equanimity. At the hospice it's not appreciably different. We sit at the bedside and we listen. We try to listen with our full body, not just with our ears. We must perpetually ask ourselves, "Am I fully here? Or am I checking my watch or looking out the window?"

Dying is not just a medical event. It's much more about relationships. At the heart of it, all we can really offer each other is our full attention. When someone is dying, their tolerance for bullshit is minimal. They will quickly sniff out our sentimentality or insincerity. There may be material that arises that we don't particularly like or even strongly dislike. Just as we do on the cushion, we need to be able to sit still, to listen not knowing what will come next, to suspend judgment—at least for the moment—so that whatever needs to evolve will be able to do so.

In a hospice there are lifetimes of stories that have been lived and are now coming to an end. They are stories of grief, of joy, of regret and reconciliation, of dreams and failures. For the person dying, as well as for family and friends, telling these stories is a way of preparing. The process of dying involves relinquishing our identities. Telling our stories can give us perspective and help move us through the process. Looking back over our life helps us to make sense of it, helps us to discover what has had meaning and value. But every story needs someone to listen.

Sometimes when a person tells his or her story, something changes. There was a very sweet elderly Italian woman, Rose, who stayed with us. She came with a prognosis of seven weeks. Seven months later she was still with us at the hospice. Volunteers kept describing the same conversation with Rose. Someone would walk in the room and say, "Rose, how you doing today?" With a tone of resignation, she would say, "I just want to die." Every day the same response. This became a running gag in the house. I told the volunteers, "We're not taking Rose seriously. We're laughing at her, and we need to listen to exactly what she is saying."

So the next morning I went into her room and said, "Rose, how you doing today?" And again she said, "I just want to die." I said, "What makes you think that dying is going to be so much better?" She looked at me as if to say, "What kind of a question is that to ask an eighty-year-old woman?" I continued to inquire, "You know, Rose, there are no guarantees that it's any better on the other side." And she said, "Well, at least I'd get out." I asked, "Out of what?" So she began to tell me the story of her relationship with her husband.

As she told her story, it became clear that in the fifty years of this marriage, she had always taken care of her husband, cooked his meals, balanced his checkbook, accommodated his moods. Now that she was sick and dying, she couldn't imagine how he could possibly take care of her. She didn't want to be a burden. Better to go to strangers to be cared for. So she moved into the hospice. After she told me her story, we spent some time talking about it. Later, she had a talk with her husband. I wasn't there for their conversation. They had been married for fifty years, so I figured they could work it out. All I know is that three days afterward she moved out of the hospice and returned home. She lived at home for another seven months before she died.

As people tell us their stories, we have to really listen, trusting that insight may well arise from the telling. There is a place in the story that will often deliver what is needed. So pay close attention. Listen all the way through. See where it is leading you.

Before Rose told her story, she was convinced that her only solution, the only way to "get out," was to die. Through telling her story, she realized that her illness and her need to be cared for—what she had imagined to be a burden—was the culmination of her life, a final gift to be shared. She made a reconciliation in her marriage and died at home with her husband and her daughter.

The basic rule is sit down, talk less, listen more, touch when it feels right. Listen to both the literal and symbolic language through which each person is trying to communicate. There was a fellow with terminal cancer who was referred to our hospice. I met him on the psych unit at San Francisco General Hospital. He had tried to take his life. He saw no purpose in continuing. So I sat next to him quietly for some time. Finally he started to speak. He said, "You've been sitting there for an awfully long time." And I said, "Yeah, I have." And he said, "People don't sit around like that here." I said, "Well, I get a lot of practice sitting. Can I ask you a question?" "Sure," he said. So I asked, "What do you want?" Without blinking an eye he said, "Spaghetti." I said, "We make spaghetti. We make really good spaghetti. Why don't you come stay with us at the hospice?" He said fine and that was the end of the admissions interview.

He moved in the next day and we had a big bowl of spaghetti waiting for him. This guy stayed with us for about three months. Near the end of his time with us, he wrote a letter to the volunteers sharing the story of his life when "pain had become unbearable" and "to cry could no longer pacify a miserable existence." He told the story of his coming to the hospice and how his life had changed there. Here's how his letter closed:

> The greatest desolation in my life was the contemplation of a very lonely existence. From the moment I arrived here I knew that a totally new experience of life was about to begin. I knew that there was something about this circle of friends that was about to reveal to me a life that most of us seek but never find, namely one of peace and kindness.

Listen to people. Most of the time they know what they need, though sometimes they may say it in an indirect way. We understood what spaghetti symbolized to this man. Spaghetti was nurturance, spaghetti was familiarity, spaghetti was home. So we served him his spaghetti made with great kindness. He, in his turn, opened his heart and rediscovered a life he believed he had lost.

Stories transport us, offer us relief. In the '80s AIDS dementia was common in maybe 75 percent of the people living with the illness. One of the things that often happens in dementia is that we have a short-term memory loss. We can't remember what happened a few minutes ago. But often, what happened several years before, or even longer, is very available to us. There are lots of ways to work with dementia caused by AIDS or Alzheimers. Generally, the most effective way is for the caregiver to remind the person of what is going on in the present moment. But sometimes it's perfectly okay to simply enter the story.

A very sweet guy came to the hospice. The most pleasure he had gotten from his life was from traveling. Now he was completely bed-bound. Martha, a coworker, tells this story: One day he'd say, " I'd like to take you to lunch." So she'd say, "Fine," and pull up a chair. "Where would you like to go?" "Paris," he'd say. And Martha, without hesitation would respond, "Let's go." So the next thing you knew, they were on the Concorde. "I've always wanted to fly on the Concorde," Peter would giggle. "Would you like some more champagne?" Getting off the plane Martha would inquire, "Where are we headed?" He'd say, "The Left Bank." So off they would go to the Left Bank. Now in a café, he would describe Josephine Baker singing in the corner. They would have an incredible lunch. Martha said that she would walk away from this experience feeling very satiated and delighted, as if she had actually just gone on a wonderful little trip. And Peter, never having actually left his bed, would be equally delighted. The next day they would decide to take a drive up the coast to Mendocino, stay at a bed and breakfast, and walk along the headlands.

Martha could have said to Peter, "Remember you're not in Paris or Mendocino. You're in your bed. You're in a hospice. There is an IV line going in. Let's get real here." She could have interjected her agenda. But these trips were as real to him as anything that was happening in the hospice. When someone is telling us a story, no matter where that story is coming from, whether it's coming from a demented mind or a clear mind, it's real in that particular moment. We have to find a way meet others in their world instead of always expecting they will join us in ours.

After having watched someone die, one might think that the reality of that person's death would be undeniable. But, in fact, it's not. Our capacity to protect ourselves is very highly developed. Sometimes, in order to truly acknowledge the death of someone we love, we need to tell his or her story.

A woman had died, and her sister had watched this process of her dying. An hour had passed after the death, and I was sitting at the bedside along with the sister. I asked her if she would like to wash the body. The sister said, "Not yet. She's not dead yet." I said, "Okay." After some time, I asked, "When was she most alive?" This was all she needed to begin to tell me her sister's story.

She started with the tale of an incredible day when, as a twelve-year-old girl, her sister had climbed down into a cave. The story of her sister's life began to unfold: how brave she was, how she later worked in political movements, then became a writer, then a traveler. As she told the story, the woman was able to move through her dead sister's life, grieving the loss along the way. The period at the end of the story was her sister's death. That's how she had to finish her story because that's where we were. Then she said, "Now I would like to wash her body."

Once or twice a year the then abbot of San Francisco Zen Center, Tenshin Reb Anderson, would come to speak with the hospice volunteers. One night he gave a very insightful talk that included the best advice I have ever heard on caregiving. He said simply, "Stay close and do nothing." That's how we would try to practice at the Zen Hospice Project. We stay close and do nothing. We sit still and listen to the stories.

From Volume 10, Number 2 (Spring 1994).

7 Gabe and the Medicine Buddha

By Rick Fields

Last November 4, less than a month after his fifteenth birthday, my neighbor Gabriel Catalfo died following a nearly eight-year odyssey with leukemia. I've known both his parents since we were all in junior high school, and for more than a dozen years we've co-owned the property on which our two families live. I watched Gabe grow up (much faster than any child should have to), and I also watched him die. Through my intimate involvement with this young man and his family during the last months of his life, I've come to learn a lot more about what the Buddha was trying to teach us about dukkha (suffering), anicca (impermanence), and anatta (egolessness). Our teachers show up in mysterious and not always asked-for ways, and I will forever be grateful that Gabe was part of my life.

I am far from alone in that gratitude. Throughout his journey, and particularly during his last months, Gabe's determination and spirit touched thousands of people. One of those people was writer and editor Rick Fields, who has played a significant role in the transmission of Buddhism to the West. Rick and Gabe became friends during Gabe's final months, and Rick's poem "Sky-Diving" was included in the printed program at Gabe's memorial service.

—ALAN NOVIDOR,

PUBLISHER,

Inquiring Mind

I don't know who it was who told the lama about Gabe's fight with cancer or how it was that Gabe started wearing the thin blue, knotted protection cord the lama sent him. But it surely seems to have been—for Gabe and certainly for me—an example of what Tibetan Buddhists call "auspicious coincidence."

Before I met Gabe I had heard about him from his father, Phil. Gabe was approaching his fifteenth birthday and had been fighting leukemia for more than seven years. I asked Phil if he thought Gabe might like a picture of the lapis lazuli Medicine Buddha who was a part of my own practice in living with cancer. I was hesitant about pushing it on Gabe or his parents, but I gave it to Phil anyway. He passed it on to Gabe, who immediately tacked it on the wall above his bed.

One day Gabe told Phil he'd like to learn to meditate. Phil and I talked about how we could arrange this since Gabe was in and out of treatment and leading a full and active life. While considering the options and difficulties in scheduling, I suddenly realized that I could teach him myself. Gabe was open to this idea, and one afternoon he came by the magazine office where Phil and I both worked. Gabe and I went into an empty room and sat down facing each other knee to knee on the floor. First we did breathing meditation. Then Gabe said he wanted to learn the Medicine Buddha practice. It involves visualizing a Medicine Buddha in front of you and the healing power of the Medicine Buddha coming to you as blessings. So we did that. Somehow he seemed to grasp both practices immediately.

A few weeks later, doctors told his parents, and his parents told him, that the cancer had come back. All they could offer was more chemotherapy, which would at best buy him a few more months, but might also do more harm than good. Gabe took this in and replied, "It's okay; I'm at peace with it. I'm ready."

Where did such wisdom and equanimity come from? Throughout the long years of chemotherapy and radiation, Gabe had continued living his life to the fullest—to the max, he might have said. For years, he refused to have a "port-a-cath" implanted in his chest; it would have made treatment much easier to bear but made it more difficult for him to play soccer and be a part of the wrestling team. He refused to give up—or give in—to the disease that had invaded his young body. He continued to attend school and hang out with his friends, wearing baggy, with-it clothes and his signature fisherman's hat.

When it came time to return to the hospital for more chemo, he said he didn't want to go. But he did want to do three things before he died. He wanted to attend one more session at Camp Okizu, a summer camp for kids with cancer that he had attended for a number of years; he wanted to go jet-skiing; and he wanted to sky-dive. When he was told that to do these three things he would have to undergo more chemotherapy, he decided to do it.

Gabe's last two wishes in particular caused his doctors and parents much consternation. Jet-skiing and ski-diving were not exactly recommended activities for someone as fragile as Gabe was at that point. On the other hand, what sense did it make to deny him these experiences, given that he may not have long to live and was now at the age where he had his own ideas and the will—and right—to make his own decisions? In the end, Gabe was able to fulfill each of his three wishes. "The coolest part of the sky-diving," he told me, "was free-falling for 1,500 feet before the parachute opened."

Later, Gabe submitted to yet another round of chemotherapy, hoping to earn another remission and buy enough time to graduate from high school. But doctors found a fungal infection under a tiny scrape on his knee and could not control it despite heavy doses of antibiotics. So he went home. When I visited him, he was resting in the bed his family had set up in the living room. The fungus was visible as a round, gray growth on his forehead. He was taking a narcotic for pain and wearing the lapis lazuli–colored Medicine Buddha T-shirt I had given him for his fifteenth birthday a few weeks before.

We watched a tape of his sky-diving. Bound to his partner, he spread his arms wide like wings and fell through the open sky. As I left, I said, "You're doing great, man."

He high-fived me. "So are you," he said to me. "So are you."

The lama who had given Gabe the blessing protection cords came to visit too. He recited the Medicine Buddha chant in Tibetan as Gabe passed in and out of sleep. Afterward, Gabe told his mom that he had been able to understand what the lama was saying—that the lama had "psychically told me the words and what they mean, and I've been saying them since then."

One morning Gabe told his mother and father that he was dying—"not today, but soon." Phil asked him if he was ready. "I don't want to leave you guys," he replied. As he had shown throughout his last few months, his main concern was how his passing would affect others. He asked his parents to promise they'd stay together as a family. They pledged to him they would, and with that reassurance he seemed to begin to let go. He died two days later, a few minutes before midnight, with his father holding his hand.

His memorial eleven days later was attended by over a thousand people. There were the kids from Berkeley High he had grown up with, kids from his cancer camp, and many others whose lives he had not only touched but changed by the generosity of his spirit and life, by the compassion he showed them. There was a shrine to Gabe in one corner of the reception room. On the shrine was a large picture of Gabe sky-diving, his floppy fisherman's hat, and at its center, the lapis lazuli radiance of the Medicine Buddha that had accompanied him on his journey.

SKY-DIVING FOR GABE

By Rick Fields

Gabe passed into
Became
The light
Last night.

At the age of seven
it began
He fought
and laughed
like the wind

free and easy
and fierce

watching it all
with an innocent awareness
that took my breath
away

One day
he asked me
to teach him
to meditate

He taught me
instead

One of his last wishes
he said
was to jump
from an airplane
into the empty sky

No one could say No
Not even the bureaucrats
at the Federal Aviation Administration

Strapped chest to chest
to his partner, he stepped into space

The coolest part, he told me
from his hospital bed
was the free fall
For fifteen hundred feet

He fell
he flew
he spread his arms
wide
like the wings
of the angel he was
and is

Now I step out
of the plane
joined to him
into the space
of groundlessness

We fall
we fly
through the clear
blue sky

No up
No down
No in
No out

No fear

And this is the coolest
part—
no doubt.

From Volume 15, Number 2 (Spring 1999).

8 Tsunami Psychologist

By Ronna Kabatznick

"Dr. Ronna! *Chuay noi! Chuay noi!*" (Help!) A Thai nurse grabbed my arm and led me past bulletin boards plastered with pictures and descriptions of missing persons. She took me to a European man screaming and kicking in anguish. His sister and thirty employees from his destroyed seaside hotel were missing and presumed dead. "What am I going to do?" he cried. I instinctively pulled his chest to mine while he wailed and then wept. My tear-drenched blouse never dried. Over the next eight days, lasting twenty waking hours each, countless mourners—parents, spouses, siblings, children, and friends—needed similar gestures of comfort as they released their suffering into the fabric of my clothes and into my being.

This was post-tsunami Thailand. On an idyllic tropical morning in this tiny area of the country, more than 5,300 lives had been swallowed and then spit out by three massive waves. Thousands more had actually vanished in the waves. The tsunami was not selective. Religion, sex, social status, and age were all irrelevant. My focus was to help survivors face what the Buddha described as the inevitable realities of life: sorrow, grief, pain, lamentation, and despair. For the previous eighteen months, I had been on retreat with Ajahn Ganha and Ajahn Anan in Thai forest monasteries. Each day I had practiced the reflection on impermanence taught by the Buddha: "All that is mine, beloved and pleasing, will become otherwise, will become separated from me." These words now took on a visceral meaning as I helped people cope with sudden, irrevocable separation from their loved ones.

After a few days in Phuket counseling traumatized inpatient survivors, I headed for the makeshift morgue in Krabi, which was actually in a *wat* (monastery). I walked into a large room to behold 500 bloated, rotting bodies. The ratio of dead to living was fifty to one. Although I was wearing a surgical mask drenched in menthol ointment, the penetrating stench of death was still sickening and unavoidable.

While on retreat in the forest, I had also been practicing body contemplation and death reflection. Death comes without warning. This body will become a corpse. This body, from the soles of the feet up, and down from the crown of the head, is a sealed bag of skin filled with unattractive things. These too were no longer abstract reflections. Lifeless, swollen, smelly bags were unsealed, and many of the unattractive things were at my feet: excrement, urine, pus, mucus, bones, and blood. It was obvious that the victims had had no chance to dress for death. The broken bags of skin were wearing bathing suits, sundresses, tank tops, shorts, and other types of leisure wear. It was unlikely that anyone had said that morning, "This could be the day that I'll die."

Next to me a small woman thought she had identified her daughter in a photograph: a swollen body black with decay, wearing flowered shorts and a T-shirt. The face was covered by a three-digit number. (Numbered pictures of the dead were being posted every two hours.) The woman and I held hands and walked up and down the aisles of corpses in various stages of decomposition, trying to match the number in her hand with a number on a face. We saw maggots crawl over bikini-clad women and worms emerge from a toddler's mouth. There were body parts everywhere, including heads dangling off necks. Before my eyes, everything was returning to the elements. It was a massive charnel ground meditation, exactly as the Buddha described it: "Here a leg, there an arm, there a head." Nearby, monks chanted. *Annica vata sankhara....* Conditions are impermanent, arising and falling away; having been born they all must cease. The stilling of all conditions is true peace.

The determined mother didn't give up when we couldn't find her daughter. At least another hundred festering corpses were left to peruse, and more were being unloaded off pickup trucks several times daily. Outside the morgue, crowded with mourners and volunteers, two brothers rolled on the ground bellowing in grief. They had just identified their sister, who lay uncovered nearby. Mingled with their heaving sobs came the ringing of my cellphone. The nurses needed me to care for a man in severe shock. This gentle-looking man stared off into space, stiff with grief. He kept repeating, like a mantra, "Dead bodies floating, dead bodies floating." A pregnant woman waddled past, hand on one hip, as her energetic son cartwheeled down the hall and the mantra repeated: "Dead bodies floating, dead bodies floating."

In the Krabi hospital lobby, survivors and family members combed through pictures of the deceased and filled out missing-person forms. They swapped suggestions on how to hasten body identification and retrieval.

"Start with pictures of jewelry: fingers with wedding rings, wrists with bracelets, and necks with necklaces. Then switch to pictures of moles, scars, and tattoos. No results? Look at the full-body pictures. Get dental records fast and fingerprints if possible. Use the Israeli forensic team. They know what they're doing. Don't go into the morgue alone."

The embassies had a mission: encourage survivors to get out of the country and discourage family members from coming in. "Everything is under control" were their buzz words. Yet nothing was under control, or ever is. While bodies were still being collected, cadaver management procedures had not been established. It appeared that many embassies had neither internal nor external resources to deal with the enormity and the sheer horror of the disaster.

Having flown twenty-four hours, a jet-lagged Euro-Asian father had come alone to find his missing twenty-nine-year-old daughter. His attention was narrowly focused on what he called "an efficient strategy." He pondered what to do first: would it be sifting through bodies or looking at pictures? But despair isn't that practical. Finally he broke down. He begged to no one, "Please don't let me go home without my daughter."

The survivors' mission was to find the dead and bring them home, to transform grief into action. The goal was to board a plane with a coffin (or coffins) in cargo. Those who couldn't were faced with not only the grief of loss but the added grief of what some perceived as a mission failed. Those still searching offered congratulations and pats on the back to relatives and friends who had made positive identifications. But the longing, and even envy, was palpable.

The news around the morgue was that dead Westerners were being refrigerated and receiving priority identifications. The Asians were being buried in mass graves to be dug up later for DNA identification. This was devastating news for the Euro-Asian father in search of his daughter. In all probability, she was already buried. Overwhelmed with sorrow, he left alone, a broken man. At such moments I remembered Ajahn Ganha and Ajahn Anan, who I knew were sending lovingkindness. Thinking about them reminded me that surrendering to suffering actually liberates us from it.

A family at the morgue needed help. A bride had been positively identified by the Israeli forensic team. Neither the groom nor the mother of the bride wanted to see the body. Would I accompany the father of the bride? After donning masks and surgical gloves, we were led to one of eight large refrigerated containers that had recently arrived. The electrical noise was deafening. "What's the number?" yelled a volunteer. The father screamed it twice. When the door slid open, a swirling cloud of cold air smacked into the tropical heat. It was a surreal few moments as two men leaped in and rummaged through the numbered and bagged bodies. "*Chuay noi dai mai?*" (Can you help us?) asked one of them. I jumped in and moved bodies so we could retrieve the right one. Two of us unloaded it onto the ground. The father unzipped the bag and stared at his frozen daughter wearing a two-piece bathing suit. Kneeling down, he shed tears on her cold corpse. Together, the grieving father and I zipped up the bag.

The following day, the groom, the parents of the bride, and I returned to collect the body. Once again we hauled it out of the refrigerator, which now had even more bodies in it. The bag was opened for the last time. The mother yelled her daughter's name louder and louder, as if she were expecting her to wake up and walk away from the nightmare. Placing lotuses on the bride's decaying face, the mother dabbed her handkerchief all over the blackened body while humming a lullaby.

About ninety-six percent of Thais are Buddhists. Although many aren't meditation practitioners, most have strong faith in the Buddha's teachings. Those who couldn't find bodies believed that the departed would receive the merit of good deeds dedicated on their behalf, with or without a body. The Thai way of grieving was quite composed and reflected a cool heart (*jai yen*). Mourners appeared to see death as part of life, not so much an injustice or a dreadful mistake, even when it was unexpected or swift. One Thai woman who lost her two children and husband responded to my condolences with "*pen tamada, pen tamachat,*" which means "this is natural, it is nature."

The Thais have been so conditioned to keep their pain private that strong displays of emotions made them visibly uncomfortable and embarrassed. When anyone crumbled in grief outside of the morgue, some giggled out of anxiety. In the hospital while people were having nervous breakdowns, a few nurses walked away. It made me realize that my task was to be a silent witness while hearts broke.

Expressing emotions wasn't an issue for *jai rawn* ("hot heart") Westerners. Many felt betrayed by the waves and the experts who didn't transmit warnings of them. Those expressing the most pain were parents who blamed themselves for not being able to protect their children from death. They confessed, "I'm a bad parent," as if they were personally responsible. Two mothers recalled premonition dreams the night before the tsunami: "If I had only listened, she'd still be alive." The tsunami had shattered their identity as parents with control over their children's lives. Questions about "bad karma" were common; what terrible things had they done to deserve this fate?

Summoned by a loud scream, I rushed to a woman bent over in grief with her husband at her side. An embassy staff member had just handed over their daughter's passport, confirming her death. Their hopes of finding her in a remote hospital or wandering in an amnesiac state had been destroyed. When I took them to their room, the screaming intensified. The mother wailed on the bed while the father leaned over the balcony ready to jump. I offered to sleep in their room.

These parents identified the body the next day. A volunteer at the morgue told me that the father was screaming "get Dr. Ronna" so I could help his wife. But the embassy staff member with my number never called, and when we spoke later, she calmly said, "Everything is under control." If we really had control, I thought, then the first noble truth of suffering would be disproved. Everyone would be able to command their minds to be peaceful and their bodies not to die.

My ability to keep people's sad stories straight finally collapsed. It was time to leave. While packing I recalled that another of my teachers, Ajahn Achalo, told me the Buddha had said that the smell of death helps keep attention focused on the fragility of life, so he recommended that monks make their robes from cloth found in charnel grounds. Not for a second did I think of taking the Buddha's advice. I had had enough of the stench of death and threw most of my clothes away.

I went to visit Ajahn Anan. On a quiet afternoon in the forest, he offered his soothing insights:

> As long as we're living in the world, things are uncertain. It doesn't matter what country we come from. Everyone wants happiness and a long life. But the world doesn't accord with our wishes and desires. Every life has suffering, and everyone has their own individual karma. When we start to think about the details of our karma, suffering arises; this is not the correct view of things. If there is birth, we have to receive the karma of death. Being conscious of death is a good thing. It may arouse a sense of urgency to be more heedful and to lead a more mindful life. When we look for happiness, we have to look for the unconditioned. If there is no birth, then there is no death. This is the nature of nibbana.

This essay is dedicated to my Dharma sister Quandow and her daughter and son-in-law, who were swept away in the tsunami, and to her five-year-old granddaughter, the sole survivor.

From Volume 21, Number 2 (Spring 2005).

III

SCIENCE OF MIND

The first verse of the Dhammapada states, "All experience is preceded by mind, led by mind, created by mind." Over the centuries Buddhists have developed and refined what the Dalai Lama calls a "science of mind." This science differs from Western psychology, as Jack Kornfield points out: instead of trying to cure the "pathologies," it cultivates positive mental states and recognizes the vast potential of the human mind. As the sciences of East and West exchange understandings, a new synthesis begins to emerge. Research psychologist Paul Ekman finds himself unexpectedly transformed through his conversations on emotions with the Dalai Lama. Susan Moon explores her depression and the ways her Zen practice does and doesn't serve her healing. Mark Epstein brings the principles of meditation into the therapist's office. Francisco Varela explains that "the brain is designed not to take Dharma seriously," a possible explanation for why meditation is so challenging. Together, the sciences of East and West may bring us new ways to both heal and enhance our mental life.

1 Beyond Mental Health
An Interview with Jack Kornfield

On any day of the week, I encounter students of all ages arriving at Spirit Rock Meditation Center where I work. They each come with their problems and their genuine search for happiness.

To my eye, the students entering Spirit Rock are not very different from the stream of visitors who came to the forest monastery where I trained in Thailand. Every day, Ajahn Chah would sit on a wooden bench at the edge of a clearing by his forest hut and receive them all—from a man whose young son just died to a semi-corrupt government official. As a young monk in the monastery, I found myself marveling at the range of questions and human problems addressed by Ajahn Chah. It was like watching a master psychologist at work. Ajahn Chah made no distinction between worldly and spiritual problems. To him, anxiety, trauma, financial problems, physical difficulties, meditative struggles, ethical dilemmas, and community conflict were all forms of suffering amenable to the medicine of Buddhist teaching. Ajahn Chah and other Buddhist masters like him are practitioners of a living psychology: one of the oldest and most well developed systems of healing and understanding on the face of the Earth.

—ADAPTED FROM *The Wise Heart: A Guide*
to the Universal Teachings
of Buddhist Psychology

Wes Nisker and Barbara Gates interviewed Jack Kornfield in June 2007 at Spirit Rock Meditation Center in Woodacre, California.

INQUIRING MIND: You suggest that Buddhism is primarily a psychology rather than a religion. That's a startling point.

JACK KORNFIELD: Some people refer to the Dharma as a psychology, but I'd rather say "science of mind," as the Dalai Lama puts it. In the West we see psychology in very limited terms—primarily focused on mental illness. But there is so much more to the human mind than pathology. "Science of mind" encompasses an understanding of the vast potential of the human psyche and consciousness.

Remember Freud's resigned vision of our capacity for happiness: "The goal of psychoanalysis is to claim a little more ego from the vast sea of id" and to change human misery into "normal unhappiness." But from a Buddhist perspective, liberation, far beyond "normal unhappiness" is possible—not just for the Buddha, but for everybody who undertakes these practices.

I should add that when the Dalai Lama calls Buddhism a science of mind, this does not deny the fact that for many people around the world Buddhism has also come to function as a religion. For these devotees, there are the belief, faith, and communal rituals that are common to most religious traditions. But that's not what the Buddha originally spent his time teaching; he taught a science of mind, what I'm calling "the psychologies of Buddhism."

IM: How appropriate do you think the psychologies of Buddhism are at this time in Western history in this culture, which so stresses the self?

JK: In many forms of Western psychotherapy there's been a great emphasis on my self—my story, my history, my problems, my getting better. At a certain point therapists will notice that even their clients are getting sick of themselves. "Enough of my story. Am I to be defined only by my story, my thoughts and my neuroses?" This is actually a tremendously important turning point, whether it's in therapy or, now, in the introduction of Buddhist practice, because it begins to turn us to other, greater possibilities, a wider identity not limited by our personal history.

Buddhist psychologies open up an enormous range of positive potential beyond what we would ordinarily think of as our mental health. We could take the DSM (the standard diagnostic tool used by mental health professionals) and reverse it. Instead of a list of twenty-five states of depression, there's a list of twenty-five states of rapture in the psychologies of Buddhism. Likewise, instead of having a list of anxiety disorders, we could have a comparable list of states of extreme trust and contentment. Instead of just focusing on psychotic hallucinations, there could be a comparable description of positive visions, all the ways that visualizations could be used, and the hearing and seeing of inner sounds, sights, and archetypes that illuminate the highest of human potential. All of what we see in Western psychopathology has a correlate in its opposite that's found in the psychologies of Buddhism.

A key principle is original goodness. As the Buddha said—this mind is luminous by nature and is inherently pure. But it is colored by the conditioning that limits it. The whole purpose of Buddhism is to return us to our original nature. A related principle is the capacity to shift identity from a vision of oneself as an injured or traumatized individual, from a small sense of self, what's called the "body of fear," to find our potential for freedom and greatness. We have the capacity to live this life as a buddha and bodhisattva.

IM: It's fascinating to consider the fundamental contrast between the two paradigms. In the Western paradigm, the essence of human nature is aggressive. But as you point out, in the paradigm of the Buddhist psychologies, practice uncovers an innate state of purity, brilliance, and goodness.

JK: In *Civilization and its Discontents*, Freud says, "Culture has to call up every possible reinforcement in order to erect barriers against the aggressive instincts of men. . . . Its ideal command to love one's neighbor as oneself is really justified by the fact that nothing is so completely at variance with original human nature as this." From a Buddhist perspective, nothing is so at variance with our original nature as the "aggressive instincts" Freud describes. In fact, aggression, hatred, and greed are seen as based in delusion and covering over our innate goodness.

If you see yourself as a limited self and you're attached to this small sense of self, this body of fear, then you will act in frightened ways—through deficiency, aggression, hatred, and greed. When you reawaken to your original nature, these fall away, and this is the liberation that the Buddha discovered.

Another principle very important in the psychologies of Buddhism is that there are systematic ways to train the mind and heart and body. Mostly in Western clinical practice, you do your work in the presence of another person, with a therapist, or in some form of therapy. In the psychology of Buddhism, you learn from teachers, you get initiation and instructions, but then you take those instructions and work with them in your own program of training. This is a whole different modality with enormous implications because it empowers us to engage in self-transformation.

Here's an example. A young man from the tough East St. Louis streets had left his gang and was introduced to Buddhist practice at one of the men's retreats I co-lead. But when both a close buddy and then his ex-girlfriend were shot and killed, his old friends pressured him to take revenge. He had to get a gun. These dangerous thoughts would have led him to kill, and then be killed, on the streets or in a prison. He knew he had to stop thinking this way.

At the retreat I gave him a skull necklace from Tibet, used by monks to remind themselves to live wisely in the light of death. We talked about the fierce initiation of one who faces death and chooses life. At first he wasn't sure he could go on. In the gangs most young people cannot picture living past the age of twenty. He had to change. So, using the Buddha's instruction on the removal of unhealthy thought, I offered him training to change his thoughts. "I will live" became one of his new intentions. "I will save the lives of young kids" was another. Through this practice and the practices of mindfulness and compassion, he learned to transform himself step by step. With the support of a strong community, five years later he has become a father and a leader for youth. The transformation of thought, a skillful means that a person can take on as a key practice, can reorient an entire life as it did for this ex–gang member. Or it can be an initial step in the process of healing.

One psychiatrist I know recommended the use of Buddhist lovingkindness meditation as a form of thought substitution for an obsessed patient. Through doing repeated lovingkindness this patient was able to transform himself. There are a multitude of skillful means which can be practiced for self-transformation.

Another principle is the contemplative dimension of the psychologies of Buddhism. One of the most important maps of awakening is the seven factors of enlightenment. Half of this map describes the activating factors: mindfulness, energy, investigation, and interest or rapture. Those qualities are quite common to Western clinical forms of therapy. The other half describes the contemplative qualities: calm, concentration, and equanimity. These qualities are mostly unknown in Western psychology. And yet, if you really want to understand your mind and develop your potential, without this contemplative dimension, you won't be able to do it.

You can see the power of this contemplative dimension in the smallest ways. For instance, if somebody comes to see me for spiritual counseling and I have her sit for fifteen minutes before I speak with her, her mind gets quiet, she gets in touch with her body, her feelings, and her intentions. Instead of being caught up with the things that just happened on the highway or at the office, she can listen in a much deeper and more insightful way. Of course, that's just the tip of the iceberg of what it means to include the contemplative dimension. It goes from there all the way to the depths of jhana practice, deep samadhi.

IM: What are some of the other contrasts between Western psychology and the psychologies of Buddhism?

JK: In Western psychology we address the power of conditioning, but in the psychologies of Buddhism the understanding is much more sophisticated, involving motivation and intention. For instance, we work with motivation when we take the precepts or the bodhisattva vow to serve all beings. We use a vision of our highest potential to set the compass of the heart, to direct our life with long-term motivation and a deep understanding of how karma unfolds.

Buddhist psychologies also have a wonderful understanding of what it means to be comfortable with the paradoxes of our human life. We learn to live in the reality of the present and understand that the past and future are contained in the present and unfold as thoughts and images out of the present. We also embody the paradox of the universal and the personal, recognizing that we have a personal and unique incarnation, and at the same time we're all part of the dream appearing out of consciousness. And both of these are true. We have to know our Buddha-nature and also know our social security number.

There's also the paradox of selflessness and self. This paradox is understood in multiple dimensions in the Buddhist psychologies more fully than in the West. Now modern neuroscience and modern research into the creation of self is finally coming to understand that self is not a fixed thing but is actually a process. In 2002 *Time* magazine explained, "After more than a century of looking for it, brain researchers have long since concluded that there is no conceivable place for a self to be located in the physical brain, and that it simply does not exist."

Most importantly, perhaps, the psychologies of Buddhism are the psychologies of the heart as well as the mind. Fundamental healing of the heart can come through Buddhist practices. In my own case, this healing has been profound. I think of my visit to see my father in the ICU after he'd had a severe heart attack. I knew that this could have been my last visit with him. He was hooked up to oxygen and a variety of beeping machines. I sat by his bedside and talked about him and our family. Then, after a few minutes of silence, I took a long look at my father: weak, vulnerable, maybe dying. I said, "I love you." His eyes got bigger. Struggling, he raised one arm, patched with tape and needles and tubes, up to his face. He pinched his nose as if to ward off a bad smell, frowned with disdain, and rolled his head from side to side, muttering, "Ugh!" Not in our family. You don't acknowledge your feelings.

It is too sentimental, too weak. For me it has taken years of training—as a monk, in meditation, in Western psychotherapy, and through the give-and-take of relationships—to reclaim my capacity to feel.

Practicing the Brahma-viharas—lovingkindness, compassion, joy, and equanimity, and with these, the possibility of forgiveness and redemption—students of Buddhism open their hearts. In these beloved practices, Buddhist trainings show how the "divine abodes" can be recovered when we've lost them or they've been covered over, and how equanimity can create a perfect balance for compassion and lovingkindness. At the highest levels, these sophisticated understandings of human well-being and healing go far beyond what we ordinarily understand in the psychologies of the West.

IM: How often do you recommend that in conjunction with Buddhist practices students go into therapy?

JK: There are many occasions where I will recommend therapy to people. I see the best of Western therapy as a paired mindfulness out loud. It uses some of the same principles of investigation and compassion as Buddhist practice, and often those who come to meditation encounter areas where therapy can really help. For instance, in meditation you might uncover a place of deep abandonment and betrayal in your early life. It's hard to be mindful of this if you are alone because it can recreate the old sense of abandonment. But if you go to that painful and frightening place in the presence of another person and can reexperience it with acceptance and love, it releases that unhealthy identity and helps to transform it. Teachers offer this healing presence all the time in interviews with students on retreat. But retreats are short. Sometimes it becomes clear that a student needs to work with somebody regularly, and I'll send him or her to a therapist. I tend to recommend therapists who have a Buddhist or a big spiritual perspective so that people don't get lost in personal history as the end of the story.

IM: What about antidepressants and other psychiatric medications. Do you recommend those?

JK: At certain times such drugs can be genuinely helpful to people. On retreats these days there are many people who are taking antidepressants, antianxiety medication, or in some cases stronger medications for bipolar disorder and so forth. On the other hand, we live in a pill-oriented culture. Half the people—I'll just say half for a round number—who are taking these pills don't need to be, or could wean themselves, or would be better off letting go of them and learning to use inner practices to transform their suffering. This is because most medications have negative side effects, and after a certain time they also have a suppressant effect, which means that people taking them don't feel their emotions as fully and are not quite as in touch with the energies of their body and mind, which are helpful in the deepest work of change.

So I have a lot more caution about such drugs than the clinics, which almost automatically dispense them when you come in with a difficulty. But if you are drowning in your experience of depression, anxiety, or fear and can't get out, medication can help regulate you to the point where you can begin to work with some degree of mindfulness and compassion.

IM: It appears to be a very pregnant moment in world history, with the wisdom and the practices of Buddhism reaching a much broader population than ever before, and our Western science starting to understand how this human mind works.

JK: It's a very potent moment. Western culture has celebrated the individual, both to great advantage and also to the great detriment of those other tribes and races that are different from ourselves, not to speak of the other creatures of the globe. Buddhist psychologies are psychologies of interdependence, rather than independence. It's extremely important in our current world to include the truth of interdependence in the way we see ourselves. And we can't just know it intellectually; we've got to make use of these inner technologies to deeply shift our consciousness. Ultimately, all of the practices of the psychologies of Buddhism are to shift from a limited identity to the sense of being nothing and being everything, to awaken to freedom and our true interconnectedness.

⋄
⋄ From Volume 24, Number 1 (Fall 2007).
⋄

2 **Mystery Remains**
A Scientist Meets a Monk
An Interview with Paul Ekman

In March of 2000 Paul Ekman arrived in Dharamsala, India, as a highly accomplished research psychologist. Dr. Ekman was soon to be named by the American Psychological Association as one of the most influential psychologists of the twentieth century. He was staunchly scientific in his views and pessimistic in his outlook on life. The Mind and Life Institute invited Dr. Ekman to participate in the eighth of a series of private dialogues between His Holiness the Dalai Lama and preeminent Western scientists. He was asked to present on his extensive research into the nature of human emotion: its universal components, evolutionary purpose, functions, and facial expressions. Although not personally interested in Buddhism, Dr. Ekman accepted the invitation.

One week later he left a different man. Frequently at these meetings, the Dalai Lama would stay at tea breaks in the mornings and afternoons to chat informally with the participants. At one such interlude, His Holiness held Dr. Ekman's hand. The scientist had an experience unlike any he had ever had before, one for which he has no easy explanation. There was, he said, a strong sensation of warmth, but more than that. In the months that followed, Dr. Ekman found that he almost never got angry, which represented a significant temperamental switch.

Since the meeting in 2000, he has had the unique opportunity to spend thirty-nine hours speaking one-on-one with the Dalai Lama discussing emotions from an East-West perspective for a book they are writing together.

Paul Ekman is now an optimist.

—MARGARET CULLEN

Margaret Cullen, Wes Nisker, and Barbara Gates interviewed Paul Ekman in July 2007 at his home in Oakland, California.

INQUIRING MIND: This seems to be an extraordinary collaboration between you and His Holiness—the scientist and the monk.

PAUL EKMAN: I really do feel like the Dalai Lama is the brother I never had. I nearly said "it's almost as if," because I wouldn't want to be seen as presuming; on the other hand, it's exactly how I feel. I told the Dalai Lama the same thing. It's a mystery to me: how two people who are so different in origins and background could feel so close. He said it was no mystery to him. But, of course, he has an easy explanation unavailable to me as a non-Buddhist, as I don't believe we could have known each other in a past incarnation.

For the sake of identification, I sometimes use the initials H. H. I have a hard time calling him "His Holiness" or "Your Holiness," because I don't think of him as *holy*. To me he's not holy at all. *Holy* refers to a saint, and I've never met a saint. I think of him as very human.

IM: What were the main topics of your discussions?

PE: We talked about mental life—issues like emotions and passion, altruism, awareness, training the mind—a lot of territory, and we ended up with very few differences. We have arrived at the same conclusions but used different means to get there. And while we both changed our positions on some things during our discussions, we ended up disagreeing about only a couple of minor points.

You know, he's a very passionate man. There isn't anyone else I know whom I can engage without worrying about the force of my arguments. It can be intimidating to people that I get so passionate, but he gets just as passionate! We both got very excited—with no anger. I told him, "It's just wonderful. Your passion matches my passion; I don't have to tone things down." He replied, "What's the point of talking if you're not excited!" Absolutely right!

So we covered the territory as well as we could, and I feel some regret that there was nothing more to discuss. He asked me at the last hour, "All over? No more? No more questions?" I said, "I'm out!"

IM: You mentioned that you each changed your views about certain things.

PE: Yes. I changed my views about forgiveness and hatred. Those are two biggies, aren't they? Hatred was the hardest to give up! (Laughs) I believe it has played an important role in my surviving a physically abusive parent—

a father who was competitive with me when I was a little kid all the way up until I fled my house. He even tried to get me arrested by claiming I had threatened his life. I hadn't; I just told him he couldn't hit me anymore: "Never hit me again, or I'll hit you back." This is a father who, when I got my first grant, wrote a letter to his congressman protesting that the grant was a waste of taxpayers' money. My father decided early on what I was about, and any contrary evidence was very disturbing to him. So for a long time, one of my motives—only recently I would have said my only motive—was to beat him at his own game. I did a lot better than he did at everything in life—from being a professor at a medical school (he was a physician) to having fourteen books published (he had none). I would think, "When he hears about this, it'll be turning a knife." Since my father died forty years ago, all this has been in my mind, but I've used the metaphor "I hope he turns over in his grave when he hears about this."

But through my interactions with H. H.—in inexplicable ways—there's been a major change in my emotional life. I couldn't get him to talk much about it, other than acknowledging he knows this happens to people in his presence. He prefers to treat it as a mystery. I said, "I think you really have more of an idea about this than you're willing to tell me." [Approximating the voice of the Dalai Lama:] "No. Mystery. Mystery."

IM: Can you describe what happened to your feeling of hatred?

PE: On an emotional level it disappeared. I don't know why; all I know is that it stopped being a preoccupation sometime after our meeting in Chicago in April 2006. We met for eleven hours over three days. We did talk about hatred, and I defended the virtues of hatred as a positive motivator. I told him that I'd saved a lot of lives in my life as a result of the work I did to feed my hatred of my father, so how can we say it's destructive? I have other examples in my book *Emotions Revealed* of hatred keeping someone together and why it worked.

But I really don't hate my father anymore. I don't even think about him anymore. He won't learn that I've been spending time with a world leader. It's an irrelevancy. He's been dead for a long time. And now I have a little bit of compassion for what a miserable life my father led, and for all he missed in being a parent that I've since experienced. He never met my children; he was dead for twenty years before they were born.

IM: What happened to your theory that hatred has value as a motivating emotion?

PE: What the Dalai Lama and I now agree to—I think this is a change in his position—is that hatred can be of short-term positive benefit but that it's a long-term poison. That's our joint view. Hatred can have some short-term benefits to you and to society, but over the long term it will corrode your nature.

We also agreed on the importance of distinguishing anger from hatred. Hatred is intrinsically the desire to hurt the other person, while the primary focus of anger is to remove an obstacle to the goal you're pursuing. If you're skilled, hurting the other person is not part of your goal. You want just the opposite: to help the other person achieve his or her ends without blocking your activity.

We became clear about the differences in terms of constructive emotion versus destructive or afflictive emotion. "Constructive" refers to an emotional episode that furthers collaboration between you and another person. Forty years ago I studied a Stone Age culture—people who never left a village of two hundred during their whole lives. They were totally collaborative; they couldn't survive without cooperation. Contrary to some evolutionary theorists, I think what's intrinsic to human social nature is cooperation.

IM: So the difference between anger and hatred is like the difference between being angry with the action instead of the actor.

PE: Which is the Dalai Lama's view exactly. As we talked we kept refining our terms. I distinguished eleven different types of anger. He loved that. He loves complication and distinction, because it brings much more focus to our understanding.

Of course, our distinctions were complicated by the fact that we were dealing with four languages: You've got Sanskrit (which is where, it seems, a lot of Tibetan scholarship comes from); then you have the Tibetan version of the Sanskrit; then you have what he calls "Buddhalogical English," which are words I think are misadopted from English to refer to the Tibetan version of the Sanskrit; and finally you have English.

IM: Is it true that the Tibetan language doesn't have a single word that refers to what in English we call *emotion*?

PE: That's right. The Dalai Lama said to me, "Well, it's becoming very clear that you have an idea of exactly what emotion is—so tell us." My definition of emotion includes about eight characteristics. For one thing, emotions can last as little as a few seconds, which distinguishes them from moods, which last hours or longer. One of the fundamental truths about emotions is that they're fleeting. So if you hold on to an emotion, you're twisting its nature. That fits very well with Buddhist views. Another characteristic of our emotional life, which I've added to my list recently, is that we are biased to see provocation and danger. People who see snakes rather than coiled ropes are more cautious, and therefore more likely to add to the gene pool than those who aren't looking for the danger.

The characteristic that's probably most troublesome for our emotional life is the fact that the evaluation process that triggers an emotion and gives rise to the impulse for action is often extremely complex, fast, and impenetrable by consciousness. Picture a near-miss car accident. We've got a mechanism in our brain for making—in literally under 200 milliseconds—complex evaluations of the speed of an approaching object and then dictating learned behavior (because cars were not part of our ancestral environment) as to how much to turn the wheel, hit the brake, depress the gas pedal. And that all happens with no awareness. Awareness comes afterward.

So we've got a mechanism that's always searching for possible danger, provocation, loss—all the things that trigger emotion. It's also attuned to all the things that we mislearned as children. (Children are bad learners. For one thing, they're very egocentric. They imagine that whatever happens is due to them. Parents get divorced, it's their fault. Rarely is it true, but that's not how kids see the world.) It's very difficult to untangle the wiring of this mechanism, to undo all of these mistaken triggers.

Here's one thing I discovered that I love so much. I always thought I was a coward because when I saw a situation coming that was going to give me a lot of trouble, I'd just try to avoid it. When I told that to H.H., he said, "That's exactly what you should try to do first. Always avoid situations that might bring forth a destructive emotion." Then, if you can't avoid them, try to use what you've learned to get yourself prepared. I've developed a whole series of exercises and mental strategies to prepare people to deal with a difficult person or situation. Preparation is essential. For instance, do a self-scan: "Am I in a state of equilibrium where I can recognize destructive impulses and not engage them? Or if I engage them, can I do it in a way that's going to be useful for the difficult person or situation I'm dealing with?"

IM: That sounds like the sort of skillful means you might hear suggested at an insight meditation retreat. Maybe you are an intuitive Buddhist.

PE: (Laughs) I developed these exercises without knowing anything about Buddhist teaching. Meanwhile, an exercise that the Dalai Lama talked about at length—which was a surprise to me but probably won't be to you—is how the Tibetans take rather simple beliefs and practice them in their minds for thousands of hours until they become what he calls an "integral conviction." A belief such as "we are all connected" becomes how your mind is furnished—to use one metaphor—or the framework from which you now view the world. It's no longer just a consideration or belief; it's now ingrained, an inescapable part of your—what's the word?...—outlook. I love the word *outlook*!

You could say that this practice is a form of brainwashing, too, and I wouldn't disagree. In the West, the only people who spend anywhere near that amount of time in a particular practice are concert musicians—and that's developing a motor skill. But these Tibetan monks are putting an unbelievable amount of time into reshaping their outlook.

IM: Do you think that science might be able to find an easier way to change our emotional life, our mental habits?

PE: At one point I asked H.H., "Suppose I could create a biofeedback technology that would allow me to create compassionate people or people who were aware of impulses before action, and that I could do this in eighty hours of training. Would you be in favor of that?" He thought it was a great idea. "If you can do that with science, do it! Then we'll make that available." He doesn't care what method one uses; he cares about what's achieved.

But he also thinks I'm a typical Westerner who's impatient and wants to see things change quickly. *He* thinks that change happens one person at a time. I say the world might not be rescuable if we do it slowly, person by person. We need a more sudden change. Maybe that's just a Western/non-Western disagreement.

See, I'm impatient, particularly at the age of seventy-three. I don't have twenty years to wait to see what's going to happen. I want to see something happen while I'm still alive. I want to have some more assurance than I do now that my children and grandchildren aren't going to live in a much worse world than the one in which I lived.

IM: What about the other "biggie" you mentioned? How were you changed in relation to forgiveness?

PE: I think forgiveness was among a number of things that were changed by my dramatic encounter seven years ago, and which over time has continued to generate change. The anger changed a lot earlier. So many different things happened that I can't untangle them.

H.H. and I talked a lot about an incident where a Chinese officer executed a sixteen-year-old boy for a crime committed by his father. And it wasn't enough to execute him. While the boy was waiting in prison for his execution, the officer came in and beat him senseless with a metal pipe. The Dalai Lama forgives the Chinese officer who did this. He said, "I forgive, but I don't forget. If I were there, I would have used force if necessary to stop the officer. But I wasn't there, and the officer will get punished in his next life." I reject the idea of reincarnation, but I don't think it is necessary to believe in reincarnation to forgive and behave ethically.

IM: But if you don't believe in reincarnation, then how did the Dalai Lama change your understanding of forgiveness?

PE: Well, I better understood his view. I think *forgiveness* is the wrong term. It's a term that often implies excusing and accepting. The Dalai Lama does hold people responsible for what they do, but he knows that harboring resentment or anger at this officer, or anyone else, will only harm himself. So he is suggesting that in forgiving someone, you don't retain a sense of anger; you don't focus on the past and harbor resentment because that would poison you. I can accept that view of forgiveness.

IM: In your many hours of meeting with His Holiness, it sounds like at times you introduced him to new terms and approaches. I know you sometimes lead workshops. Did you describe any of your exercises to him?

PE: Yes. He thinks they're pretty good for a nonmeditator! (Laughs) I have a whole series of exercises; they aren't rocket science. For instance, an exercise I'm focusing on at the moment is the self-scan. It's a way to bring yourself back to a state of equilibrium. The military has asked me if I would be willing to develop a technology to help people return to equilibrium in high-stress situations such as warfare. I suggested setting up a little telephone box somewhere in the field where soldiers could sit down and choose among three or four different ways to decompress. You want people like soldiers and police to be able to make good decisions. I emphasize that you do a self-scan before you enter a situation of potential danger. And if you can't do it, then your partner has to help you and say, "Take ten deep breaths" or whatever. Different things work for different people.

IM: You recently attended two insight meditation retreats. What was your impression?

PE: It was the hardest thing I've ever done other than quit smoking.

IM: Did you find it to be a useful training of the mind, perhaps an exercise or practice you would prescribe for people to intervene between the impulse and the action?

PE: I think the practices were of some benefit. But it seemed to me that the teachers' understanding of the mind is fifty years out of date. (I'm talking about their Western understanding. Their understanding of Buddhism, I presume, is really good.) We've learned so much in the past few hundred years. The Dalai Lama gets very excited about scientific discoveries. He now is quoting Darwin back to me. (Laughs) I gave him a quote in which Darwin says, "The highest moral virtue is to be concerned about the welfare of all sentient beings." He loved that. That's why you'll hear him say, "Darwin says..." Isn't that wonderful?

I'm reminded of when I told him I didn't believe in reincarnation. He said to me, "The Buddha was an empiricist who instructed his followers that if it didn't fit their experience, then reject it." That's a scientist! I like that. That's really good.

When I finished my training in 1958—that's fifty years ago—there were a lot of things that were either misunderstood or mysteries, which we now understand. The Dalai Lama and I differ in that he thinks there are things that will forever be mysteries and I don't. Neither of us will live long enough to find out who's right, because we're not going to be here in another fifty years.

IM: But don't you think some things in life can't be explained? What about your transformations in your meetings with the Dalai Lama?

PE: I have my own theory on that. I've talked to seven other people who had similar experiences with him. I was about to retire, others had just gone through a divorce, some had survived a life-threatening illness. All of us were in transition. Also, we all had an emotional wound in early life. I had my mother's suicide. I think the Dalai Lama senses that a person is open. In transitions you're much more open to change. And when there's a wound, he senses it. He focuses and radiates goodness, and that heals. I don't know if we have a way of measuring it, because no one has tried.

I'm not talking about a metaphor; I'm talking about something that is palpable. When I had this experience with him—it was an eight- or nine-minute period—he was talking to my daughter and he and I were holding hands the whole time. My body was filled with a sensation that I'd never felt before. I have small versions of it now whenever I'm with him. In fact, when I'm sitting at the computer editing what he said, I get little versions of it. But that first experience was extremely intense. I think I was feeling that goodness. And it did heal something. A mystery?

⋄⋄⋄ From Volume 24, Number 1 (Fall 2007).

3 Two Person Meditation
Psychotherapy with Mark Epstein

The publication of his book Going to Pieces Without Falling Apart *in 1998 confirmed Mark Epstein as one of the preeminent synthesizers of the wisdom of East and West. The following interview reveals how as a psychotherapist Epstein applies Buddhist ideas and practices to the needs of his clients. It was conducted by Wes Nisker and Barbara Gates in 1998.*

MARK EPSTEIN: I think about therapy as doing a two-person meditation. So in a therapy session, I try to give the same kind of impartial attention to everything there is to observe, making the entire space a field of meditation. As I see it, the best psychotherapy, whether or not it is labeled Buddhist or meditative, is creating the kind of space that I'm describing. As it is conventionally practiced, however, most psychotherapists have their own agendas for their patients. They are trained to look for conflict and to draw it out of the patient in a particular way. That process will often support the therapist's view of how change is supposed to take place rather than how it might naturally occur.

For instance, in working with anger, a lot of therapists—and also a lot of patients—believe that what is most important is to express that anger. Upon seeing the hint of anger in a patient, a therapist with this kind of agenda might encourage the patient to express the anger, act it out, get angry at the therapist, try to exhaust the anger through expression. My training in Buddhism has taught me something different, which is basically that anger is bottomless, and that the way to transform it is to create enough space around it so that the anger can come and go on its own. So while I'm very attentive to anger in a patient during a therapy session, I don't necessarily encourage expression of it but only an acknowledgment of its presence.

Most therapists these days are also trained to look for what's called *transference*, that is, all the ways the patient brings some earlier relationship to bear upon the relationship with the therapist. So when the therapist gets a sense that the patient is treating him the way the patient must have treated his mother or father, the therapist is trained to focus the attention on the transference relationship and to make interpretations, such as, "Oh, you must be experiencing me like your mother." The conventional strategy is to feed the transference, to consciously try to turn the patient-therapist relationship into a transference relationship and then to resolve it. Then, presumably, the therapy is done.

I've been wary of doing that with my patients. I try to be attentive to the transference, but then just to allow it to dissolve so that we can have a real relationship, meaning a direct, in-the-moment relationship between the two of us as we actually are, instead of encouraging a fantasy transference relationship.

IM: In that way do you feel that you come to a different sense of a person or find a different kind of healing?

ME: I believe that I am finding something more immediate and playful, which therefore has the potential to be more liberating than bringing up and going over the old, conditioned, patterned relationship. I'm not saying that I don't work with the transference, only that those old patterns are usually so obvious they don't need to be developed and promoted in the way conventional psychotherapists are taught. These patterns can be talked about as they come up, and then they can be let go of right in the moment. It is precisely that letting go of the transference from moment to moment that is so much like meditation, and it can free the person in the same way meditation can.

IM: In *Going to Pieces Without Falling Apart* you say that your patients' most common fear is that they will be overwhelmed by their feelings; the ego is afraid it will lose control in anger, fear, or sorrow.

ME: Most of the people who come to see me are having some trouble around emotions, and they usually have one of two basic strategies in trying to cope with their difficult feelings. One is to push the feelings away because they are afraid of being overwhelmed by them. The other is to be overindulgent with the feelings and to act them out too much without ever really experiencing them. Because of my Buddhist training, I know that it is possible for someone to create an internal environment in which any feeling can be experienced without either having to express that feeling or become overwhelmed by it. This requires an understanding of what feelings really are.

What I have noticed, in myself to start with, is that although we may be able to talk about feelings, we don't readily understand the extent to which our emotional states are physical experiences. I think the defensive strategy that most of us adopt is to jump away from the physiological sensations and into our minds. We try to turn our feelings too quickly into thought, which means that the bodily aspect of the emotion is being pushed away. That's how people become estranged from critical aspects of themselves. When we learn to experience the complexity of our emotions in our physical being, they become more understandable as well as more tolerable. Therapy can then become a kind of practice ground for knowing and exploring our feelings.

IM: Many people discover in meditation that they are much more aware of their thoughts than they are of their feelings, and yet it seems as though feelings most often are leading in the dance.

ME: I believe that feelings do lead. I've been especially drawn to the ideas of the child analyst D.W. Winnicott, who describes in great detail how a child develops an over-reliance on thinking. Winnicott explains that when a child has to cope with either an impinging or an ignoring environment, the most common defensive strategy—perhaps just because we are humans with brains—is to go up into the mind and to start thinking about how to manage the situation. That strategy takes the child away from her feelings and leaves her, as one of my patients put it, spinning in the eddies of the mind.

I believe that what Winnicott says is true for most of the people who have come to me for therapy. I think that over-reliance on this defensive, coping mental energy stays with us from childhood. I've also noticed that all the thinking usually has a certain kind of sadness attached to it, the sadness of a child who is either not being seen or not being left alone enough. What can happen in therapy or meditation is that by paying attention to all that obsessive thinking, we begin to feel the sadness beneath it, often only noticeable as a subtle physical sensation. I believe that to contact this sadness is often to get at the root of all the thinking.

IM: Some Buddhist teachers encourage the practice of staying with a feeling so that a meditator can experience it fully and become familiar with it, while others instruct you just to let the feeling go, saying that it's only another experience arising and you needn't pay any more attention to it than you might a fly buzzing by your ear.

ME: I think there are times when the advice just to let go is very skillful. Some Buddhist teachers would also advise countering a disturbing emotion with its opposite, hoping to quickly balance it out. That strategy can also be useful, showing people that their minds are made of more than just negative emotions. But ultimately, I think the real freedom comes from the ability to allow whatever feeling is arising to appear, play itself out, and leave on its own. That is the training of true equanimity.

IM: Most conventional Western therapy seems to be based on the notion that the psyche can be "fixed," and once it is fixed we can live happily ever after without any negative emotions. In contrast, the Buddhist approach is that the psyche or self is a mixed bag by its very nature. That's the Buddha's perspective, the first noble truth.

ME: I feel that the materialism that is endemic to our culture has infiltrated our way of thinking about psychology. So we idealize a perfect self and believe that by building it up—through self-improvement, self-knowledge, self-discovery, self-esteem—we can create a self that won't suffer anymore. What the Buddha says, and many great psychoanalytic thinkers would agree, is that any notion of a concrete, inviolable, nonsuffering self is an illusion. In the Buddhist view, in order for a person to be happy the ego has to keep unraveling. So the ego comes into existence briefly when it has to accomplish something and then dissolves. The self is always forming and de-forming, evolving and devolving. If we can make way for that process instead of getting in the way of it, then we can start to experience ourselves as we really are. That's really the meaning of the title of my book, *Going To Pieces Without Falling Apart*.

From Volume 15, Number 1 (Fall 1998)

4 The Worst Zen Student That Ever Was
Reflections on Depression and Buddhist Practice

By Susan Moon

I want to tell you about coming apart, wanting to die, and returning at last to myself, and about how my Buddhist practice both helped and hindered me in this zigzag journey.

Although I was suffering from severe depression, I didn't call it that for most of the several years I was in and out of it. I thought depression was for lethargic people who stayed in bed all day. But my pain was as sharp as an ice pick. Restless in the extreme, I paced and paced, looking for a way out. The visible cause was the drawn-out and difficult end of a relationship with a lover. The invisible causes were old griefs and fears, and other conditions unknown to me.

It's taboo to be depressed. When I was feeling really bad, I still went to work, though I was barely functional. If I had a case of the flu and had been in a fraction of the pain I was in, I would have called in sick. But I didn't call in "depressed." One day I threw a whole issue of the magazine I edit into the computer's trashcan, thinking I was saving it. Then I emptied the trash. I had to hire a consultant to look for it in the virtual garbage, and eventually I got most of it back. But it was myself I wanted to put in the trash.

Physical pain is hard to describe, and psychic pain is even harder. I was in intense, moment-by-moment pain, and all I wanted was to get away from it. The pain was in the thoughts, which I didn't (and couldn't) recognize as just my thoughts. A voice in my head repeated what I took to be "The Truth": that I would never again love or be loved by another person.

I spent hours every day on the phone. Once, during the forty-five-minute drive from my lover's home back to Berkeley, I had to stop and call a friend from a pay phone by the side of the road so that I could drive the rest of the way home, even though it was only fifteen minutes away. "I just got off the Richmond Bridge," I sobbed. "I'm afraid I don't exist."

"You exist," she said. "How could I love you if you didn't exist? Come over right now, and we'll take a walk on the Berkeley pier."

I've gained some understanding of what it must be like to have an invisible illness, like lupus or chronic fatigue syndrome. I wanted to wear a sign around my neck—"I might look okay, but I'm sick!"—so people wouldn't expect me to be functional.

I couldn't eat—a common symptom of depression. It wasn't just loss of appetite. Chewing itself was unbearable. A blob of bread was scary because it got in the way of breathing, and breathing was already hard enough to do. Liquids such as hot milk with honey and Earl Grey tea were more manageable. It occurs to me now that I'd regressed to the stage before I had teeth, when the only kind of eating I could do was sucking.

Like many other depressed people, I didn't sleep well. I clutched my pillow and called out to the flapping curtains for help. I took sleeping pills— sometimes they worked, sometimes they didn't. I couldn't read in the night (or the day, either, for that matter) because I couldn't get past the fear to concentrate on anything.

Waking in the morning was the worst of all. The moment consciousness returned, the pain came with it. Oh no! I have to breathe my way through another day.

I didn't like getting into the shower because I didn't want to be alone with my skin. To feel my own skin and imagine that nobody would ever touch it again was unbearable. Better to swaddle myself in layers, no matter what the weather, so the skin didn't have to notice it was alone.

One of the worst things about being so depressed is that one becomes totally self-absorbed. I could hear other people only when they were talking to me about me: recommending homeopathic remedies, interpreting my dreams to me, telling me they loved me.

During my depression, one of my adult sons had a serious bicycle accident, and my fear for his well-being snapped me out of my self-absorption for the five days that he was in the hospital. I sat all night in a chair beside his hospital bed, hyper vigilant, watching him sleep. I put a cool cloth on his forehead. I prayed to whomever was listening; I made a promise I couldn't keep—not to be depressed if only he would be all right.

He came home to my house from the hospital with one leg in a full cast. One day I walked into the living room where he was reading on the couch, and he said, "My god, what's the matter? You look like a ghost!"

Dry-mouthed with panic, I told him I had to go see my lover; we had to decide right then whether to break up. "Do you think I should stay with him?" I asked.

My son looked at me with an expression I'll never forget—a mixture of despair and love. "I don't think you should be driving in the state you're in. Why don't you just stay here and be my mother?"

But I couldn't. I drove out to see the man, compelled by an irrational sense of urgency, with my son's stricken face burning in my mind.

I had been a Zen Buddhist practitioner for over twenty years. I assumed that my meditation practice would steady me. What could be more comforting than forty minutes in the peaceful, familiar zendo with the sweet smell of tatami straw matting? But it didn't help. This is what I want to say: at times it made things worse. The demons in my mind took advantage of the silence. They weren't real demons, but they didn't care whether they were real or not; they tormented me anyway.

My Buddhist teachers urged me to keep on sitting zazen. "Don't turn away from your suffering," they said. "Just watch the painful thoughts arise, and watch them pass away again."

When I sat down on a zafu, the painful thoughts arose all right, but if they passed away, it was only to make room for even more painful thoughts. I'll die alone. And, adding insult to injury: After twenty years, I'm the worst Zen student that ever was.

When I told my teachers I was disappointed that zazen didn't make me feel better, they told me. "You don't sit zazen to get something. You sit zazen in order to sit zazen." But didn't Buddha teach the Dharma in the first place to alleviate suffering? Did all those other people in the zendo really get up out of bed at 5 A.M. for no particular reason?

Still, I kept going back, hoping that if I meditated hard enough, I'd have some sort of "breakthrough." I signed up to sit Rohatsu sesshin, the week-long meditation retreat in early December that commemorates Buddha's enlightenment. He sat down under the bodhi tree and vowed not to get up until he saw the truth. It took him a week. I had sat many sesshins before, but maybe this would be my week.

The first day was bad. Each day was more difficult. On the third day, during a break, I snuck away to a pay phone down the street and called my sister in Philadelphia. Choking on my own words, I told her I didn't know who I was. The fourth day was worse yet. A nameless pressure mounted inside me. I couldn't stay another second.

Driving away from the zendo in the privacy of my car, I shouted: "This is the worst day of my life!" (There would be other days after that when I would say it again: "No, this day is worse.")

I drove into Tilden Park and walked into the woods where no one could see me. I screamed and pulled my hair. I lay down on the ground and rolled down the hill, letting the underbrush scratch and poke me. I liked having leaves get stuck in my hair and clothing. It made me feel real. I picked up a fallen branch from a redwood tree and began flailing myself on the back. The bodily pain was easier to bear than the mental pain it pushed aside.

But I scared myself. How could I be spending my sesshin afternoon beating myself with sticks in the woods? How had it come to this?

I picked the leaves out of my hair and went home. The next morning, the fifth day, I called the Zen Center and said I wasn't feeling well—an understatement if ever there was one—and wouldn't be sitting the rest of the sesshin. I didn't sit zazen for some months after that.

I thought I had failed in my practice—twenty years of it!—and was bitterly disappointed in myself. Only after the depression subsided did I see what a growth it was. Choosing not to sit was choosing not to be ruled by dogma, to be compassionate with myself, to take my spiritual practice into my own hands.

Buddhism teaches that we have "no fixed self." There is nothing permanent about me. During the depression, I wasn't my "self," as we say. I didn't seem to have a self at all, in a way that cruelly mimicked this central point in Buddhist teaching. You'd think that it would be painless to have no self, because without a self, who was there to be in pain? And yet there was unbearable pain. Like a wind-up doll, I went stiffly through the motions of being Sue Moon, but there was no person present, no aliveness—only a battery that was running down.

I felt angry at Buddhism, as if to say: You told me there's no fixed self, and I believed you, and look where it got me! I'd lost track of the balancing truth that there was no separation.

I couldn't have gone on like this indefinitely; I was tearing up the fabric of my life. As I was weeping to my friend Melody on the phone one afternoon, speaking my familiar litany, she suddenly shouted at me: "Stop it! You've got to save your own life! Nobody else but you can save yourself, and you can do it! You just have to be brave." This was an important phone call: she startled me into finding a stick of courage, and I held on to it by reminding myself of her words.

Still, the misery continued, and I finally decided to try medication. I consulted a psychiatrist, who prescribed Prozac. I took it for about a week and felt much worse, something I thought wouldn't have been possible a week before. The psychiatrist had me stop the Prozac and try Zoloft. I felt it kick in after a couple of days. I didn't feel drugged—rather as though a deadly fog was lifting.

Zoloft is supposed to be good for people who have trouble with obsessional thinking, and I seem to be one of those. Zoloft did what zazen didn't do—it quieted the voices in my head: "I hate him. I hate myself." It didn't shut them up entirely, but they weren't as loud, and I was sometimes able to turn away from them.

I had a lot of resistance to taking medication. I thought my unhappiness had two parts: negative circumstances in the outside world, which Zoloft obviously couldn't fix, and negative attitudes inside my head, which I thought my Buddhist practice should take care of. Besides, the monks of old didn't have Zoloft. But some of those monks probably obsessed their lives away in misery; others may have left the monastery because they couldn't concentrate. Buddhist history doesn't tell us about the ones who tried and failed, the ones with attention deficit disorder or clinical depression.

I was learning to trust myself. Taking Zoloft and stopping sitting were both acts of faith in myself. So, too, I learned to construct my own spiritual practice.

Every morning as soon as I got out of bed, I lit a candle on my little altar and offered a stick of incense. I made three full bows, then stood before the altar, my palms pressed together, and recited out loud my morning prayers, starting with a child's prayer a Catholic friend had taught me:

Angel of God, my guardian dear,
To whom God's love commits me here,
Ever this day be at my side
To watch and guard, to rule and guide.

Then I took refuge in Buddha, Dharma, and Sangha, saying the words out loud whether I felt anything or not.

That I had shaped this practice for myself gave me confidence. And the early morning incense smoke, though it was thin and drifting, provided a hint of continuity for my days. They seemed, after all, to be days in the same life. One person's life—mine.

Now I can say this: there are times in life when nothing helps, when you just have to feel terrible for a while. All you can do is go through the agony and come out the other end of it. It's a gift, in a way, to hit the bottom (though it didn't feel like a gift at the time!). If you lie on the grass, you can't fall down.

Once, when I called Zen teacher Reb Anderson in despair, he came to Berkeley to see me. We sat on a park bench in a children's playground, and he told me, "The universe is already taking care of you." I said this mantra to myself over and over: "The universe is already taking care of me."

I remember a turning moment when, at the end of a hard summer, I was visiting friends on Cape Cod. One late afternoon I walked barefoot and alone down the beach and into the salty water. There were no people about, so I took off my bathing suit in the water and flung it up on the sand. I swam and swam and felt the water touching every part of me. I was in it—no dry place left. I wasn't afraid to be alone with my skin because I wasn't alone; there was nothing, not the width of a cell, between me and the rest of the universe. I did a somersault under the water and looked up at the shiny membrane above me. My head hatched into the light, and I breathed the air and knew that I would be all right. No, not would be, but was already. I was back in my life.

I still don't know why I suffered so much, or why I stopped. I can neither blame myself for the suffering nor take credit for its cessation.

I sit again—I mean on a zafu—but not as much as I used to. I also bow and chant and pray. I've stopped taking Zoloft, though I'd return to it without shame if I thought it would be useful.

I practice curiosity. What is it to be born a human being? What does it mean to be embodied in your separate skin?

I now admit that I sit zazen for a reason: I want to understand who I am (if anybody), and how I'm connected to the rest of it.

From Volume 17, Number 2 (Spring 2001).

5 | What A Relief! I Don't Exist:
Buddhism and the Brain
An Interview with Francisco Varela

One thing that distinguished Francisco Varela from others in the field of cognitive science is that he was a student of Tibetan Buddhism and brought the wisdom of that tradition to bear on his study of the mind and brain. Before his untimely death in 2001, Varela was considered among the leading cognitive scientists in the world and served as director of research at the French National Research Council and head of the Laboratory of Cognitive Psychophysiology at the Hospital of the Salpétrière in Paris. Along with Humberto R. Maturana, Varela co-created the "Santiago Theory" of cognition and authored The Tree of Knowledge. *Varela's* The Embodied Mind, *written with Evan Thompson and Eleanor Rosch, grew out of Naropa Institute's Science Program and was a seminal work in exploring and contrasting the Buddhist and Western scientific models of mind and self. In the introductions to both* The Embodied Mind *and his last book,* Ethical Know-How, *Varela gratefully acknowledges his teachers Chögyam Trungpa and Tulku Urgyen.*

Wes Nisker spoke by phone with Varela at his home in Paris in the summer of 1999.

INQUIRING MIND: The convergence of Dharma and Western science seems to be entering an exciting new phase with the current revolution in biology, and especially in your field, cognitive science. This exchange of understanding seems likely to have even more import than the well-explored interface between physics and Dharma.

FRANCISCO VARELA: Absolutely. There was a glamour that came with the physics interface, because physics has long been considered the baseline science, talking about very fundamental things such as matter, atoms, and gravity. But the understandings that come from physics don't have much relevance or direct application to everyday human life and experience. To most people the concepts are just too abstract. The natural sciences and cognitive science, on the other hand, are about our bodies, our minds, our moment-to-moment experience. The teachings of Dharma have very little to say about physics but a lot to say about mind and body.

IM: One of the most interesting and somewhat shocking conclusions currently emerging from cognitive research is scientists' apparent inability to find a "self" or director in the brain who runs our personal drama.

FV: That is precisely what we were trying to articulate in our book *The Embodied Mind*. With few exceptions, cognitive scientists have come to understand the egolessness of self. What is surprising, however, is how little their scientific conclusion is taken personally, or really applied to an individual's life. Buddhism does not focus on a general theory of the brain but points to the fact that it's about you, about your life. Many cognitive scientists close the door of the lab after studying all day about the selflessness of the brain, and they go right back to their normal, self-absorbed life.

IM: Perhaps the crucial difference between scientists and meditators is in the direction of their respective gazes—the scientist looking outward and the meditator inward.

FV: Why not look in both directions?

IM: Right. And that leads to the question of how new scientific understandings can be useful to people engaged in meditation practice, or to people's lives in general.

FV: What science *can* do is to give the notion of selflessness a stamp of authority or validity. In some cases at least, this may motivate people to look at themselves more closely, with fresh eyes. Even then, there is still that mysterious leap people take when they decide to study the Dharma, to come to a transformative understanding of themselves.

IM: Why do you think it is so hard for people to be transformed, even after learning of the scientific research or after having a personal experience of no-self?

FV: My hypothesis is that evolution has shaped human beings to disregard the basic sources of our being. We were built to forget how we were put together. Being aware of that process would make us slightly hesitant toward ourselves and our behavior. It is like a centipede looking at itself walking; it might very well become all tangled up. So we are born with a bias to pay no attention to the original sources of the self and to simply operate in the world. That is why you can have an intellectual understanding of egolessness, or anatta, while the emotional root that weaves that understanding into your life remains absent. In some sense, a heightened degree of self-awareness is anti-evolutionary.

IM: Otherwise we'd be second-guessing ourselves at every moment: who is deciding to buy a house or have a child?

FV: That's right. Every decision would be suspect. So evolution has designed you so that you just want to hurry on with your solidified self. That is what the sense of being a separate organism is all about.

IM: I'm reminded of what Richard Dawkins says, that the brain is designed by evolution not to believe in Darwinism. (Laughs)

FV: Yes, and the brain *is* designed not to take Dharma seriously. (Laughs)

IM: If we are to accept the idea that the brain is a self-organizing system that works without a director or "self," then how are we to understand the idea of a meditator who develops mindfulness? How do you understand the sense that some independent agent exists that can alter the way the brain works or change how consciousness sees itself?

FV: You put your finger on what is still to me a big gap in our understanding, which is that funny flip-over into being self-reflective. Mindfulness practice is based on a spontaneous human capacity that is normally occluded by our evolutionary drive to solidify. But my sense is that consciousness is not just consciousness of something. It also contains an element of pure presence or pure awareness, and this consciousness is always there. So in mindfulness practice, rather than constantly engaging with objects one discovers that little entry point into the awareness that is always present. And then you practice, practice, practice until this presence is more thoroughly deployed.

Actually, one way of talking about this distinction is by differentiating an awareness that goes to an object, and is therefore intentional, from an awareness that is not intentional because it is just there as bare awareness, as pure awareness. We might think of it as some kind of pre-reflective, pre-conscious awareness. You sort of bring it forth from the edges into the center. How that shift happens is where the interesting questions lie for me right now. I think we have a good grip on how consciousness of the world comes about, or at least very good glimpses of it; however, consciousness of itself is still pretty much an open question.

IM: If we see clearly how the process of mind is taking place without any self, and therefore see very little free will within the process, we could certainly be led to a kind of despair or futility.

FV: Well, one possible reaction is to say, Oh, my God, I don't exist. But from a Dharmic perspective you might say, What a relief! I don't have to hold on to the illusion of self. One of the things you realize in meditation practice is that once you let go of the belief in self, there are no terrible consequences. You do not cease to function or even thrive. In fact, there is a kind of a peaceful presence untouched by any of the ideas you have about it. The problem does not exist once you can become at ease with the actual experience of no-self. If you realize the end results of giving up on the illusion of a solid self, then it is not as much a problem as it is a solution.

◇
◇ From Volume 16, Number 1 (Fall 1999).
◇

IV

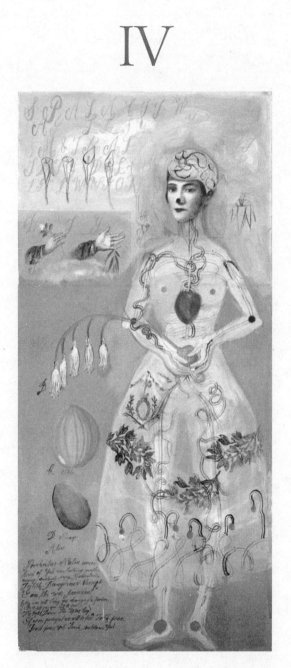

THE DHARMA & THE DRAMA

Drawing on the canon of the Sarvastivada, an early school of Buddhism, Zen teacher and poet Norman Fischer revisits the myth of Siddhartha's renunciation and his wife's birthing of their son: "It's quite clear that it is the whole situation—both the outer birth and the inner turning—that describes the fullness of the path. Leaving home and staying home, renouncing the world and accepting the world, are seen here as parts of a seamless whole." Here are stories of the dramas of life—at home, in cooking, in a red-neck bar—seen through the lens of Buddhist teachings. In her unexpected dinner with Carlos Castaneda, monologist and writer Nina Wise learns to appreciate her ordinary life. At a month-long meditation retreat, Charles Johnson, one of the few African Americans in attendance, faces memories of his near-lynching years earlier. Cook and Zen teacher Ed Brown suffers over his rhubarb dessert, which goes untasted by his U.S. senator Dianne Feinstein. When we walk the path, our experiences and encounters become more than drama; they are also lessons in Dharma.

1   The Sacred and the Lost

By Norman Fischer

In the middle of the night Siddhartha prepares to leave the palace. But as he passes his wife Yasodhara's room and sees her sleeping figure, he is overcome by her beauty and his love for her. He can't leave. He goes to her, without telling her of his resolve, and they make love, conceiving their only child. Yasodhara senses Siddhartha's impending distance. "Lord, wherever you go, take me with you," she pleads. "So be it," he replies, "Wherever I go, I will take you." By morning, he is gone.

From that night on Gautama's spiritual quest is mirrored by the course of Yasodhara's pregnancy; both go on for six years and culminate during the same fateful night. Both Gautama and Yasodhara, in their very different circumstances, practice austerities, eating only one sesame seed, one grain of rice, and one pulse pod a day. And for both the period of asceticism is grim and unsuccessful; Gautama nearly dies and Yasodhara almost loses the child. When Gautama accepts solid food again, Yasodhara does too, and the child is saved. Gautama sits under the Bo tree full of strength and determination; Yasodhara enters labor. Gautama is then tempted by Mara while Yasodhara, in the palace, receives a messenger from Mara who tells her that her husband has died, and she, overcome with grief again, almost loses the child. But at the moment when the former prince is about to enter enlightenment, Yasodhara hears the truth, recovers, and gives birth to their son, Rahula, at the eclipse of the moon.

—ADAPTED FROM John Strong's article "A Family Quest: The Buddha, Yasodhara, and Rahula in the Mulasarvastivada Vinaya"

Being human is a tough proposition. The world is wonderful, colorful, and bright. But it is also overwhelming, and embedded within it, as the very essence of its beauty, is the seed of suffering. As the *Dhammapada* says, the flower is beautiful, but within the flower there is an arrow pointing right at us. In our experience of the path we find the world quite often too much for us. Too distracting and powerfully seductive. It pulls us in and eventually pulls us down.

But to set the world aside isn't the answer either. Even imagining some-how a Shangri-La where we can be truly quiet, peaceful, and fulfilled (sup-ported somehow by an inheritance), we will still have ourselves to contend with and all the worlds of our own minds. Wars, storms, disgust, and rage will be with us, even if the world is not. And even assuming we could somehow subdue all of this and find contentment, I think we would soon discover that that contentment was shallow without some way to express our gratitude for this body and life. So we would be very soon turning toward the world again, the world as a sacred place, a field for the activity of our practice. And so we would, with a new sense of things, be confronted again with our human dilemma.

Let's consider the world as sacred. *Sacred* means set apart. The sacred is the exclusive; its sacredness comes from what it excludes from itself and is manifested in its very difference. There's a built-in difficulty with this idea, of course: the very exclusivity, which renders the sacred, in the end, violent. For it seems as if the sacred, in order to be the sacred, must scapegoat the profane, must, in fact, see to it that there is a profane in order to scapegoat it. The exclusivity of the sacred is its downfall.

But perhaps there is another dimension to the concept of the sacred. What is separate or exclusive is also particular and distinct. It has a strong integrity in and of itself. It is this thing, not some other thing. So perhaps the essence of sacredness need not be exclusivity but rather particularity. Sacred particularity implies a powerful sense of commitment to something very con-crete and specific. It involves a certain sense of vowing, of letting go of things outside the vow, outside the particular, of giving ourselves completely to one thing.

In fact, through total devotion to the particular we come out into the open space of our living. When we walk down the corridor of the particu-larities of our life we come out finally into the wide field where we can meet everything. Powerful practitioners I have met over the years achieve union with the universal in just this way. These people, through total dedication to a particular thing throughout the course of a lifetime—whether that thing be a relationship, a skill or an art, a practice tradition, or perhaps most radi-cally, each and every moment of living—have been able to somehow tran-scend that particular thing. In other words, they've been able to include everything within it, acquiring in the process an ease and a graciousness that looks quite a bit like enlightenment.

A traditional Sanskrit Buddhist term that might be useful for extending our discussion here is *tathata*. It means "thus," "just," "merely," or "as it is" and indicates the real nature of things as they actually are, without additional projections, elaborations, or improvements. Seeing the world just the way it is sounds like a good idea—we all aspire to truth rather than falsehood, to accuracy rather than fuzziness—but it is a radical idea that requires more of us than it seems to at first sight, because the world as we know it is nothing other than the world of our projections and confusions. The very idea of "myself" is the biggest projection of all, the screen beyond which I cannot see. Everything in my experience is colored by it; everything I cherish and desire is created by it.

And "things as they really are" is constantly passing away, coming and going, free from our desires. Things as they are, from a human perspective, requires an acute appreciation of loss—total loss, loss of self, and loss of world. This is what freedom means. This is the real shape of the sacredness of the world, the union we find within the particularity of each moment of our lives.

In other words, it is not a question of holding on to the world or transcending it. The real world is its own transcendence, and our dilemma is conceptual. It is language and thought that imprison us, not the world, not even our own desire. In order to be free, we need to be free in relation to this transcendent world, because there isn't any other way. There isn't anywhere else to go.

A monk once asked Yun Men, "When there's no thought inside and no thing outside, what is it?" Yun Men replied, "Upside down!"

Our world is upside down. We long for peace outside of activity, but there isn't anything outside of activity. We want to hold on to the world, but the whole world in its real form is nothing but loss, moment by moment. And there's no hope for this. There's only the appreciation of it for what it really is. With this appreciation we can once and for all respond to conditions as they arise. With this point of view the whole world and our particular place within it is the field for our practice.

How to practice then? Didn't the Buddha, facing a choice, leave home, renounce the world and his family, and devote himself to a life of dedication to Dharma? And don't we as practitioners face a similar choice?

The story of the Buddha's renunciation comes to us through the Theravada canon, one of several versions of the canon that were handed down in the various schools that existed after the Buddha's time. That this particular version of the story is the one that has been given to us in the West is simply an historical accident. It is not the "official" version nor is it in any way the best or the truest version. It is simply the one we happen to have given our attention to over the years.

I'd like to discuss a different version of the renunciation story (condensed above), which exists in the canon of the Sarvastivada, another major early school. After the Buddha makes love to Yasodhara, conceiving their only child, the story proceeds remarkably and mythically along a dual track. All of the events of Buddha's quest are matched exactly by the course of Yasodhara's pregnancy, which, like Buddha's journey, lasts for six years. In the Theravada version of the story the word *rahula* is etymologized as *fetter*, but in the Sarvastivada version it is said to derive from the word meaning "Moon God," because the dual event of the Buddha's enlightenment and Rahula's birth takes place on the night of the eclipse of the moon.

This story, as I understand it, is about sacredness and particularity and the loss these entail. The Buddha does leave home and Yasodhara does stay. They give each other up, and each must pursue his and her own path with full devotion. As a result of this opting with full commitment to the path taken, fruition comes about: inner and outer birth ensue. But I think the story, read on a structural level, is not simply about, on one hand, the Buddha and his solitary heroic quest for enlightenment, and, on the other hand, the girl he leaves behind. Structurally, the story is clearly presented as a single narrative with two halves. The implication is that the enlightenment of the Buddha isn't something that happens to him or is effected by him alone. Nothing in the way the story is told here privileges Siddhartha over Yasodhara. It's quite clear that it is the whole situation—both the outer birth and the inner turning—that describes the fullness of the path. Leaving home and staying home, renouncing the world and accepting the world, are seen here as parts of a seamless whole. We can't have it all. Our path is particular and, as such, always involves renunciation. In the story, the Buddha is a renunciate. But so is Yasodhara. The Buddha gives up the home life, but Yasodhara gives up the homeless life. Together, through loss of each other and devotion to the particularity of their own paths, they create the whole of enlightenment. Both appreciate the world as it really is.

From Volume 14, Number 1 (Fall 1997).

2 Luck Disguised as Ordinary Life

By Nina Wise

My fortieth birthday was approaching like a tidal wave. I was single, child-less, and questioning the value of being a performance artist with a cult fol-lowing but no steady income. I was living without the requisite evidence of adulthood—a couch, a dining room table, a matched set of dishes, a sound system. I tried to convince myself that this was due to the fact that I had sep-arated from a relationship and nearly all of the furniture and electronic devices I had used for seven years belonged to my ex-lover. But I knew the real dilemma was that I'd dedicated my life to my work and I wasn't getting famous fast enough. There were no book contracts, no movie deals, no tel-evision appearances coming my way. I needed help, a guidebook for the mid-life moonscape of defeat.

One of the great benefits of disappointment is that it drives you to reli-gion. Usually not the one you were raised with; if that had worked you wouldn't be in this condition. Exorcism was the only methodology to stave off the demons that had caught wind of my approaching birthday and flicked their icy tongues in my ear, chanting a liturgy of symphonic discontent. I decided to learn to meditate, discovered a vipassana Buddhist teacher in my neighborhood, and began to sit every morning on my purple zafu.

One afternoon my friend Isabel called to tell me the Dalai Lama was coming to Santa Monica to give the Kalachakra Initiation. I'd met Isabel when she came backstage after one of my performances.

"That sex fantasy with the refrigerator was so *divine*," she told me at one of her Pacific Heights dinner parties, while butlers serving smoked salmon and caviar toasties on silver trays waded through a bubbling crowd of envi-ronmentalists, publishers, writers, and philanthropists. Isabel had grown up in Argentina, where it was traditional among the wealthy to create an international milieu of royalty, intellectuals, and artists. Her warm brown eyes exuded confidence, her cheeks were aphrodisiac, and she wore a silver streak in her brown hair the way teenagers wear nose rings, to show that even though she was holding forth on a white rug arrayed with priceless antiques, she was really a rebel. Over champagne, Isabel and I discovered that we both were seekers. We began going to retreats, Dharma talks, satsangs, and darshans together.

"Do you want to go to Santa Monica with me and be my roommate?" Isabel asked over the phone.

The Kalachakra Initiation is one of the most esoteric and advanced practices in the Tibetan Buddhist system. During the initiation, participants take vows to devote their lives to altruism, to become bodhisattvas, enlightened beings who, instead of stepping off the wheel of incarnation upon their death, return to this Earth to serve all living beings. Normally these teachings are only given to students with years of preliminary practices under their belts, but because the world was in such an escalated state of environmental devastation, the Dalai Lama had decided to offer this transmission to anyone who felt moved to participate. Many of my friends were heading for Southern California for this event. And yes, yes, I wanted to go.

When I arrived at the Shangri-La, an upscale art deco hotel on Ocean Boulevard, Isabel was spread out on the king-sized bed balancing *Mothering* magazine on her stomach, which rose like a whale from a calm ocean. She was expecting her fifth child after a twelve-year pause, and she needed to get current on parenting. I lay down next to her and pulled out the forty-page text we'd been given for the five-day initiation process.

From this time until enlightenment
I will generate the altruistic intention to become enlightened,
Generate the very pure thought,
And abandon the conception of I and mine.

"Isabel, what is the 'very pure thought'? I'm not sure I'm following this," I said, eager for an in-depth Dharma discussion.

"It doesn't matter. We'll get it by osmosis. Do you think I should get a diaper service?"

"Definitely," I said, turning back to the incomprehensible text.

In the morning we waited in lines that stretched around the block until it was our turn to take three mouthfuls of saffron-blessed water and spit out our mental and emotional toxins into an enormous white plastic bucket. "I'm going to throw up," Isabel groaned, covering her eyes so she didn't have to look at the frothy urine-colored spittle.

We did three prostrations as we entered the hall, one for the Buddha, one for the teaching, and one for the community of seekers. Searching for our places in the crowded 2,000-seat auditorium, I tried not to stare at the celebrities. We settled into velvet seats, pulled out our books, and studied the stage, where monks in one-armed, wine-colored robes and scarlet chicken-comb headpieces chanted their multi-octave, deep-throated drone, and the Dalai Lama recited detailed instructions in Tibetan.

"What page are we on?" I asked Isabel.

"It doesn't matter," she said, waking from a nap. "Breathe. Meditate."

"But we're supposed to be visualizing some deity with green arms and a flower on his forehead."

"Relax," she said as she closed her eyes, stretched out her legs, and leaned her head back on the top of her seat.

I couldn't relax. This was my opportunity to receive an important transmission. I struggled to follow the text.

Within the great seal of clear light devoid of the elaborations of inherent existence,

In the center of an ocean of offering clouds of Samantabhadra
Like five-colored rainbows thoroughly bedecked . . .

At the break people dashed into the lobby, where men in denim and polo shirts paced outside in the Santa Monica sunshine, their cellphones pressed against their ears.

"Did you get the address of Richard Gere's party for the Dalai Lama?"

"Has my agent called?"

"He said he would sign? Fantastic. Maybe this stuff works."

At the sound of the gong, people rushed back into the art deco auditorium, which resonated with deep-throated chants. Isabel and I settled ourselves into our plush seats and joined the 2,000 seekers praying to be truthful, kind, compassionate, taking vows to dedicate our lives to the well-being of others.

On the way home, Isabel whispered in a conspiratorial hush that her friend Carlos Castaneda was coming to the hotel to join us for dinner.

"Don't tell anyone; it's just for us. He's a bit finicky about who he hangs out with."

We only had thirty minutes. Like college roommates getting ready for a double date, we took turns in the shower, hovered shoulder to shoulder in front of the bathroom mirror with our blow dryers and lipstick, finessed each other's outfits. Our wrists were still moist with Isabel's French perfume when we heard the knock. Isabel glided to the door with cultivated poise. Wide-eyed, I examined a short gray-haired man in a wrinkled polyester suit and dusty cowboy boots embracing her in the doorway.

That cannot possibly be him, I thought. I had imagined him tall, with broad shoulders and a swatch of thick dark hair, someone with an air of Mexican aristocracy steeped in shamanism and desert ravines. I had read all of Carlos Castaneda's books when I was in college, and they had affected me more than any other writer I had ever studied. Castaneda's accounts of his encounters in Mexico with the Yaqui Indian sorcerer Don Juan Matus had informed my entire generation. I would quote Don Juan to my friends, who would quote him back to me. "Follow a path with heart," we would tell each other. "Keep death over your left shoulder." We were taking psychedelics and changing the world into a place that prioritized human love above materialism and magic above science. Castaneda and Don Juan were our guides through a terrain outside the law, one that our parents were too conservative and too terrified to explore. Castaneda was our surrogate father, Don Juan our spiritual teacher, our prophet.

"Carlos, this is Nina," Isabel smiled with a seamless grace. "Nina, Carlos Castaneda."

Like earth opened by a plow, Carlos's furrowed face fell into a wide grin as he shook my hand. His palm was as warm as a chicken's nest. He sat down in a floral-print easy chair and asked for a glass of water. I could hardly believe I was in the same room with this man.

"I've been waiting to ask you for ages, what really happened to Don Juan?" Isabel dove in. "Did he die?"

"No, no," Carlos chuckled, "he didn't die. He disappeared. He went to the other place. I am learning this too to become immortal. This is my work now, which begins after dark. Most people think that their work is what they do at their jobs, during the day, but the real work happens after midnight.

"After Don Juan left, La Gorda became my benefactor," he went on, leaning forward, looking us both directly in the eyes as if fishing. "She was fat and ugly, with coal-black hair and dark eyes. I was completely under her spell."

I was completely under Castaneda's spell now. The lilt of his voice, the Spanish accent cradling an impeccable English, hypnotized me. His eyes glowed with the victory of our capture.

"And anything La Gorda wanted me to do, I had to do it. So one day she told me to go to Tucson. She said I should work as a cook in a cafe.

"'No,' I said to her. 'I like my life in Los Angeles. I like my friends. I'm not going to Tucson. I don't know how to cook.'

"I got into my truck and I drove off. Six hours outside of Nayarit, I was thinking, 'My life in Los Angeles isn't that great.' Twelve hours outside of Nayarit I was thinking, 'My life in Los Angeles has its ups and downs.' Eighteen hours outside of Nayarit I found myself on the border of Arizona, heading for Tucson, thinking, 'My life in Los Angeles is completely miserable.' I pulled up to the first greasy spoon cafe I laid my eyes on and I walked in. I asked for a job."

Carlos crossed his arms over his chest and deepened his voice.

"'Do you know eggs? Ya see, hamburgers and fries are easy, but we serve breakfast all day and you've got to know eggs.'"

He uncrossed his arms and let his voice soften.

"I found a studio apartment and I practiced cooking eggs for two weeks—scrambled, over easy, over hard, soft boiled, hard boiled, omelets, poached. I went back to the cafe.

"'Do you know eggs?' the boss asked me again.

"'Yeah, I know eggs,' I said.

"I got the job. After a month they promoted me, put me in charge of hiring and firing. And this young girl named Linda came in and wanted a job as a waitress. So I hired her. We got to be friends and she told me that she was a fan of Carlos Castaneda and she gave me a couple of Castaneda's books to read. I didn't know what to say. I took the books and a couple of days later I gave them back. I told her I didn't really understand."

Carlos chuckled, enjoying the story. I sat on the pink hotel couch with my legs crossed and studied his face. The media had recently discredited Castaneda's claims to have apprenticed to a witchdoctor in Mexico. Sympathetic critics had suggested it was poetry, important fiction. Harsher critics had accused him of fraud. I listened to Carlos's story like a detective, looking for factual flaws. I examined his brown and wrinkled face for evidence of deception. But I couldn't hold myself back; I fell into the story as if carried away by rushing water, seduced by Castaneda's enthusiasm, his sunny chuckle, his intelligence, and the understated grace of his gestures.

"One morning Linda came into the cafe and she was very jumpy.

"'What's going on?' I asked. '¿Qué pasa?'"

Carlos sat up straight in his chair, pulled his knees tightly together, and spoke in a high pitch.

"'He's here. Carlos Castaneda. In the alley. There's a tall dark Mexican man sitting in a white limousine with the air conditioning on and the windows rolled up and he's scribbling notes on a yellow pad. I'm sure it's him. There are rumors that Carlos Castaneda is in Tucson. What should I do?'"

He relaxed his knees.

"I didn't know what to say. I told her to just go out there and introduce herself. She thought she was too fat. And that Castaneda would never fall for a waitress at a greasy spoon cafe. I looked at her standing there in her cap and apron. She looked beautiful to me, radiant. She was young and lively and had a quick mind.

"'You're perfect, just the way you are,' I told her.

"She put on lipstick and fixed up her hair and went out into the alley. Two minutes later, she came back with tears streaming down her face.

"'What happened?' I asked her. She could hardly talk through her tears.

"'I knocked on his window...and he rolled it down...and I said...hi and told him my name...was Linda...he just rolled the window up...he wouldn't even talk to me.'

"I felt real bad," said Carlos, a sadness darkening his eyes. "I knew he wasn't Castaneda; I was. But I thought maybe she'd meet some guy who'd take her out to dinner. I didn't know what to do. I took her in my arms and I held her." He paused, looked out the window at the silhouettes of palm trees lining the street.

"Her shoulders heaved gently in my arms as she tried to stifle her tears, and then I started to cry too. I'd come to really love this girl. We'd been best friends for nearly a year. I wondered if I could tell her who I was. But I realized she'd never believe me. She'd think I was making it up to make her feel better. You see, for all this time she'd known me as Joe Gomez."

Carlos Castaneda, the man she dreamed of meeting, was holding her in his arms, but she didn't recognize him. Love slips by with an alias as the Sirens of disappointment captivate our imaginations. I'm Linda, I realized, thinking that what I long for is something other than this life unfolding moment to moment in ways I could never plan or even fantasize. Outside, seagulls cried as the sun began to sink and colors marbled the sky.

Carlos paused and looked directly at me, his face aglow with the pink light of sunset. No one moved. Then he let his eyes fall.

"When I got back to my studio apartment, La Gorda was sitting there, waiting for me. I don't know how she got in. She always got in, always found me. I told her what had happened. I asked her what I should do.

"'*Vámanos,*' she said.

"'But I can't just leave,' I told her. 'I have to give two weeks notice, train a replacement, say goodbye to my friends.'

"'What's a matter,' she said. '¿*Tiénes miedo?* You're afraid no one can cook eggs as good as Carlos Castaneda? *Vámanos.*'

"We got into my truck and drove off."

Carlos got up to go, shook out his pant legs, extended his arms. I walked right into his strong hug.

"You're perfect just the way you are," he whispered into my ear.

I could hear him whistling as he strode down the hall.

From Volume 11, Number 2 (Spring 1995).

3   A Love Letter to Garbage

By Barbara Gates

A mound of refuse or the sweepings of a street,
Old kettles, old bottles, and a broken can,
Old iron, old bones, old rags, that raving slut
Who keeps the till. Now that my ladder's gone,
I must lie down where all the ladders start,
In the foul rag-and-bone shop of the heart.

—WILLIAM BUTLER YEATS
from "The Circus Animals' Desertion"

Garbage. It's an unlikely calling. Somehow, though, it has become mine. I've been taking walks at the Berkeley Marina, built on landfill. Once marshlands, mudflats, and bay, the marina is "filled" with construction debris, old bricks, old glass, municipal waste. What better arena to reflect on garbage and to encounter the heat and churn, the scrape and stench of refuse in the heart.

It was a shock when, at the age of fifty-eight, I found myself drawn into intense inward churning of the sort I'd assumed I'd left behind. I thought I'd successfully dumped a lot of old garbage and found a graceful rhythm in these middle years—a settled home life, steady husband, sweetly growing teenage daughter, daily grounding in exercise and sitting practice. But this summer, for no apparent reason (or was it postpartum upheaval on completing a seven-year book project?), I found myself at the mercy of an inner chaos of self-recrimination, almost despair—feelings and thoughts, long ago crammed away. And this in a world rapidly destroying itself—a world to which, in this state of self-preoccupation, I could barely attend.

Maybe no one else knew. I did keep giving book talks, ferrying my daughter to school and soccer, making daily calls to my eighty-three-year-old mom. But in the center of my office, a seven-year mound of papers and books, maps, bills, and cancelled checks continued to heap up in an unruly mess, threatening to topple. I couldn't force myself to touch it, barely to look at it. I could hardly get myself to do the dishes or the laundry or to make a dinner for my family. I couldn't even get myself to take walks (a favorite pastime had been long, usually solitary walks) without the support of a friend. In fact, no matter what it was, without support I couldn't do it. This included meditation. For twenty-eight years I'd struggled, and often failed, to sit every day. It was only in the last several years that I had settled into daily practice. But now I couldn't get myself to set my buttocks on a cushion.

It was in the early morning of a day of a particularly toxic inner onslaught that I headed toward the Berkeley Marina with Jeannie, a new Wednesday walking partner. We circled Cesar E. Chavez Waterfront Park, where for about twenty years the City of Berkeley dumped 300 tons of municipal refuse a day. Jeannie began to talk about a Tibetan *ngöndro* practice. Surprising myself—ordinarily ritual-adverse—I found myself urging her to teach me the words recited as part of the practice.

She began by calling on the guru, reassuring me, the no-frills agnostic, "What you're really doing is calling on the active part of your Buddha-nature, your Buddha within." I'd heard that phrase many times. But that morning, unaccountably, it moved me to lengthen my spine, to feel inside a kind of broadening, to open my eyes and listen. I watched Jeannie's gold earring glint in the sunlight, the flash of her ring as she strode along. I tried to focus on the verses, heard fragments. "Samsara is an ocean of suffering... unendurable and unbearably intense.... Recognizing this, my mind turns toward the Dharma."

Little did Jeannie know what agitation competed with her words. Neither could she know that these phrases felt like a life preserver. When she stopped speaking, I watched her feet, heard the crunch crunch on the gravel, sensed the pebbles under my own sneakers.

Maybe with some help from my friends, I could start sitting and walking again. I remembered a friend who sat in the early mornings at the Berkeley Buddhist Monastery. I called her up and made a plan to meet her the next morning at 6:15 for the meditation. I'd already called another friend and arranged to meet her at the footbridge to the Marina at 8:30 so I could force myself to walk. Luckily, neither friend number one nor friend number two showed up. There I was at the monastery at 6:15, challenged either to leave or to muster whatever it took to go inside. Somehow I entered, found myself a cushion, and sat down—with all my agitation. Likewise, two hours later, when I was stood-up at the footbridge to the marina, I mustered all of my discipline, walked across the bridge on my own, and circled the park.

As I walked, my mind kept revolving at a crazy pace. Attempts to remember the Buddha within had scant results. As I hurried along, I barged through thoughts; I felt like I did as a kid, shouldering off crowds in the New York City subway. I tried to pay attention to what was right there. Notice my fingers, cold; notice the gravel under foot, the chill wind smacking my face. Notice the ground squirrels, slick and fat, racing toward the rocks along the shore, the cormorants flying low over the water. Notice the walkers with wool hats, with earphones, with strollers, with dogs. Through a mess of thoughts, I heard the chime of navigation bells, the long bass note of a foghorn.

I hiked on, past the flare station linked to wells throughout the park that collect highly flammable methane gas. Just then I remembered that I was walking on landfill made of decomposing garbage. The fire of decay seemed to match my own inner turbulence, the landfill garbage to match what I felt inside. This resonance lit my imagination, jiggled my preoccupation with my self, began in some unaccountable way to open my view to include the world.

In the following weeks, I found myself unexpectedly fascinated by the history and troubles of the landfill itself. One morning I tracked down Patty Donald, who had worked for twenty-five years as a naturalist at the marina. Eighteen years earlier, she'd founded the Shorebird Nature Center, which is where I found her. I followed Patty and her dog, Tigger, around the marina area, talking garbage.

Not only was the landfill made of household waste, slag, sand, construction debris, and dredged spoil, but each day new refuse continued to wash up and spill out onto its shores. We began at a tiny beach where the culvert of School House Creek emptied out into the bay. "Some refuse," Patty told me, "is washed up onto the beach from the bay—needles and other medical waste, garbage dumped off the sides of Navy and cruise ships, pesticides and herbicides carried to the bay from Central Valley agriculture by the Sacramento and San Joaquin Rivers."

The shore was also mucky with washed-up trash and excretions from the culvert: leaf litter, an empty oil can ("One of these can pollute 250,000 gallons of water"), fertilizers, pesticides, herbicides, soap, Styrofoam, plastics. "The garbage comes from us," said Patty, baldly.

Tigger bounced ahead of us through a section called the Berkeley Meadow. "Look how it's taken on a life of its own!" Patty gestured toward native coyote bush, California sage, and non-native fennel and dock. Witnessing life recovering itself here in a meadow that was once garbage, I felt in some way excited.

We got down on our knees, and Patty showed me the tiny shrimp in vernal pools. "See here how the meadow has become a vernal wetlands. In the winter, water collects in shallow pools ('not even an inch deep'), and the water hatches the seed shrimp. The shrimp attract dabbling ducks, and there are other predators eaten by birds like egrets and great blue herons.

"Maybe it's through the creek culverts that rabbits, ground squirrels, voles, and raccoons have found their way across the freeway into the meadow. Kingfishers, kestrels, red-tailed hawks, and white-tailed kites thrive on the rabbits and voles, blue-bellied lizards, and gopher snakes." Again a tremor, a sense of possibility, that when allowed to flourish, the natural world has a tendency to heal itself.

In counterpoint with the walks at the Marina, I continued to get myself to the monastery each morning. I didn't miss a day, afraid to lose my momentum. One morning when I was sitting in silence at the monastery, a thought came up: Nothing should be thrown away. A moment later, another thought followed: Of course, nothing can be thrown away. Noxious chemicals in landfill sites leach back into our groundwater. And isn't the mind the same way? Thrown-out feelings return unbidden, driving our actions.

A few days later, listening to the radio, I heard scientists talking about tiny microbes found in the environment that can transform hazardous waste. The microbial life which surrounds us and of which we are composed is adept at eating and breathing some of our most dangerous toxins. The geobacter microbes, metal-breathing bacteria first found by scientists in the mud of the Potomac River outside of Washington, can "breathe" various radioactive metals, including uranium, technetium, cobalt, and plutonium. Most amazing to me, the geobacters are natural constituents of almost all soils. Normally, they would be relatively low in numbers, but by simply sprinkling soil with vinegar, a food that they like, scientists can get them to become extremely numerous. They breathe the toxins in and out and in the process change them from a very soluble to an insoluble form.

While meditating, it had come to me that nothing can be thrown away. Now I took another step: nothing can be thrown away, but it can be transformed. We can be nourished by the garbage. We can "eat" it or we can breathe it in and breathe it out changed.

This picture of bacteria transforming garbage, like that of the landfill meadow healing itself, became a catalytic image for me. I imagined teams of toxin-gobbling bacteria eating and digesting the trash and turning it back into Buddha fields. What I loved most was the thought that microbes are natural constituents of most soils, and that, allowed conducive conditions, the landfill moved naturally toward life and healing. Not so different from the healing of the heart through meditation.

I felt a sense of intrinsic possibility—that our basic nature, if approached with finesse, can recover itself. Whether we're grappling with the garbage of place or of heart, we can tap into a natural propensity to express a fundamentally wild nature—spontaneous, self-propagating, freely manifesting, intrinsically orderly, naturally coherent.

Several months into my regime of sitting with the garbage, walking with the garbage, studying the garbage, I noticed that, without my realizing it, some of what had felt so stymied in my life had indeed changed. I had finally sorted, reshelved, and filed the remains of my book project; I was meditating every day, first at the monastery, and most recently, after I had cleared space in my office, at home; and I was once again taking exploratory walks on my own.

Each day I continued to walk around Waterfront Park. One morning I watched the ground squirrels standing tall on their hind legs, front paws together, at attention; from their lookout rocks they called out warnings each to each. All along the shore, in brown robes with paws in prayer, they looked to me like monks from the Order of Interbeing, standing alert and still, taking care of each other. I was reminded again of that potential of the world, so easily squandered, to take care of itself.

As I walked back toward the footbridge that morning, a breeze blew in from the bay, across the tidal mudflats, past the long-legged shorebirds, riffling through the reeds and cattails, and, as I felt it, ventilating my inner landscape. After all of those months of walks around the landfill, of allowing myself to breathe with that rotten sludge of feelings in the chest, something was clearing inside me, an open breezy space where the bay wind could blow free. I felt a wide clarity. The heart can love. That's how it came to me.

◇
◇ From Volume 20, Number 2 (Fall 2004).
◇

4 Looking at Fear
Memory of a Near Lynching

By Charlie Johnson

While waiting for the registration process to begin at a month-long vipassana meditation retreat, I saw that I was going to be one of the few people of color, maybe the only African American. This had been true at my previous retreat as well. My job as an engineer at a major oil company frequently put me in similar situations. As far as I was aware, this did not raise any particular anxiety, and certainly nothing like what I was soon to discover.

At the beginning of this retreat, I found to my surprise that I could not get comfortable during the meditation periods. I had been meditating and doing yoga since the early 1970s, but I was just beginning to attend formal silent vipassana retreats, first a people-of-color retreat, then a ten-day retreat in the desert, and now this month-long. Over the years I had become accustomed to sitting cross-legged on a cushion and could typically sit for hours without significant discomfort. However now, no matter what I tried, nothing worked. I tried using a bench, a chair, and a zafu. At various times I sat with pillows under my knees, thighs, and buttocks. Everything was sore. Of course, all of this discomfort was affecting my meditation. I couldn't figure out what was wrong.

During a walking period toward the end of the first week of the retreat, a realization seemed to come out of nowhere: I was not at ease in this sea of unknown white people. Surely, my discomfort in meditation was a physical manifestation of the fear churning unconsciously inside me. Five minutes earlier I would have said that being one of few people of color at the retreat was not a significant issue for me. I had no idea that fear could impact me in that way or so unconsciously. Over the next several days, I sat with the emotional impact of my sudden realization. And although there was fear, I was okay with these feelings and could allow space for them without being

overwhelmed. It was getting easier to sit in comfort, and in general I was set-
tling into the retreat. It seemed as if the whole issue, although still present,
had been diffused.

Then one night toward the end of the second week, upon returning to
my room to go to bed, I found an anonymous note on my door. It was from
someone asking me to do something about my snoring, which was keeping
him/her awake. Initially I did not think much of the note; I put it on the table
and went to bed. Then I began thinking: I do not snore, at least not signifi-
cantly. My wife has never said anything about it. At the last retreat I had a
roommate and he hadn't said anything about it. On and on I went. After a
while I began to wonder if the note was really intended to be about snoring.
Or was it an opportunity to hassle Charlie? I dismissed that thought.

But my mind would not let this go and continued to race for the next
hour or so. Then, all of a sudden, I became very frightened, almost to the
point of panic, as I had a flashback to something that had happened over
thirty years earlier. A white coworker and I were having a drink at a bar close
to where we worked. This bar was in a lily-white rural area, and normally I
would never have gone there. However my friend had repeatedly invited me
to go with him, and after a considerable amount of urging he convinced me
it would be safe. For several weeks it was.

On that particular night things seemed to be going as usual. Then one of
the waitresses, with whom we had become friendly, informed us that she had
overheard some guys discussing how they were going to get my friend and
me after the bar closed. Hastily, we paid our bill, and as we began walking
toward the door we heard a voice from the back of the bar say, "Hey, nigger!
I'm going to get you and your nigger-loving buddy." My friend was able to
get to his car and leave. I was not so fortunate. Although I remember only
bits and pieces of what happened that night, I do recall being hit in the head
as I was trying to get into my car and later being huddled on the ground while
I was kicked and punched from all directions. It seemed like hours before the
police came. I thought I would not survive the night. According to the police
estimates there were around eighty people hitting me. Luckily, I was not seriously injured physically. However, as I am now learning, the ordeal left deep
unconscious emotional scars.

As I was lying there in my bed at the retreat, all of the emotions from that
earlier encounter exploded in my consciousness. Even through the fear, my
rational mind was saying I was just being silly, no one at the retreat was out
to get me. But a nanosecond later I was thinking about what I could do if
someone did want to attack me. They could come right into the room; there

were no locks on the door. I was on the second floor with the only window opening to a downward-sloping hill. If I jumped out, I would only lie injured on the ground below, easy prey for those who would harm me. The only way out was the door. If someone came into the room with the intent of doing me harm, there was no way I could escape. A few moments later I'd think no one was going to come in here after me, that this was nonsense. Just go to sleep. I'd cover up, take a deep breath, and close my eyes. Then I realized I didn't have my clothes on. That left me even more vulnerable. My next thought was that I'd really gone too far. Nonetheless, I got up and put on my pants.

Ultimately, I decided to go home. It was about two o'clock in the morning when I packed my bags and took them down to my car. But my car was blocked in, and I couldn't get out. I considered sleeping in my car, but that would have been more confined; I'd be less able to defend myself than if I stayed in my room.

I decided to go to the meditation hall. It was a large room with lots of doors and windows, so there were escape paths if needed. There were also lots of chairs that I could throw at my attackers. Concluding that I could defend myself if necessary, I stayed there.

At first light, I got the retreat manager to have the cars moved that were blocking me in, scribbled a quick note to the teachers telling what had happened, and left. I clearly recall the cacophony of thoughts that surfaced during my one-and-a-half-hour drive home. There was relief at being away from the perceived threat, anxiety about what I was going to tell my wife, and uncertainty about what I would do next on my spiritual journey. The group with whom I thought I had found a spiritual home emphasized long residential retreats. But if people-of-color retreats were the only ones I was going to be able to attend, I would have to look elsewhere.

After arriving at my house I decided to do what I call house-cleaning meditation. Ever since I was very young I have cleaned house when things are weighing heavily on my mind. I am not sure exactly how this works because while I am cleaning I am fully into cleaning. It's not as though I am consciously thinking about anything other than the spot on the window or the dust on the floor. However, when I finish I am usually in a different relationship with what was troubling me when I started.

With the space created by this unusual meditation, the regular sitting and walking meditation, and the sensation of being at home, I had a different perspective on the retreat. I appreciated how insidious and resilient fear can be, affecting us in ways that do not leave a clue that fear is the root cause. It was also clear that I was transferring feelings from a real-life threatening situation onto circumstances which, although the source of some uneasiness, were rather benign. It came to me that I could and should return; that the feelings around being in the sea of unknown white faces, the fear resulting from my experience at the bar, and personal peace of mind could all coexist.

The next day I got a call from one of the retreat teachers, who wanted to make sure I was okay. After some discussion I was given permission to return. Although given the option of taking another room, I wanted to keep the same one.

Walking up the hill back to my room at the retreat center I was filled with fear, hope, and embarrassment. The fear was there because even though I felt different toward the demon that had driven me away, there was no way to know whether the change was real until I tried to sleep in the same room with the unlocked door again. I was hoping the shift I believed was there was real. It was with a sense of embarrassment that I looked into the inquisitive faces of the other retreatants as I walked by them on the way to my room. Clearly they were wondering what had happened to me. I was glad it was a silent retreat; it would have been difficult to talk to them at that point.

It took me a day or two to get settled back in, however I was able to do so without too much difficulty. During the meditation periods I was able to get comfortable. At night I felt safe in my room and was able to sleep soundly. From time to time I would get flashbacks to the feelings I'd had the night I left the retreat, but I was able to watch them come and go without supplying them with the energy I had earlier.

I have attended a number of retreats since this one. Except for the people-of-color retreats, there have been few people of color present. I very seldom get the same fearful thoughts, but they do still arise. When they do, I have been able to just watch them go by. I wonder if this is what true fearlessness is—not the absence of fear but rather the courage to look at fear just as it is, without giving it energy and without letting it take control.

From Volume 19, Number 2 (Spring 2003).

5   Rhubarb

By Edward Espe Brown

My friend Ronni asked me if I would help out with a benefit for the nursery school she heads. Right away I said, "Yes, of course, by all means. For you, Ronni, whatever you want." After all, Ronni had been coming to my meditation group for years, and I knew she adored me. Plus, I loved the way her clothes fit.

"We are going to have a 'Magnificent Mingle,'" she said. "We are asking celebrity chefs to plan a menu together, and then each one will cook their dish. Would you be willing to do that?"

That sounded pretty simple to me. No problem.

Later Ronni let me know that the plan had changed. Senator Dianne Feinstein and her husband, Richard Blum, had decided to hold the event at their house in San Francisco and to underwrite the catering. The senator, it turns out, is Ronni's boss's mother. So the new plan was for the celebrity chefs to provide desserts. Was I still willing to participate? Ronni wondered.

Here a whisper of doubt surfaced. I'm not much of a dessert chef, especially when it comes to presentation and flourish. Nothing like you might expect from a fancy high-class restaurant. "Rustic cuisine" is what I call my cooking. That way there is plenty of leeway for dishes to turn out the way they do, rather than the way they should.

"Ronni," I hesitated, "you know, I'm not really much of a dessert maker, and I'm sure that compared to the others—who are actual pastry chefs—whatever I make will not really measure up. I don't know…," my voice trailed off.

"We'd still really like you to participate," Ronni responded. She sounded so earnest, but I still didn't believe that "we" particularly cared one way or another, so I told her that I didn't think my participation would be so important after all.

"Maybe not, but it would be wonderful for me if you were at the event. It's going to be fancy dress-up, and I'm not used to socializing like that. Couldn't you come for support?"

"Okay, but fancy dress-up? What will I wear? The only dress-up clothes I have are my Buddhist robes."

"That would be perfect!" was Ronni's animated reply. "Wear your Buddhist robes. Come as my priest. Keep me company."

It's easy to be intrepid when the event is months away.

A few weeks passed, and Ronni told me the plans had changed again. "Remember how I told you that you would bring the dessert and serve it? Now the caterers are going to serve all the desserts. You can just deliver your dessert to them, and they will take it from there."

"Fine," I said. "Easier for me to enjoy the evening in my black dress."

The event was to be held in February, and even though that sounds early for fresh fruit, I decided to make a strawberry rhubarb tart cake. I thought I would leave the chocolate to others as well as the frills. Since I'd never seen a recipe for anything like this, I figured that while it might not turn out spectacular, at least it would be original. Besides, if I'm going to cook for 150 people in my modest home kitchen, I definitely like to "keep it simple, stupid." A layer of tart dough, a layer of fruit, and cake on top. Instead of cute petite tartlets taking up pan after pan, I'd make it in sheet pans and cut it into individual servings. I figured it all out: four half-sheet pans with three rows of fifteen servings each. Nothing to it.

As the time drew near, I thought I had better try out my dessert at least once before making it for the masses. I like to think of myself as daring, willing to take risks, and I had a pretty good idea it would work, but I went ahead and tested it out the Monday before the event. Rapturous. We loved it. And from my home-scale trial I could easily extrapolate the quantities needed for my weekend shopping list. Once in a while I even dared to hope that my homey dessert would be a big hit.

That was before Saturday, although Saturday started well enough. By eight o'clock I had the rhubarb cooking, and shortly after that, Susan and Stork, two other people from my meditation group, came by to help. I thought I had the baking well-organized and my anxiety pretty well concealed. It's not easy cooking with people who know me as a meditation teacher. A lot of performance anxiety. I had to stay calm and keep it together. At least that's what I imagined was expected of me. Everything had to go smoothly, and if it didn't, well, I'd be at least as buoyant and unflappable as Julia Child when she dropped the suckling pig on the floor on live television. Let it come and let it go like clouds in empty space. Sure thing. Nothing to it.

For several hours everything went like clockwork. At about two o'clock the trays of strawberry rhubarb tart cake began coming out of the oven in an appetizing shade of brown, giving off absorbing aromas of butter, sugar, and flour accented with vanilla and freshly ground anise seed. I spent some time figuring out the exact details of how to cut the tart cake into triangles rather than diamonds, squares or rectangles. I was pleased with my ingenuity. "Haven't seen that very often," I gloated.

Then came the unexpected. As Susan and Stork were getting ready to go, I thought I would give them each a few pieces from the ends of the trays. I inserted my handy-dandy triangular metal spatula and lifted out a piece of fragrant tart cake. I tilted the spatula to let it slide off. Nothing happened— except immediate, intense anxiety. The tart cake was sticking to the spatula. So I gingerly tilted the spatula more steeply and began to shake it in order to loosen the dessert. The top layer of cake with some fruit on the bottom slid off onto the plate. Stuck to the spatula was the crust with more of the fruit. My anxiety doubled, but I was still able to contain it.

I tried more pieces. Same result. My dessert for 150 of San Francisco's social elite was going to be unservable. I had miscalculated. Compared to my test run, the crust on the bottom was too thin and hadn't been prebaked long enough to be solid. The fruit on top was so thick that the moisture had turned the crust underneath into a mush. That's when I lost it. I started screaming and wailing. With my whole body and mind. As a Zen teacher, I don't do things half-heartedly.

Not that I get involved in blaming people. I know better than that. I blame the universe for being organized the way it is. To humiliate me when I am trying to do something of benefit. What's its problem? "Fuck the universe!" I screamed. I try to do something generous, something kind, something good, and just get fucked over. What kind of a world is that? Pretty soon my raging shifted to preverbal intensity: wordless, but extremely loud and piercing. It's embarrassing to be over fifty and yet throwing such a massive tantrum.

My students stood there in stunned silence at first and then began to suggest that things weren't that bad. The dessert was really delicious. Maybe it would be easier to serve it when it cooled off more. But I knew.

"It's easy enough for you to say that things will be fine. You're not going to have to stand up in front of San Francisco's social elite at Senator Feinstein's house." I wouldn't let up. I was inconsolable. My high-volume wails continued.

Once my students realized that I was not to be consoled or quieted, they headed for the door. I couldn't blame them. They had worked hard. There was nothing else they could do but leave. I saw each of them to the door with their dessert-to-go, calming down enough to offer thank-yous as best I could, expressing my appreciation for their taking the time to help out. Then I went back to ranting.

After cleaning up the kitchen I lay down on our recamier. (Okay, I can't find it in the dictionary either.) It's a marvelous recliner sofa, higher at the end with the pillows. Maybe it's a "fainting couch," just what I needed. I stared at the ceiling, acknowledging that my life was over, done for. I'd worked hard, done my best, and messed up. There was nothing left to do but face the end that was in store. Oh well. I made a cup of coffee, half decaf, with warmed half-and-half. Lay there and slowly revived myself, took a shower, and put on my Buddhist robes. White jibon, beige kimono, black koromo— the flowing dress, the layered look. Tied on the black rope belt. Adjusted all the collars. At least I would be formally attired as I met my fate.

I rarely get anywhere promptly, but amazingly, even with traffic, I was one of the first guests to arrive at the party. I parked just a few steps from the Feinstein residence and carted my trays of dessert into the kitchen, where the caterers found a place to put them. I was ready to party. Almost immediately a glass of champagne appeared in my hand and Dianne Feinstein herself, my senator, was there to greet me. "Hello, how are you? Good to see you again. How nice of you to contribute a dessert to our benefit. Please, make yourself at home."

Then her husband, Dick, was there to say hello. As a fellow Buddhist he swept me right up. We hadn't spoken in years, but he was friendly and graciously offered to show me his Buddhist art from Nepal and Tibet. I was so happy to be with him, and walking through the upstairs of his house in the quiet company of exquisite statues and *thangkas*, my heart went out to him. Silently to myself, I wished him all the health and happiness this world has to offer. On the spur of the moment, he offered me a beautiful turquoise ceramic trivet shaped in the syllable *om*. "Here," he said, "you could probably find some use for this. I'd like you to have it." I slipped it into the "pocket" of the sleeve of my kimono. Then it was back downstairs into the maelstrom of people I didn't know, people I'd never met.

The catering crew was attentive, and trays of appetizers came by, along with refills on the champagne. I began to feel I was in exalted company— a reach of my hand and food is there, my empty glass fills. Then the meal was laid out in the dining room, and we paraded around the table spooning food onto our plates. I managed to find a chair and visit with someone while I ate. I forgot my apprehension. Whatever will be will be. Let the caterers deal with it.

I helped myself to seconds before the food disappeared from the dining room. Then I heard that desserts were being served in the very special–sounding "solarium." The moment of judgment was at hand. I cruised through the living room to the solarium, and as nonchalantly as possible I sauntered around the table where the desserts were displayed. Cookies, cakes, tarts in all their magnificence, plate after plate, met my eye. Any moment I expected to see some of my tart, but it was nowhere in sight. My spirits started to sink, and the more desserts I saw which were not mine, the further my mood plummeted.

"What's the story?" I wondered. "Has someone decided it is not fit to serve? My dessert is not that bad." In my mind I rushed to its defense, "It may not look that great, but the flavors are terrific. Really, you should give it a try." But nobody heard my soliloquy. The guests were happily helping themselves to desserts and chatting away. A huge wave of humiliation washed through me. I had anticipated that people might find other desserts preferable, but now I was devastated to suddenly realize that mine wasn't being presented at all.

Dazed and bereft, I began searching the house for Ronni, looking for an explanation. I couldn't believe how I had been so upset earlier at the thought that my dessert was not perfectly enticing. How shameful to have been so distraught, when not having it served at all was even more distressing. Two times through the house and I couldn't find Ronni, so I headed for the kitchen to see if someone could serve my dessert.

The kitchen was bright and already cleaned up and fresh-looking. I found a handsome gentleman plating rich-looking round chocolate "bombs," garnishing them with fresh raspberries and a mint leaf. In response to my inquiry he said he was from one of the restaurants. When I consulted one of the caterers who was cleaning up, she knew nothing about serving my dessert and referred me back to the chocolate server. No help here. I considered serving my own dessert, but my formal robe has two-foot-wide sleeves which extend past the wrists, and even if I "tied back" the sleeves, serving-up would have been awkward, especially considering the champagne I'd drunk. So I went in search of help.

After a while I found my way outside and around the back of the house to a downstairs staging area. Two long folding tables were set up, replete with desserts. A whole crew of people was putting them on plates. It was the staff from Boulevard, a large upscale restaurant in downtown San Francisco. They couldn't make up their mind which dessert to contribute, so they brought their entire dessert menu. "What would you like?" they asked.

In this world of overabundance could there possibly be any significance to a simple home-made dessert? Now I recognized an old feeling of betrayal: "What I want, what I wish for, doesn't matter. It never has, it never will. You thought somebody cared about what you had to offer, but they can do just fine without you." I wandered back upstairs, lost and confused.

In the vast foyer I was suddenly face to face with my senator, who startled me with her gracious and solicitous inquiry, "Ed, are you all right?" "Yes, fine, thank you," I lied, not wanting to admit how completely devastated I was that my contribution to the benefit was not being served. But my senator was not blind. "Is there anything I can do for you?" she asked sincerely, "anything at all?"

My United States senator was asking me if there was anything she could do! Shouldn't I ask for something important? Saving the redwoods, filling the hole in the ozone, storing nuclear waste, reforming campaign financing? I couldn't decide, but I was convinced that it would have been really petty and selfish to ask that my dessert get served. "No, that's okay," I stammered, and ducked away before I started to cry.

The guests were beginning to leave by the time I finally found Ronni and explained to her that my dessert was not being served. She said she would look into it and returned shortly to explain there'd been a misunderstanding, that the chefs were serving their own desserts after all, not the caterers. I should have known. Some behind-the-scenes arrangements, perhaps even my senator's request, led to a few slices of my dessert being served.

What a fiasco: a dozen or so plates of strawberry rhubarb tart cake sat forlornly in the dining room, a house-length away from the solarium where the other desserts had been offered, while the last half dozen guests said their good-byes. There was nothing left to do but pack up and go home. My life as a celebrity chef hit bottom. I felt so empty. The message I heard from the world was, "It's not that we don't like your cooking. We're just not interested. You and your cooking are irrelevant."

I know that's not what happened. I know there is no one to blame and that no one actually said that. But that's my story, and I'm sticking to it. What a bummer.

Three and two-thirds trays of tart cake accompanied me home. My neighbors were delighted. They can't get enough of that wonderful stuff.

❖ From Volume 17, Number 2 (Fall 2001).

V

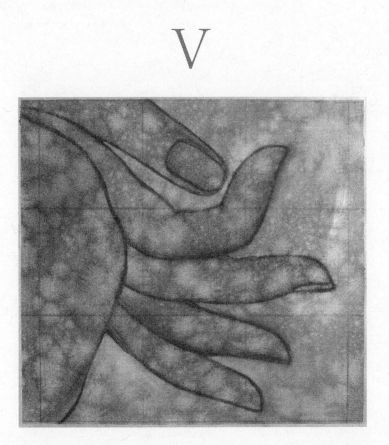

COMPLEMENTARY PATHS

As the Asian wisdom schools have flowed into the West, they have merged and created tributaries, exotic mixtures, and an abundance of riches. Western Buddhists can walk the path of the elders, attend Zen sesshins and Tibetan empowerments, or explore the nondual schools of Advaita or Dzogchen. Some, such as author/teacher Stephen Batchelor, have studied vipassana as well as Zen and Tibetan practice. Batchelor begins this section by comparing these three major Buddhist traditions.

As other teachers testify, following complementary paths can sometimes yield serendipitous results: Ram Dass discovers that vipassana meditation enhances his Hindu devotional practice. Dzogchen teacher Tsoknyi Rinpoche finds that vipassana meditators show potential in "nonmeditation." Theravadan students and teachers seek the wisdom of Advaita master Hari Lal Poonja, who turns the questions back on the questioners. Zen teacher Yvonne Rand, Tibetan nun Tenzin Palmo, and Theravada nun Ajahn Sundara exchange insights and find sisterhood in their complementary paths.

1 Complementary Paths
An Interview with Stephen Batchelor

Stephen Batchelor is a writer and Dharma teacher who has spent many years as a monk, both in the Tibetan and Zen traditions and also trained in the Theravada. He translated Shantideva's Guide to the Bodhisattva's Way of Life, *and he is the author of many books including* Alone with Others: An Existential Approach to Buddhism, The Tibet Guide, *which won the Thomas Cook Guide Book Award in 1988, and* The Faith to Doubt: Glimpses of Buddhist Uncertainty. *His most recent book is* Living with the Devil: A Meditation on Good and Evil. *Batchelor lives with his wife, Martine, in France.*

The following interview was conducted by Wes Nisker and Dan Clurman in Berkeley, California, in the Spring of 1991.

INQUIRING MIND: As someone who has practiced Tibetan Buddhism, Korean Zen, and South Asian Theravada Buddhism, how would you describe the essential differences?

STEPHEN BATCHELOR: Both Theravada and Tibetan Buddhism operate within a framework of Indian metaphysics. In these traditions, the path is seen as a series of linear stages that you pass through. It's understood that if you apply the techniques correctly, you're guaranteed success. Practice is a very predictable, almost scientific endeavor which presupposes that consciousness is a linear phenomenon that occurs within a cause-and-effect framework. Meanwhile, in Zen there's an acknowledgment that insight can erupt unpredictably or suddenly. You will find the use of the term *sudden* in Zen, and sudden is an acknowledgment that insight or illumination can occur at any moment.

IM: So Zen teaches that enlightenment is innate within us, but covered over by the more rational, analytic faculties of mind?

SB: Not exactly. Zen might say that the rational, analytic mind is just one part of a much greater whole, which Zen sometimes calls "the big mind," and this big mind includes the part that is already enlightened. We've just sealed ourselves off from that mode of awareness. In Theravada and Tibetan Buddhism, enlightenment is seen as something distant or transcendent, something "other." Whereas in Zen, enlightenment is seen as something that is immanent; it's already present within our consciousness, and if we press the right button or open the right door, there it is.

Zen recognizes that human consciousness and human life function multidimensionally, and that we live as temporal human beings in a linear history, and also as poetic, mysterious creatures. The practice is one that involves both dimensions.

IM: In your book *The Faith to Doubt,* you discuss the attitude of doubt as one of the basic elements of Zen practice. How would you describe that quality of doubt, and how is it cultivated?

SB: The doubt I am describing is a complement to faith. In Zen, you have the idea of great faith and great doubt as mutually supporting poles of spiritual practice. In fact, the three main aspects of Zen practice are Great Faith, Great Doubt, and Great Courage. Usually we tend to think of faith and doubt as opposites, that we need to get rid of doubt and hold on to faith, not recognizing perhaps that you cannot have one without the other.

The kind of doubt we speak of in Zen is not something that is leading you to a nihilistic or purely cynical point of view, but rather one that maintains faith in the possibility of awakening. There is actually a direct correspondence between the depth and the extent of one's perplexity and the depth and the extent of one's enlightenment or understanding. If one's doubt is merely intellectual or philosophical, then that will give rise to no more than an intellectual or philosophical enlightenment. But if your doubt is existential, gut level, which is what I'm talking of here, then it's something that resonates through the whole of your body and mind. That doubt will be the locus for a corresponding insight that will also reverberate throughout your body and mind.

IM: Would you say that enlightenment is the end of doubt?

SB: Not really. The doubt I'm talking about has to do with mystery, and I don't believe that enlightenment demystifies the world. If anything, it makes it more mysterious, more wondrous, and more awesome. That's the direction in which this doubt-perplexity is moving.

IM: The doubt you talk about does seem to be more prevalent and cultivated in the Zen schools than in the other schools of Buddhism. In Theravada, for example, you are encouraged to have an investigative attitude, but early on you are given a framework for practice so that you know what you are looking for. You are instructed to notice impermanence and emptiness of self. You are pointed toward the insights.

SM: Zen has its own subtle way of providing a framework for practice. For example, there are numerous terms in Zen that correspond to the concepts of impermanence, emptiness, and so on. In Zen you have terms such as *true mind* or *true person* or *Buddha-nature*. In the records of the Zen masters, you find these terms being repeated again and again. But in actual practice you are indeed expected to suspend all expectations of having any specific insights or experiences.

Imagine that you have a garden or a park full of children. With an Indian approach—Theravada or Tibetan—the teacher says to the children, "Look, there's a red ball and a blue cross and a green puppet out there. Now go and find them." You are told what it is you are supposed to find, and then you can go out and look for it. Whereas in Zen, it's as though the teacher says, "There is something hidden in this place. See if you can find out what it is."

IM: Speaking of "hidden," the koan meditations are very fascinating to many of us who have not practiced in that method. "What is the sound of one hand clapping?" "Does a dog have Buddha-nature?" How does the koan system work and how do these puzzling, unanswerable questions lead to the insights of Zen?

SB: The koan, at least in Korea where I was taught to use it, is basically a device, a sort of springboard to throw you into a state of doubt or perplexity. Once the doubt or perplexity is alive within you, then the form of the koan can be discarded. It's not important. The idea is that through working with the koan, your mind takes on a quality of uncertainty, of unknowing, of inquiry, perhaps even bewilderment about what is actually happening in your life from moment to moment.

But the koan also serves another function, and that is to concentrate the mind. So by focusing your attention single-pointedly on the koan, you also cultivate a degree of tranquility and concentrated awareness.

IM: When you're working with a koan, isn't there an element of analysis that takes place? After all, you're being given a riddle.

SB: You do start out analytically. You start out with a question or koan such as the one I used in Korea: "What is this?" Very quickly that question becomes, "What is it that asks 'What is this?'"

IM: Basically the koan starts questioning you.

SB: Right. The teacher I worked with used koans that ask "What is it?" or "What is this?" as a way of asking what is this consciousness, what is this mind? But he would emphasize that by *mind* or *consciousness* we don't mean the intellectual mind, the mind that is aware of sense objects. So right away the question gets thrown up in the air.

IM: Does the Zen master ever explain at the beginning that what is really being questioned is the self and the nature of consciousness?

SB: Some of the teachers do. The actual text itself just says, "What is this thing?" "What is it?" without specifying. The Zen master's role is to shock you into at least a preliminary awareness or an intimation of what the question really refers to. That is often done by example, by metaphor, by poetic suggestion. But again, in terms of practice, it's something that you work out for yourself. In Korea, you're left very much on your own to work these things out. It's a very difficult practice, and there's not a lot of guidance from the teacher. A Chinese Zen master of the twelfth century said that koan study is like gnawing on an iron stake.

IM: The mysterious is not only the province of Zen. For many people, Tibetan practices seem quite mysterious, perhaps because of the complex symbolism and ritual involved. You studied Tibetan Buddhism for eight years, so perhaps you could enlighten us a bit on some of the mysteries of Tibetan practice as well.

SB: When we talk of Tibetan Buddhism, we're actually considering a vast range of schools and practices, so one's understanding depends on which specific Tibetan school one enters. I studied in the Gelugpa tradition, which emphasizes study in order to develop a firm foundation in the basics of Buddhist philosophy and psychology prior to getting into any yogic, tantric, or meditative practice. I feel this study of Buddhist philosophy is a unique and very important point of departure. You start by reflecting deeply and repeatedly about what it is you are doing; you begin cultivating a Buddhist worldview.

IM: How do you do the reflection?

SB: It's important to understand that it's not just thinking about something every now and again. It's systematic reflection, which is a practice that I don't think exists in any other Buddhist school. It's analytical meditation, really. You sit on a cushion and you settle your breath, and then you reflect on death, the value of life, the meaning of refuge, or the meaning of suffering. Through this systematic reflection, you not only work toward a Buddhist understanding of life in the world, but you challenge your own cultural assumptions as well. So it's a two-way process for a Westerner.

I think this reflection practice is one of the great strengths of Tibetan Buddhism. In both Zen and vipassana, we too often reduce Buddhism down to a form of meditation practice, and the philosophical and metaphysical context remains in shadow. Furthermore, just consider for a moment that the noble eightfold path starts out with right view and right thinking; it doesn't start out with right mindfulness or right concentration. Those come at the end of the list somewhere. The Buddha didn't put right view and right thinking at the beginning just because they were the first things that came to mind. The Buddha had his reasons, which the Tibetans respect and incorporate into their practices.

IM: And where does the Tibetan practice take you after reflection?

SB: The range of practices embodied within Tibetan literature is vast, but in all the schools there's a strong momentum toward tantric practice. This always includes some type of concentration practice, perhaps initiation into various mandalas, visualizations, or mantra practice, and then ultimately yogic practices. In some of the traditions, however, like dzogchen and mahamudra, there's a more immediate immersion into a Zen-like or vipassana-like meditative practice.

IM: In Tibetan visualization exercises, students are given very complex images and mandalas, sometimes multi-armed and multi-headed deities, and they practice holding these images in their consciousness. Beyond development of concentration, what is the effect of these practices?

SB: The visualizations are much more than concentration exercises. They have to do with a reconstitution of perception. When you do these visualization practices, you are actually working to undermine your ordinary perception, your ordinary thinking. You are substituting a divine Buddha-world for the ordinary world. You replace the mundane with deities and mandalas. And in doing that, you are working with the basic dynamics of perception, the very matrices of consciousness that determine how you perceive the world.

IM: We assume you're not talking about the creation of a fantasy world, which you then try to inhabit.

SB: No, not at all. It's a world that you create and then deconstruct over and over again. You construct it, then deconstruct it; construct, deconstruct. You don't give it any kind of solidity.

IM: In *The Faith to Doubt*, you say that while you were studying Tibetan Buddhism, you took the opportunity to go on a vipassana meditation retreat with S.N. Goenka, and it threw your whole Tibetan practice into doubt. Can you describe what happened?

SB: Well, after giving that very positive assessment of Tibetan Buddhism, I'd have to say that I found a certain rigidity in the tradition. They're locked into a causal sense of how things should progress, inherited from Indian metaphysics, so that over the centuries they have become hostage to their own system. For example, many Tibetans believe that whoever you are, you must go through fifteen years of scholastic training. They don't seem to take into account other possibilities of the human mind, or the twenty years of education a Westerner brings to practice. You must understand that most Tibetans come to Tibetan Buddhism as we would come to primary school: to begin a liberal education. Meanwhile, most Westerners come to Tibetan

Buddhism with a superfluity of education, and then are expected to go back to grade one. I think as Westerners we can work through some of the preliminary Tibetan practices in a much shorter length of time.

Furthermore, most Tibetans assume that meditative experience cannot be had until you've done all the preliminaries as prescribed in their system. So, let's say you go on a Zen or vipassana retreat, as I did, and you get deep meditative insights about the mind-body processes and the nature of reality. Some Tibetans wouldn't even accept this as a possibility, since you haven't done your preliminaries yet. Nonetheless, after ten days in a vipassana retreat, you can understand anicca and dukkha in a way that is completely unexpected in a Tibetan framework. If you have a direct meditative experience before going through all the steps and preparations—as I did at the vipassana retreat with Goenka—it can throw the whole Tibetan system into question. Perhaps that's one of the advantages of being a Westerner and having access to the different schools of Buddhism. We have both the perspective and cultural detachment to question the forms themselves. We can see each system for what it is.

IM: In assessing the character of each system, would you say that one Buddhist tradition emphasizes more engagement with the world than the others?

SB: I think that, in general, Zen emphasizes engagement. For one thing, Zen tends to be more sensitive to nature. Zen monks are prepared to work the land, and that relationship to growing crops inevitably affects their understanding of the world in which they live. But I also feel that we have a popular image of Zen as "in the world" that does not necessarily represent the tradition as it exists. For example, the Zen tradition in Korea today is criticized, especially by Christians and secularists, for not being engaged. In eleventh-century China, the Confusians had a similar criticism of Zen.

So "in the world" is a tricky phrase that means different things to different people. If it means being actually engaged with social and political and environmental issues that are pertinent to the lives of ordinary people, then I think Buddhism has fallen short, as a rule, in its response to those issues, Zen as much as any other school. Mahayana will talk about saving all sentient beings, but that doesn't mean anyone necessarily goes out into the street to save them. And Zen can be expressed in everyday life, provided you live up in an idyllic little mountain retreat in some obscure province of China or Japan. In Mahayana Buddhism, the bodhisattva ideal is constantly reiterated, as in the last of the ox-herding pictures, when the enlightened one goes back into the market with gift-bestowing hands: he returns to the world for the sake of all sentient beings. But in practice, the bodhisattva ideal is not often realized. I think that is the challenge in our culture: to realize that metaphor.

IM: How might the different schools of Buddhism complement each other, especially as they take root in the West?

SB: It seems to me that every Buddhist tradition we encounter in the West today has developed certain specializations. Theravada Buddhism, for example, preserves the value of the Vinaya and the monastic life as the Buddha described it. In Theravada we also find the very powerful vipassana meditation practices, leading to direct insight into the essential characteristics of life: suffering, impermanence, and selflessness. Meanwhile, Tibetan Buddhism has a comprehensive quality. It integrates the whole range of Buddhist philosophical development, from early so-called Hinayana through the Mahayana, and on top of that maintains and develops the tantric tradition. It's also rich in presenting the Dharma through symbolic imagery. Meanwhile, Zen is very good in sustaining the force of uncertainty and mystery. Zen also has great reverence for nature. In Zen you find painting and poetry are actually encouraged as part of the spiritual practice. Even tea drinking. Can you imagine a Theravada bhikkhu putting any value in painting as an expression of the Dharma? It's certainly not very common. In Tibetan Buddhism you don't find much poetry either, and although there is painting, it is very formalized.

I want to make it clear that I do find Zen and the Indian traditions complementary. They are simply coming from different perspectives, operating within different models of consciousness. We can, as Westerners, appreciate the full range of qualities fostered in the various traditions. So what we are confronted with when we consider Buddhism is not something monolithic but rather a complexity of styles and traditions, each of which has its own strengths. And many people, like myself, do not feel entirely satisfied with any one of them. I find that I mold my practice according to the needs I have, both personally and culturally, as a Westerner, as someone whose conditioning is very different from that of a Thai or Tibetan or Korean.

IM: There are many teachers who would say there's a real danger in that kind of mixing and matching of practices.

SB: I would agree with that. It's essential that one's practice be grounded in one of the traditions, both experientially and philosophically, before moving on to a different school. If one does a two-week vipassana retreat, and then a few Tibetan mantras, and then a course on Zen swordsmanship, one won't get much out of any of them. But I also think there's a danger in the other extreme, when one narrows one's vision and identifies completely with a cultural form that has evolved to address the needs of an Asian people with whom one may have very few affinities.

IM: Perhaps the reason that vipassana practice has become so popular in the West is because it was introduced here with less of the Asian cultural trappings than the other traditions and practices.

SB: I think that's certainly one of the strengths of vipassana. It's very commonsensical and practical. While I wouldn't want to define vipassana purely as an application of technique, I would say that it can be almost scientific in its methods. And there's a subtle danger in the emphasis on technique. As Westerners, we have a tendency to reduce all our thinking and feeling capacities to some kind of technology. One could argue that to adopt a Buddhism that likewise defines itself in terms of techniques and technologies, we risk falling for the very illusion that is at the root of a lot of our spiritual malaise.

IM: Of course, the vipassana technique does lead to an opening of the heart and the mind and can nurture a person's intuitive and poetic faculties. So in their retreats Theravadan teachers often recite Zen poetry and will sometimes use methods borrowed from Tibetan schools.

SB: Exactly. And this is an example of how the different traditions can complement each other as they develop in the West.

IM: Do you think Buddhism is really here to stay, and if so, how do you expect it to change its dress and manners as it takes root in the West?

SB: I see Buddhism as a vital force in my own life, and by implication, out of whatever sense of compassion I have for others, I would like to see it become a vital force in other people's lives. I think that's natural. That's my categorical imperative. But I don't know if it's even possible for us to say at present whether Buddhism is here to stay. I think Buddhism is still a very marginal phenomenon in the West, even though it touches a considerable number of people. It is still marginal to our cultural mainstream, and I don't think it has penetrated very deeply. So perhaps it could be just another fad for the West, like theosophy was in the nineteenth century. But if Buddhism does take hold in our culture, then it will certainly change as it has in every country and culture and era through which it has moved.

IM: As it takes root in the West, do you think Buddhism might be able to help change our current culture and way of life?

SB: Buddhism could be a valuable counterbalance. But Buddhism may not be able to save Western culture.

IM: Perhaps it's for the best. (Laughter)

From Volume 8, Number 1 (Fall 1991).

2

Devotional Practices and Vipassana
An Interview with Ram Dass

Ram Dass has been a spiritual pioneer and guide for a generation of Western seekers. Through psychology, drugs, and spiritual disciplines he has explored the human psyche and consciousness and returned with maps for the rest of us. There have been some wrong turns, but his honesty and ability to laugh at himself have enabled us all to learn from his mistakes. There is a large Sangha in the West for whom, without Ram Dass, the journey would be more difficult and far less enjoyable.

The primary focus of Ram Dass's spiritual life has been the Hindu practice of guru kripa with his teacher Maharaj-ji (Neem Karoli Baba), whose basic message was to love people, serve them, and remember God. Ram Dass has also been a regular practitioner of vipassana meditation. He began studying with S.N. Goenka in the winter of 1970 in Bodh Gaya, India, and over the years has done several intensive vipassana retreats. In June of 1984 Ram Dass sat for a month at the Insight Meditation Society with the Burmese master U Pandita Sayadaw. His retreat was cut short by the illness of his father, but Ram Dass was attracted to the method and wanted to continue, so he applied for a visa to go to Burma to practice further under U Pandita's guidance.

This interview took place on June 1, 1985, at Dominican College in San Rafael, California, on the occasion of the annual board meeting of the Seva Foundation, a service organization involved in many worthy projects but primarily dedicated to ending unnecessary blindness in the world. At this meeting Ram Dass was chosen as Chairman of the Seva Foundation Board.

INQUIRING MIND: How does vipassana meditation fit in with your devotional practices with your guru, Maharaj-ji?

RAM DASS: I first started practicing vipassana in Bodh Gaya with Goenka-ji fifteen years ago. After forty days or so, I remember escaping from the retreat and rushing back to Maharaj-ji for a bhakti hit—for a shot of love. I felt that the vipassana method was dry and lacking heart. Then a year and a half ago I was at Dhammagiri sitting with Goenka for about a month. I went in feeling that I was in such a good bhakti space that I could handle the dry up. But then at the end of the month, as my mind got quieter, I felt a deeper quality of devotion to Maharaj-ji than I had ever felt before. I thought, isn't this interesting, it took fifteen years, but I'm in a different space and, therefore, the vipassana method is serving me in a different way. Then when I sat with U Pandita at Barre last year, that process continued and intensified.

IM: You found that the training of the mind can lead to an opening of the heart as well?

RD: Right. My basic method is guru kripa, devotion to the guru and the grace of the guru. I surrender my life to him to lead me to God. I realized that the quieter my mind, the more clearly I can hear that part of me, that higher part of me that is Maharaj-ji and me in dialogue. So you could say I am going to Burma to sit with U Pandita again in order to get closer to Maharaj-ji. You see, I am extremely attracted to U Pandita's method as a way of extricating myself from identification with thoughts and sensations that are increasing my distance from God, or the source, the "one." I find U Pandita to be an absolute master, analytic technician, scientist of the mind.

The way he works is through a fifteen-minute individual interview every day, and I like that form. I'm not that inner-directed, and I work best under some kind of social pressure to keep me going. It's not about meditating with other people; it's the form of reporting to the teacher that is very important to me. First you're under the vow of truth. Then you walk in, and the first thing you're asked is, "In the past twenty-four hours since our last meeting, how many hours did you sit and how many hours did you walk?" There is an accepted number, which is sixteen hours or something like that. If you didn't do it, there's just a raised eyebrow and that's enough. It's like, well, if you took a nap, or took a walk, and didn't play the game all the time, then perhaps you're not sufficiently motivated to do this method. It's a fierce sadhana: four hours of sleep, no food after noon, and all those hours of sitting. But when you really want to go into your mind, what else have you got to do anyway?

Then there is U Pandita himself. You see, I am so used to conning people; I'm so used to being so charming and charismatic. People always want something from me; it can be just a smile, but they want something. U Pandita didn't come out of this culture. I was just another fifty-year-old guy with a mustache and a mind. That's what he saw. He didn't see Ram Dass. So when I met him, it didn't work. I couldn't charm him. It was so delicious to me. You don't know how desperately I wanted that experience of not being able to charm somebody. Because the minute I charm, that paranoia begins: they don't really know the real me.

IM: What about the technique itself, the precise observation and labeling? Did you find that difficult?

RD: Yes. Very difficult. At first I felt I should proceed very fast, so I kind of conned myself into thinking that I was staying with my primary object longer than I was. I reported it, and both U Pandita and the translator laughed at me. I was glad they busted me. They busted me within two days. That was wonderful.

But then I got increasingly agitated because the pressure was so intense. I couldn't get my mind to stay on the primary object more than twenty, thirty, or forty seconds before it would flick away somewhere. The reporting was expected to be very exact. For example: I'm going to report on a sixty-minute session that happened at 6 P.M. last evening. I was following the rising and falling of my breath. I brought my awareness to the rising, I noted it as "rising," it had the quality of elasticity. I brought my awareness to "falling," I noted it as falling, it had the quality of fluidity. After thirty seconds my awareness was drawn to the sound of a bird, I noted it as "listening." Then U Pandita breaks in and says, "Did you hear the bird on a rising or a falling?" and I say, "I didn't notice." And he says, "Well, please try to do better." That's an example of the game, and I couldn't get in tight enough. It was like going into a tighter and tighter space, and for three weeks I got more and more agitated until I would go into the bathroom and I would be biting my hand to keep from screaming. I was in such agony. I was like a cornered rat. At one point I ran out in the woods screaming the Hanuman *chaleesa* as an act of rebellion. I so longed for a bhakti hit. Then I ran back so I wouldn't lose much meditation time. I was caught in that bind.

Then at some point I was sitting alone in the dining room, and I thought, what the hell am I doing? I'm on the wrong side of this game. I'm fighting him and the method and myself. Why don't I surrender? Why am I identified with the mind that's going off instead of the mind that's staying with the primary object? It was as if there was some release at that moment, and by the next meditation session I was starting to stay twenty, thirty, forty *minutes* on my primary object. I walked in, and he says, "Well, I think you're beginning now."

IM: And after that breakthrough the process became easier?

RD: Then I began to see that it was now an effortless method. Whole niches started to open before my eyes with no effort at all, and I realized what he had been saying in his lectures, that once you get neighborhood concentration, once you stay with your primary object a little bit, it will all happen automatically, you don't have to do anything anymore. I had been so busy doing, and now I was just along for the ride. It was a whole different orientation toward the process, which I assumed all the other meditators were well into. But for me this was a major breakthrough, because there was no more struggle in meditation. About four days later, when it was just opening like a lotus flower for me, my father fell and broke his back and I had to leave. I went to U Pandita and said, "You're my teacher, whatever you say I will do. My father has had this accident and he needs me, and I can treat that as another attachment." He said, "No you must honor your father; you should go."

IM: It sounds as though you were surrendering to U Pandita just as you would to Maharaj-ji, relating to him as if he were your Hindu guru rather than your Buddhist meditation teacher.

RD: Yes, but at that moment, when you take on a retreat, you surrender to the teacher. He was my teacher and I wouldn't have gone if he hadn't given me his permission. In my gut I felt I should go home, but I didn't trust my gut. He knew my mind at that point better than I knew my mind. He had been listening to minds for thirty-five years, and what he saw in me was like a computer printout of mind. He saw where my mind went—memory, fantasy, planning—the whole structure. I had never had that intimacy with a teacher before. I had intimacy with Maharaj-ji, of course, but it was a different quality.

IM: Perhaps with U Pandita you had "impersonal intimacy," or some such crazy contradiction.

RD: Yes. Incredible. It was an intimacy with the mechanics of my mind and not the content, and that was the difference.

IM: One of Maharaj-ji's fundamental messages to you was to love and serve others, and you have always been involved in some kind of service: the dying project, the prison-ashram project, your book *How Can I Help?*, and your current work with the Seva Foundation. How does vipassana meditation practice affect your work in the world, the quality of your service? Is there any connection there?

RD: It affects all of my relationships in the world. For example, when I go to Burma people will say, "Send me love, think of me now and then." I say, "I hope not." I was just chosen to be chairman of the Seva board, but I hope not to think of Seva at all. When I sit in Burma, my business is extricating myself from forms, from thoughts, from sensations. That's my business when I'm there. My assumption is that truth waits for eyes unclouded by longing, and that if my mind is quiet, I will be able to see more clearly and serve more purely, and that it will all happen automatically. My Dharma will be defined by my karma. Much more, as my meditation gets deeper, I feel much less that I'm doing anything. It's just like my heart is beating and there is this work that is appropriate to do. I'm even amazed at how much less ego there is recently in giving talks and lecturing.

IM: It always seemed as though you were a relatively clear channel when you were giving talks.

RD: I've achieved that effect through drugs. I've smoked grass to give lectures, for years and years and years. Because I always felt that I wasn't enough without it. That people expected me to be way out there, and I had to get out there, and I wasn't. Now something's changed, where I'm saying, "Whatever it is, it is." There's more trust. When I'm doing the vipassana practice intensively, I feel like I can let go of the world to be in the world instead of feeling like if I let go of the world I'm going to lose the world. It's like trusting at the mythic level.

⋄
⋮ From Volume 2, Number 2 (Fall 1985).
⋄

3 Dzogchen and Vipassana
An Interview with Tsoknyi Rinpoche

I first met Tsoknyi Rinpoche in 1993 when he was leading a nine-day meditation retreat in the practice known as dzogchen. At that time he was twenty-seven years old. As you might know, sometimes during silent meditation retreats people can look very grim and determined. One day when I was walking down the hall and passed Rinpoche, he just reached out and tickled me in the ribs. He had that kind of playfulness and joy throughout the retreat. In fact, one of his opening meditation instructions was: "Be happy, be cheerful."

Tsoknyi Rinpoche's teachings of Buddhadharma were among the clearest and most profound that I had ever heard, and I wondered how such teachings could come from a twenty-seven-year-old body and mind. I came to understand this better after hearing Tsoknyi Rinpoche's history. He is considered to be the third in a line of reincarnate lamas, the first of whom was a lama in Eastern Tibet in the last century. The first Tsoknyi Rinpoche was known for perseverance and effort in his meditation practice, and he also founded a large nunnery. The current Tsoknyi Rinpoche is the son of one of the most renowned dzogchen masters of this century, Tulku Urgyen Rinpoche. Tsoknyi Rinpoche was recognized at age eight by His Holiness Karmapa. At age thirteen he began twelve years of very intense formal training. After hearing this history I came to understand Tsoknyi Rinpoche better: you take a previously enlightened mind-stream, give it the genes of a renowned dzogchen master, recognize the qualities at an early age, train that intensively, and you get Tsoknyi Rinpoche.

—GUY ARMSTRONG

This interview was conducted in 1998 by Guy Armstrong, Sally Clough, Wes Nisker, Barbara Gates, Mary Ann Clark, and Terry Vandiver in Woodacre, California.

INQUIRING MIND: We would like you to begin by describing the essential teachings of Tibetan dzogchen for the readers of *Inquiring Mind*, many of whom know Buddhadharma primarily through the elders' tradition of Theravada Buddhism and the methods of vipassana meditation.

TSOKNYI RINPOCHE [*speaking primarily through his translator, Tony Duff*]: Having gone through all of the practices connected with the mind, in Tibetan Buddhist practice one finally arrives at dzogchen, which goes past the mind. Many traditions depend on mind in meditation. No matter how far you go with them, you still end up with a subject and object. There is still a meditator present, even though its presence might be very, very subtle. Dzogchen provides the means to break through the duality.

IM: Do you believe, then, that dzogchen adds to, or somehow completes, the path of insight from the elders' tradition?

TR: As you might know, the Tibetan tradition does incorporate the various practices of shamatha (concentration) as presented in the Theravada. Shamatha practices do not abandon conceptual mind. You might go very deeply into those practices and make conceptual mind very, very subtle, but it still remains. Even at the most subtle level of those practices, there is still some kind of grasping at a meditator. You are in the present moment but are dwelling there with a subject and object still involved.

IM: Are you saying that in dzogchen there is no meditator meditating? No sense of someone who is doing something?

TR: When we speak of meditating, we take it to mean that you are creating a state with your rational mind that ceases when you stop meditating. Thus, meditation does not get to the natural clarity but to a clarity that is constructed by the mind. In that case you have a stoppage. Where are you stopped? You are stopped in whatever you are creating with your conceptual mind. On the other hand, if you don't meditate but just allow yourself to be distracted, you are just an ordinary person. (Laughs) In the dzogchen method there is no meditation, and in that nonmeditation there is no distraction. These two together are crucial to the way of dzogchen.

IM: In vipassana practice, the meditation object is often the breath, in which case it would seem that the meditator is present with what is real rather than something created by the mind. How is that different from dzogchen?

TR: What you say is true. Breath is a natural phenomenon. However when you focus on breath, you are setting it up as an object that is separated from the knower of the object, so you are maintaining the subject-object duality. You still have not gone to the other shore. The method is good, but you are still using a method. From the dzogchen point of view, you must destroy the method too.

IM: Dzogchen is usually taught in your Tibetan tradition as the final fruition of a very long and arduous path, requiring many years of practice. Now you are teaching dzogchen to senior students of vipassana. Why do you think they are qualified or ready for these teachings?

TR: The American students who have done a lot of vipassana practice have reached the point where the subject-object dichotomy is quite subtle. In fact, if you do vipassana meditation for long enough, the distinction between subject and object will naturally dissolve. The dissolving of subject and object through the application of insight is likened in the Tibetan tradition to the wearing away of both knife and whetstone when a knife is sharpened. The dzogchen teachings can make that happen a little faster. Dzogchen can be like a match that will ignite the situation. Rather than needing twenty years of practice to gain insight, you might only need fifteen.

I am also very comfortable teaching vipassana students because they understand meditation. If you don't know about meditation, instructions about nonmeditation won't make any sense. Generally, people who have practiced vipassana can go smoothly into dzogchen because when I tell them to let go of the meditation, they really know what needs to be released.

IM: Please describe the dzogchen teaching of the world as emptiness and appearances.

TR: Just look around you at all of the different things and people in your environment. You see all of these things here, but the fact is that not one single one of them has any true basis whatsoever. Nothing has any true existence. The sun, moon, solar system, the world—look at anything and you realize that you don't really know what it is, finally. You can describe the process that is taking place very well, but you can't say anything about its beginning or where it ends. You might say the beginning was the Big Bang or something like that, but you don't know what came before that or who created it. How did it "big bang"? The fact that there are so few answers to these questions is a sign of the illusoriness of appearances due to their being empty.

Also, if you really look carefully into whatever there is, whatever there might be, you can never find any root to it. Nothing is permanently established. Therefore behind everything is emptiness and all things are only appearances. There is only an effect happening.

IM: It is easy to imagine that someone who was not familiar with Buddhism or had not done any meditation practice might get confused or upset by that teaching.

TR: That is why the dzogchen teaching is not given at the beginning of the path and why it isn't something that we broadcast throughout the world. On the other hand, I think this teaching is especially good for Americans. Everything here is considered too real, too serious, and because you think everything is very real, you get crazy. You have a "real" problem. (Laughs) You want real life, real happiness, real meaning, real, real, real. You are too greedy, and even though you know that about yourselves, you don't know how to let go of it. Dzogchen can cut that very effectively.

Moreover, I see that you have high-class confusion in America. (Laughs) I can see it in people's eyes. Generally, when I see people who live in poverty and have no opportunity to work, I see a dull confusion in their eyes. When I see Americans, who are confused with so many things to do, so many things to have, so much intellectual this and that, I see that their eyes always look outward. Their eyes show a speedy, intellectual, high-class type of confusion. Dzogchen is very useful for dealing with that type of confusion.

IM: Some people in the West are concerned that Buddhist teachers are ignoring the problems of a planet very much at risk. Specifically, they are worried about these teachings that say the world of phenomena is only appearances arising out of emptiness. They say that such teachings could undermine the motivation for action around such issues as human rights or environmental pollution.

TR: Once you clean up your inner pollution, there will still be a motivation left to clean up the world's pollution. The Buddha spoke of that pure remainder as compassion. At this moment you are affected by illusion pollution. Therefore you have to first clean up the illusion pollution from the illusion. (Laughs) Having done that, you will have pure compassion in your mind, and that pure compassion contains within it the intention to do something about suffering beings. Beings are suffering in a dream-like existence, so you do try to help within the dream. But at the same time you need to understand that all is illusion, including yourself.

As part of the dzogchen teachings we make many dedications and aspirations to benefit the external world, focusing on a healthy environment and peace and harmony for everyone. However if we are going to talk about Dharma, we must talk about how things really are. The actuality of all things is emptiness occurring simultaneously with appearances. The teacher has a responsibility to express that reality as it is. It is then the responsibility of the students to hear what is taught and not be stupid about it. If a student doesn't look deeply into the teaching and understand it properly, then it won't help the student or the world.

From Volume 14, Number 2 (Spring 1998).

4 Who's Asking the Questions Here?
A Non-interview with Hari Lal Poonja

I have always wanted a Hindu guru to call my own, a Jewish mother-type with whom I could just hang out and laugh. He wouldn't give me any difficult meditation exercises but would simply embody the great realization, transmitting it through his aura or by patting me on the head now and again. I turned down a chance to meet Neem Karoli Baba back in 1970 and have suffered a bit of guru envy ever since. So after listening to glowing reports from various vipassana teachers and yogis about a profound Indian master living in Lucknow named Hari Lal Poonja, I decided to go to India to see for myself.

It seems that Hari Lal Poonja, or Poonja-ji as he is affectionately known, was born with the deep passion for realization that resides in many an Indian breast. The story has it that when he was a little boy he became fascinated with a statue of the starving Buddha and went through a period in which he wouldn't eat. Instead, he took his food into his bedroom and threw it out the window to the dogs. As a young man, Poonja-ji's devotion to Krishna became so intense that he would dress up in women's clothing as the goddess Radha, Lord Krishna's consort, in the fervent hope that Krishna would appear to him and reveal his divine face. Poonja-ji later became a disciple of the venerated Indian master Ramana Maharshi, and in subsequent years completed his spiritual search.

Poonja-ji's realization and teachings come out of the Hindu Advaita Vedanta tradition, which features radical inquiry into the nature of self. Such inquiry is carried out in individual dialogues with the teacher in the presence of the satsang, *a Hindi word for a group of disciples, literally translated as "the community of truth." Poonja traveled worldwide giving talks and leading satsang sessions until he decided to remain at his home in Lucknow and let the world come to him. He became quite well-known in Western spiritual circles, partially due to the fact that two of his disciples, Andrew Cohen and Ganga-ji (Tony Varner), began teaching in the West. As a result, hundreds of Westerners traveled to Lucknow to be with Poonja-ji himself.*

When I first went in to see Poonja-ji, I gave him a copy of my book Crazy Wisdom. *He picked it up, looked at the cover for a few minutes, and then turned to me and asked, "Who gave you your name?" I thought he was referring to my nickname Scoop, so I explained to him how I was given that moniker as a radio news commentator. "No, no," he said, "who gave you the name Nis-ker?"*

"That is my real last name," I replied. "My father gave it to me."

"Oh, this is a very good name," Poonja-ji said. "In Sanskrit Nis-ker means 'non-doer.'"

Poonja-ji gives out a lot of new names. During one satsang session I saw him give a woman the name Nirvana. Later I saw this woman at my hotel and couldn't help but ask her, "How's Nirvana?" She laughed and said, "Wonderful!"

I personally had no desire to get a new name from Poonja-ji, but I certainly do appreciate him telling me what my own name means. How appropriate, I thought. Non-doer is a name that I would gladly live up to, relax into, become one with. Non-doing is something I'd like to know more about. It turned out that I received an elementary lesson in the meaning of my name during an interview with Poonja-ji for Inquiring Mind. *I went in to see Poonja-ji with a list of what I thought were important questions. I was the journalist desiring the "inside" story from this man. I wanted the "real scoop" about the differences, say, between Buddhism and Hindu-based Advaita Vedanta, and whether meditation practice is useful for certain psychological types, and whether, if we are really all one with everything, who or what is it that awakens? However, rather than answer my questions, Poonja-ji went after my mind. I would ask him something, and he would just turn to me and say, "Who is asking this question?" Ever try to do a decent, respectable interview when the interviewee is busy deconstructing your ego?!*

For a while I tried to get control of the conversation. I wanted to flip Poonja-ji into my frame of reference, the plane of relative reality, so that the vipassana community could learn why some of their teachers of Buddhadharma were going to hang out with this jolly Hindu guru. I wanted to say to him, "Poonja-ji, you know, journalists are supposed to ask five questions when they are out on a story, 'Who, what, where, when, and why?' Now, those are basically the same questions you are asking of your disciples. Journalists will ask those questions about a government or a car accident, and you ask those questions about the nature of the 'self' and the accident of the universe. Although I may be playing in relative reality, Poonja-ji, I am asking these questions as a journalist of the spiritual quest, for the sake of all sentient beings, and all that other good stuff. I know the rules and I accept the fact that we can't really talk about any of this, but just for now let's pretend that we can. My next question is…"

Eventually I had to let go of my attempts to direct things, and finally I just relaxed into the conversation. However, as I left Poonja-ji's house I felt disappointed, thinking that this interview had not produced much that would be useful for Inquiring Mind *readers. Later, when I listened closely to the tape, I began to hear more and more. You can judge for yourself.*

—WES NISKER

This interview was conducted by Wes Nisker in Lucknow, India, in the winter of 1991.

HARI LAL POONJA: First I want to ask you a question about the title of your book. What is this thing you call "crazy wisdom"? Wisdom cannot be crazy. Maybe some other word should be used.

INQUIRING MIND: Crazy wisdom is only crazy to the ordinary mind. It looks crazy, but it is actually true wisdom. That's what the term means.

HLP: When mind is rooted in the ego, then it is crazy. When it is related to some object of the senses, then it is a crazy mind. But first of all we must know what the mind is. Mind is nothing but a thought. You can't separate thought itself from the mind. So first you have to find out which is the first thought that arises from the mind. Which is the first thought?

IM: "I."

HLP: Yes, "I" is the first thought. This "I" is ego. When we use the word *I*, then there is ego, then there is mind, then there is a body, then there are senses, then there are sense objects, and then all manifestation arises.

IM: And then there is suffering.

HLP: Of course. Where there is a separate being, there is suffering. Where there is union, there is no suffering. So understand where this "I" arises from. The question is this: "Who am I?" Keep alert and then you will know. Pay full attention and then wait for the answer. Keep quiet and wait for the answer. It only takes one instant of time. Question where the I is arising from now.

Previous notions and concepts will not help you. This is the question you have not yet asked yourself. You ask questions to others about something else, but not this question to your own self.

IM: I think that in fact I have asked this question.

HLP: "I think I have." Who thinks that I have? Again, you will have to solve this in order to solve everything.

IM: I am using the term *I* in a relative sense, just to . . .

HLP: "I" am using. "I" am using. Here is the I again.

IM: You are telling me to ask "Who am I?"! And that is exactly what I have been doing in my Buddhist meditation practice for the past twenty years. I have been investigating "Who am I?"

HLP: Yes. "I" have been investigating, "I" have been investigating. But you have not really investigated. Investigation means to go in.

IM: Now? You want me to do it now?

HLP: Yes, now. Don't run away from now. Just catch hold of this now. You can try to step out of this now, but it will follow you—behind, in front, this side, that side, up and down. So what do you see in this now?

IM: I see me.

HLP: "I see me, I am me, I am now": what does it mean? Who is the seer, and who is the seeing? Tell me what you see? "I see me." Is it an object or is it a subject? What is the form? What is the form of I?

IM: (Pause for some investigation) This "I" I am referring to doesn't seem to have a solid form.

HLP: When a word has no solid form, then there is no more word. The previous I you were using is no longer there. Now you have come to the real I. Now you are working from now. This previous I was a fake I. That I represented the body and was the egoistic I. But just now, when it went and jumped into the beyond, it was finished. And now this "now" is finished. You have to start afresh all over again.

IM: Every moment I have to start over.

HLP: To see the real I means to see total consciousness, which in reality is representing emptiness. Before, the I you were using was from the body, ego, mind, and senses. But when it is arising from emptiness, it is emptiness itself. And this is the fathomless I. When you see this I then you will see everything as I. Then there will be love, then there will be wisdom, then you will see your own reflection, in animals, in birds, in plants, in rocks.

Now what about the twenty years of your practice of investigation? What have you been doing for these twenty years?

IM: I've been looking in. I feel like I have experienced emptiness, and have dissolved into emptiness during meditation. I have seen the emptiness of all phenomena...

HLP: That emptiness you have been seeing was full of egoism. That was not emptiness. That was only a word, a concept. The emptiness which I am speaking about is not even emptiness. Emptiness has got nothing to do with where I am taking you, but I am using the word. I don't allow you to use the word *emptiness* even. Where did you learn this word *emptiness*? You must have heard it from some sutras.

IM: Many Mahayana sutras talk about emptiness.

HLP: But that belongs to the past. It has nothing to do with this emptiness that I speak about. Now I tell you, don't use the word *emptiness* either. This emptiness is the finger pointing to something else. You have to reject the finger to see the moon. Now reject this word *emptiness* if you want to go beyond!

IM: So, do you think my twenty years of vipassana meditation practice was wasted effort?

HLP: No. Those twenty years have brought you to me. (Laughs) And not only twenty years have you been doing this, but for thirty-five million years. But there's no time wasted. In emptiness there is nothing existing at all. This is the ultimate experience. *Emptiness* is only a concept. To have this concept is just the pride of the mind. Once you touch the word *I*, simultaneously time will arise and you will have past, present, and future. When the I ceases, everything ceases. "Nothing ever existed" is the ultimate truth. It is something unspeakable and it will remain unspeakable. Buddha spent forty-nine years speaking, speaking, speaking. And I don't think he touched the point. Why should he speak for fifty years after enlightenment?

IM: He said he taught in order to end suffering. To free people.

HLP: He was trying to express that which he could not.

IM: We all try to say it in order to pass it on. That is why the Buddha gave out various practices.

HLP: Yes, but this is all from ego. In all practices you are working from ego. You identify with the body and say "I am so and so," and you separate yourself from the ultimate truth. The absolute is something else altogether, and in any kind of practice you miss it.

IM: Would you say that all sadhanas or practices are a hindrance? And is this true for all people?

HLP: Sadhana is not for freedom. It can remove some old habits, such as identification with the body. But sadhana is not for freedom, not for truth, not for the absolute. All the time you are doing sadhana the truth is standing in front of you, smiling at you. The barrier in practice is your past concepts, such as the idea that you are bound. You say to yourself, "I am bound, I am suffering." And you are only doing sadhana to remove the suffering. Not for freedom. Freedom doesn't want any practices. It is there as it is. And you are already free.

IM: You tell people to just be themselves. It sounds like the Zen masters who say, "Just be ordinary."

HLP: Be ordinary. Yes, just remove the doubt that says you are not awake or not enlightened. Because you are, and it's that simple.

IM: Poonja-ji, finally, would you give me some advice about how to open my heart and love the world more?

HLP: To love the world you have to first learn how to love your own self. If you love yourself, then you love the whole world, because your self includes everything.

IM: Some Zen Buddhist master once said, "Now that I'm enlightened, I'm as miserable as ever." In other words, you get the understanding, you get enlightenment, and still you have to live in the world.

HLP: Maybe the Zen master said that because he suddenly realized that he had suffered needlessly for thirty-five million years, when all that time he had actually been free. (Laughs)

IM: So then, how would you define enlightenment? I think a lot of people believe that they can achieve a steady state of realization, always living in "now," always in emptiness. Is that how you would define enlightenment, or does it come and go?

HLP: Whatever you do and whatever you don't do is all empty. Every day I am seeing people who have had many different teachers and have done all kinds of practices, and they say, "We are here seeing you because you don't give us any teaching, and you don't give us any practices. Now we don't have anything to do. We just laugh." (Laughs)

From Volume 9, Number 1 (Fall 1992).

5 On Fearlessness and Fear
A Conversation with Tenzin Palmo, Ajahn Sundara, Ajahn Jitindriya, and Yvonne Rand

Sparked by the visit to the San Francisco Bay Area of Tenzin Palmo, nun and author, a remarkable group of women teachers came together to discuss the themes of fearlessness and fear. Originally from England, Tenzin Palmo ordained in 1964 as a nun in the Tibetan Buddhist Kargyupa lineage and undertook eighteen years of retreat, twelve of them in a Himalayan cave. Welcoming her and hosting the discussion at Goat-in-the-Road Center in Muir Beach, California, was one of America's leading Zen teachers, Yvonne Rand, an ardent spokesperson for the feminization of Buddhism. Two Theravada nuns joined the group from nearby Abhayagiri Monastery. French native Ajahn Sundara was one of the first four women novices at Chithurst Monastery in England in the late 1970s, and Australian-born Ajahn Jitindriya took anagarika ordination in 1988.

This forum was convened by Barbara Gates and Dennis Crean at Yvonne Rand's Goat-in-the-Road Center in Muir Beach, California, in early 2003.

YVONNE RAND: In my experience, at the bottom of virtually all reactive emotions is fear. If people drop down deeply enough they will discover that fear is what is fueling or triggering other emotions.

TENZIN PALMO: Yes, fear is the last boundary of the ego. Particularly since September 11, fear has been on everybody's mind. In the question-and-answer sessions following my talks, again and again people raise questions about how to deal with their own fear. When they ask what they should do physically to feel safe, this is difficult to answer. But when they ask how to respond emotionally, it is easy to answer. We should all respond with compassion.

INQUIRING MIND: What are some practices to allow us to move from anger or fear into compassion?

YR: For a long time, I've been teaching a meditation on five aspects for working with strong, highly energized, reactive emotions. The whole practice is really contained in the first step: to hold the emotion and accompanying body sensations at the heart chakra with the tenderness of a mother with her only newborn child. You let the attention rest on the breath as it rises and falls, and include awareness of the emotion and the accompanying physical body sensations that are arising in the moment. Hold the emotion with tenderness, with the hands held at the heart-center. If the emotion is particularly strong, as it is with both anger and fear, I find that it works best, at least initially, to do the practice during walking meditation instead of while sitting. When I do this practice without forcing it, I realize that the emotional state has the mark of impermanence. I then begin to take the emotional state less seriously, and I can gain interest in the causes and conditions for the arising of the emotion. Doing this practice, I am struck by the capacity to uncover, and to be with, what one has previously thought one couldn't stand. That shift can be extraordinarily powerful.

TP: Sometimes I say to people, "Hold yourself like an injured animal." In Dharma circles there's a lot of talk about the evils of self-cherishing and how we have to drop the ego. But for many people, the ego is fractured and in pain, and we can't just drop something which is injured. So first we have to heal. After we are balanced and healed by holding ourselves in compassion, then we can see through the ego and learn to go beyond it.

IM: How might an average person unfamiliar with techniques of meditation move from that fear reaction into compassion? After all, compassion is not something that you can impose on your heart.

TP: Take the response to terrorism or war. Even people who don't meditate can use their imagination to see themselves as ordinary Iraqis at this moment. They are just trying to live and enjoy their lives. How would we feel if we knew that the greatest power on Earth was about to attack us? Although we hadn't personally done anything wrong, how would it feel to know we might get bombed because other countries don't like our leader? [During the time of this conversation, the United States was regularly bombing Iraq.] All we have to do is put ourselves in other people's shoes; then we can imagine their plight. That is compassion.

AJAHN SUNDARA: In addition to compassion, I found that patience is key to understanding how fear affects us. Usually we refuse to experience fear. We try either to get rid of it or immediately resolve the situation that triggers it. So with patience, we can witness the mind running through its reactive, patterned responses to fear.

At the beginning of a long retreat some years ago, Ajahn Sumedho said in one of his teachings, "If you think you have a problem with fear, you will keep recreating fear." I had been struggling with fear for weeks, and as he said this, I understood how much I had identified with fear as "my problem."

So I vowed that if fear arose, however convincing it might seem, I would not try to resolve it, "let it go," or anything but simply be aware of it. By the end of the retreat, as the fear came and went, my heart was at peace with it. The anticipation, aversion, and desire to control it had been the real causes of suffering, not the fear itself. This was when I learned the importance of patience in uncovering all the layers at the root of my fear.

TP: Did the fear come back?

AS: Oh, it's there; this body is a fear body. The fear comes back but not in the same way.

IM: Do you think there's a relationship between compassion and fearlessness?

TP: Yes. Sometimes people imagine compassion as being passive and kind of wimpy, but genuine compassion is fearlessness. The other side of Avalokiteshvara, the bodhisattva of compassion, is the fierce-looking Tibetan deity Mahakala, with flames coming from his head. Those are the flames of wisdom, while Mahakala's heart is compassion itself. There are times when compassion means standing in strength, but it's not ego power and it's not based on anger. Compassion is actually the most fearless emotion in the world.

AJAHN JITINDRIYA: I once heard Pema Chödrön say, "Being fearless is not being without fear. Being fearless is feeling the fear and stepping forward anyway."

TP: In the Tibetan tradition, we have practices in which we try to arouse a strong emotion like anger, greed, lust, or fear, bring it up, and then look at it until we really see it. If we look at it with a relaxed but penetrating awareness, instead of appearing solid, the emotion becomes quite transparent. On the Vajrayana path, that's what we mean when we talk about using our negative states as the path. That doesn't mean we indulge them. It means that underlying fear, anger, or lust is a very powerful energy, and if we can tap into it at the moment of its arising, it self-liberates into a clear, penetrating insight.

AS: In the forest tradition, the teaching encourages us to go to the body itself, to witness and to feel those emotions—anger, greed, hatred, fear. These emotions manifest in the body because the body is, in a sense, our biggest receptor and our most solid karmic formation. After facing a fearful situation, the mind may be able to dispel the mental energy, but physically, we may still be shaking. The body carries the memory of our fear. If we can stay with the sensations of fear in the body, we don't have to follow our compulsion to run away or struggle with fear. As we bear with fear with kindly acceptance and awareness, we can let it go and free the mind.

Many years ago, before becoming interested in Buddhism, I was struck by Krishnamurti's statement, "Thoughts are fear." This resonated so deeply that it prompted me to investigate for the first time my own thoughts. To my surprise, most of them were the result of some form of fear—fear of losing the comfort of my habits, fear of the unknown and the uncertainty of the future. I began to recognize the compulsion of the mind to think ceaselessly and how little control I had over it. So I would ask myself the questions: "What am I thinking? Are my thoughts really fear?" It was fascinating to witness thoughts directly and the way the mind related to fear. This interest was one of the main factors that brought me to this path.

TP: The practice of taking refuge also creates protection. In the Tibetan tradition, before we start any practice, first we take refuge in the Buddha, the Dharma, and the Sangha. Then we take the bodhisattva vow, meaning that we are not doing this practice for ourselves but in order to benefit all beings. We follow this vow with guru yoga, meaning that we visualize the lineage starting from the primordial Buddha all the way down, master to master, each one handing down the flame, until we see our own teacher above our head. Then the lineage absorbs into the teacher, who, in the form of Vajradhara, the cosmic representation of our Buddha-mind, absorbs into ourselves. We realize that our own mind and the Guru's mind are one. We are not his personality, but we are his genuine realization, which is Buddha-nature. From that sense of oneness with what is at the core of our being, we begin meditation. Whatever comes up, we know it's okay; we are protected.

AS: In Theravada Buddhism taking refuge is not described in such great detail, with visualization of the lineages or being surrounded by these wonderful forces—which I'm sure must feel like an incredible protection. We emphasize the protection that comes from taking refuge in the Buddha, Dhamma, and Sangha. We are taking refuge in the qualities of wisdom, truth, and virtue that are inherent in all of us. My teacher often pointed out that mindfulness is our real protection. When we encounter fear and simply know it as it is, fear is transmuted. The experience is transformed into one of strength and confidence.

IM (TO TENZIN PALMO): In the chapters of your biography describing the twelve years you spent in a Himalayan cave, your remarkable fearlessness comes through. One might expect that great demons of fear would have been aroused, or that you might have experienced a realm of pure terror. However, that was anything but the case.

TP: There's not a lot of time for fear. For one thing, living in a cave we have to be in physical reality. For six to eight months of the year, it's snowing, so we have to clear snow. We have to chop wood. We have to melt the snow to get water. We have to cook food. So we're not spacing out while we are there. We are dealing with common, everyday realities. Also, in the Tibetan tradition that I study in, we do certain set practices four times a day; there are three-hour sessions and we don't vary from the routine.

Living completely alone, I gradually began to shed layer after layer of identities I had held when relating to other people. I worked with the questions, "Who am I?" "Which bit of this experience is *me*?" The more I went inside and looked, the more my identities fell away. One of the first that went was a sense of gender, because when you're all by yourself, male or female, what's the difference? Of course, later these identifications came back.

I was also very happy. People always imagine, "Oh, living in a cave all alone! What austerity! How frightening!" But I stayed there because I couldn't think of anywhere nicer to be. As to the lack of fear, I myself was surprised—especially after a weeklong blizzard when the cave was completely buried under snow, and I was sure that I was going to die. It turned out that there was enough oxygen in the cave, but I didn't know that at the time. I was in a tiny, completely black place, and I was convinced that I was going to be asphyxiated. But strangely enough, it didn't worry me. I just got myself prepared. I thought back to things in my life that I had done wrong and said I was sorry. I aroused gratitude for myself for the things I had done right. Then I really took refuge. I realized that in the end, the only thing that mattered was the Lama and that the Lama was really a part of my deep mind. I was surprised at how ready I was to die. Of course, I don't know how I would have reacted in the last moments.

Another time, I woke up in the night and felt a big, black, evil entity trying to suffocate me. My immediate reaction was, "Excuse me! I am protected by all the buddhas and bodhisattvas of the universe. What are you thinking? Get away immediately!" (Laughs) I felt humorous indignation—that this naughty little third-class evil entity was trying to frighten me. At that, it went "shoom!" and shrunk from a huge, heavy presence into a tiny little black spot and flew out the window. I just laughed: "Cheeky devil!" You just can't know how you will react.

IM: How does the capacity to laugh relate to fearlessness?

TP: I always think that the sense of humor should be the seventh paramita. The ability to laugh at oneself and at external events keeps us sane and balanced.

AS: I used to ask my teacher, Ajahn Sumedho, "How can you not go crazy on this path? You are the one who is deluded, and you are the one who has to train this deluded being, all the while knowing that there is really nobody here that is deluded." (Laughs) It really is hilarious, isn't it?

AJ: Laughter is a great release of tension. Once you get the right perspective, you can laugh about anything! So much of our suffering is laughable.

YR: After the fact! (Laughs)

AS: The ego only thinks one thing: "I'm the center of the universe." It's really a kind of humorous mechanism.

TP: That's because it takes itself so seriously!

AJ: Fear is the essence of the sense of self. It separates. If there's no separation, who's there to be afraid?

IM: Well, I'm afraid we're out of time. Are there any last thoughts before we resolve this fear?

AS: Yes. I'd like to express my great delight at being with Tenzin Palmo for a few hours.

TP: It is always good for nuns to get together and share stories from our lives. Perhaps that is why the Buddha started the Sangha. (Laughter)

From Volume 19, Number 2 (Spring 2003).

VI

PRACTICES

P ractice, practice, practice," says Professor Robert Thurman. "All I hear is Buddhists talking about practice. What I want to know is, when do we get to the performance?!" Start here. Bow your way from San Francisco to Los Angeles with Reverend Heng Sure; go into deep absorption and "taste the mango" with jhana teacher Ayya Khema; or take a fantastic voyage through the Buddha's cosmos with Joseph Goldstein. In this section you will also learn to track your breath (This one!) with Santikaro, and learn from vajrayana expert Miranda Shaw how to gaze steadily into the eyes of a tantric partner until you see the divine. If none of this interests you, Professor Thurman will turn your essential impermanence into bliss. There are many gates to the gateless, and here are a few of them, swinging open for us.

1 Why I Meditate
(After Allen Ginsberg)

By Wes Nisker

I meditate because I suffer. I suffer, therefore I am. I am, therefore I suffer.
I meditate because there are so many other things to do.
I meditate because when I was younger it was all the rage.
I meditate because Siddhartha Gautama, Bodhidharma, Marco Polo, the
    British Raj, Carl Jung, Alan Watts, Jack Kerouac, Allen Ginsberg,
    Alfred E. Neuman, et al.
I meditate because evolution gave me a big brain, but it didn't come with
    an instruction manual.
I meditate because I have all the information I need.
I meditate because the largest colonies of living beings, the coral reefs, are
    dying.
I meditate because I want to touch deep time, where the history of
    humanity can be seen as just an evolutionary adjustment period.
I meditate because life is too short and sitting slows it down.
I meditate because life is too long and I need an occasional break.
I meditate because I want to experience the world as Rumi did, or Walt
    Whitman, or as Mary Oliver does.
I meditate because now I know that enlightenment doesn't exist, so I can
    relax.
I meditate because of the Dalai Lama's laugh.
I meditate because there are too many advertisements in my head, and I'm
    erasing all but the very best of them.
I meditate because the physicists say there may be eleven dimensions to
    reality, and I want to get a peek into a few more of them.
I meditate because I've discovered that my mind is a great toy and fun to
    play with.

I meditate because I want to remember that I'm perfectly human.

Sometimes I meditate because my heart is breaking.

Sometimes I meditate so that my heart will break.

I meditate because a Vedanta master once told me that in Hindi my name, Nis-ker, means "non-doer."

I meditate because I'm growing old and want to become more comfortable with emptiness.

I meditate because I think Robert Thurman was right to call it an "evolutionary sport," and I want to be on the home team.

I meditate because I'm composed of 100 trillion cells, and from time to time I need to reassure them that we're all in this together.

I meditate because it's such a relief to spend time ignoring myself.

I meditate because my country spends more money on weapons than all other nations in the world combined. If I had more courage, I'd probably immolate myself.

I meditate because I want to discover the fifth Brahma-vihara, the Divine Abode of Awe, and then I'll go down in history as a great spiritual adept.

I meditate because I'm building myself a bigger and better perspective, and occasionally I need a new window.

From Volume 23, Number 1 (Fall 2006).

2 Technology of Breathing In and Out

By Santikaro

With mind spinning "got to finish this," worrying about that, irritated with something or another, hurrying to meet a deadline—yes, monks and nuns also fall into this stuff; after all, we are human, too—the bell for evening meditation rings. It's a loud bell, loud enough to penetrate postmodern samsaric mind. Struggling with the temptation to blow off the sitting, I manage to turn off the computer, finish the cup of tea, and get out the door. Fortunately, it's a bit of a walk to the meditation hall. Blessed with the trees of a small forest on what was once a sand bar beneath the Gulf of Siam, the short walk to the open-air hall fosters a shift, a slowing down, even if I have to hurry to be on time.

So ended many an evening work session during the later part of my fifteen years as a monk in Thailand. I'd often begin the meditation with walking, enjoying the soft crunch of the sand beneath bare feet and the gentle movements of arboreal friends next to the hall. I'd pace back and forth rather quickly at first to contain the leftover energy—though it revs up quick, it seldom goes away so fast—mind following the breath in and out, in and out...in...out, with frequent lapses back to the unfinished article, e-mail debate, or monastic problem to solve. These lapses were easy, I learned, because the stirred-up breath didn't foster quiet and stability, it perpetuated agitation. The breathing reflected and had been provoked by what had been going on in mind.

Such breathing jarred body, which perturbed mind, which messed with breathing—a nasty circle of causality. Shallow, quick breath pushing the chi up and cerebral. Tight, stressed breath denying the relaxation and joy of a nice walk. Hot, irritated breath radiating throughout mind-body. Tired, sluggish breath weighing me down. Loopy breath making it easy to space out.

Erratic breath from sleep deprivation and caffeine stimulation. Many times, many breaths. All mirroring what mind has been up to and caught up in. Unhealthy breath patterns built up by mind-body imbalance and reactivity. Distorted breath sustaining any imbalance, agitation, weariness, or stuckness. It goes on for years.

Now living in America, I use the Internet a lot and sometimes wish I had DSL or cable instead of poky 56K. Yet something about mindfulness has sunk in over the years of practice so that when a webpage comes up slowly or e-mail downloads in trickles, I can take a few relaxing breaths. Slow connections become a slowing in order to connect body and mind through breath. When the computer is really slow, I can stretch or get off the chair for a shoulder stand. Maybe slow is beautiful. This paragraph came to mind while I was downloading a big upgrade and walking my breathing on a veranda overlooking Missouri hills and fields.

Speed seems relative. Wanting something fast makes for slow. Reacting to slow speeds up mind. To chat online with a friend on the other side of the globe through the slowest web connection is still a lot faster than pony express or clipper ship, let alone walking over there on foot.

As a recent returnee to the Land of the Free,[1] I continue to stumble upon and stagger past things that amaze. In airports, obese white folks line up for fast food while people of color serve from the other sides of counters. Layers of stunning amazement! Consumerism, foodism, racism, classism… I feel sadness, disgust, anger. Not too strongly but enough to buzz around in the mind and tighten up body with breathing that's indignantly extra-strong. Still, mindfulness comes home to breathing and follows it in and down. Relaxing down into belly, lightening up the breathing; relaxing down into legs, regaining balance. Then, breathing up through the heart, softening and remembering that these folks munching on tacos and rubbery pizza are my pals in birth, aging, illness, and death. I can smile a bit—they aren't my enemies—yet remain concerned by the blatant racial inequality and unhealthiness of what I see. Mindful, too, that I am not outside the mess looking in; I am participating in it willingly when I drink Starbucks coffee and unwillingly just by being alive in the globalization era. How to make that participation beneficial?

In many suttas the Buddha taught *anapanasati*, a systematic training of heart and wisdom through mindfulness with breathing in and out. This comprehensive practice contains sixteen "lessons" that cover and perfect the four

---

[1] Actually, *Thailand* means the same thing, so I've gone from one "Land of the Free" to another. I wonder if they are the same kind of "free"?

foundations of mindfulness. Usually, the Buddha started with "getting to know long (deep, healthy) breathing," followed by "getting to know short (shallow, unhealthy) breathing." Through experience, one learns whether breathing is long or short, relaxed or tight, natural or unnatural. Then comes "experiencing all bodies," that is, the relationship between the quality of the breathing and the quality of the body. These three preliminary steps culminate in "calming the body-conditioner," which means cultivating naturally deep and subtle breathing that fosters inner peace, stability, and joy. From there, the feelings of satisfaction and joy arising from this practice are investigated and released. Then mind is explored and trained in various ways. Finally, the whole hog of breathing, body, feelings, and mind are revisited from the vipassana angles of impermanence, dukkha-ness, and not-self. If it's real vipassana, profound letting go takes place and liberation occurs.[2]

Though simple, the early steps ought not to be taken for granted; after all, there isn't any vipassana when the mind isn't calm and clear. Fortunately, Ajahn Buddhadasa, under whom I studied for a decade and for whom I served as translator, stressed the importance of long breathing and wasn't namby-pamby about it. He didn't mind "controlling" the breathing if it brought healthy results, so I also found creative ways to foster—not force—long breathing, and through it internally massage tightness and tension in chest, solar plexus, back, and abdomen. The easing and lightening could then spread throughout the body. Increasingly, these developed without conscious effort. However they might arrive, the results were delightful: Body more relaxed and light, whether walking or sitting. Mind much more settled and clear. Pleasant feelings. Happiness. Maybe that's why the Buddha talked about these things specifically instead of giving the watered down "watch your breathing." He even taught us to experience satisfaction and joy as we breathe in and out.

Artful breathing only happens through the training and development of mindfulness. To fully plumb the subtleties of breathing, a refined awareness is needed. Not just counting ins and outs, the breathing artist-technician explores all kinds of breathing and how they interrelate with various conditions of body and mind. As the mutual conditioning becomes clearer, possibilities for deeper calmness, centeredness, silence, and concentration open up. This is not Wal-Mart stuff, nor will it show up in espresso joints or on TV.

---

[2] The *Anapanasati Sutta* (Majjhima Nikaya 118) and *Satipatthana Sutta* (Majjhima Nikaya 10) are primary examples of this teaching. See also various suttas in the Anapanasati-samyutta of the *Samyutta Nikaya* and Buddhadasa Bhikkhu's *Mindfulness with Breathing* (Wisdom, 1988; tr. Santikaro Bhikkhu).

It's the realm of mind that has taken its inner life seriously cum playfully, softened up toughly, and jumped in carefully. As we pay attention through deepening levels of refining awareness, the foundations of mindfulness grow into factors of awakening (as described in the Anapanasati Sutta).

Breathing is something I genuinely need. It's free and has no packaging to fill up landfills. I can enjoy it right now and won't get e-mails to upgrade. My RAM was sufficient at birth to follow it in-down and up-out. It connects me to inner strength that no political charades can disempower. When my appetite is stimulated, I can calm around the belly to see if the hunger is coming from there or is concocted by sensual reactivity. Again, slowing down, relaxing, softening, and centering give me space to ask the questions: Do I need this? Do I really want it? Who will it benefit? Awareness gets a toehold and wisdom gets a chance.

Technology of mindful breathing not only has wonderful benefits, it is cheap and simple. Breathing and mindfulness can be applied anywhere. They're free. This technology is fun and playful. Everybody can do it. That makes it "real tech" in my book, beyond mere high- and low-tech.

It wasn't for nothing that the Buddha hung out in "the dwelling of anapanasati" and taught it in more depth than any other meditation practice.

From Volume 19, Number 1 (Fall 2002).

3 Biting into the Mango
Doing Jhana Practice with Ayya Khema

Ayya Khema was born in Germany, educated in Scotland and China, and later became a citizen of the United States. She was ordained as a Buddhist nun in Sri Lanka in 1979, and in 1982 established Parappuduwa Nuns Island in southern Sri Lanka as a training center for Buddhist nuns and women wishing to lead a contemplative life. As a Dharma teacher, Ayya Khema became well known for her focus on the meditative absorptions, or jhanas. She taught meditation retreats internationally until her death in 1997.

INQUIRING MIND: You are one of the few Western teachers in the Theravadan tradition who emphasizes the so-called jhana practices, the meditative absorptions. Describe for us how a meditator enters into an absorption or jhanic state.

AYYA KEMMA: We begin with a concentration practice. It doesn't matter whether we watch our breath or visualize a Buddha statue inside of us or use colored discs (*kasinas*). Each of these are methods of calming the mind, and in jhana practice it is important to calm the mind to the point where thinking stops. People who are patient and steady in their meditation will eventually stop thinking.

Once we have completely calmed the mind—stopped thinking and reacting—then we can step over the threshold into our inner being, where everybody really belongs. What we experience at that moment of entry is utter delight. That is an indication that we are in the first jhana. Immediately after feeling this utter delight, the first reaction of the mind usually is, Hey, what is this? And then the absorption is broken. At that time people need a teacher who will tell them, "That's fine, do it again." I've heard that when vipassana students accidentally enter the jhanas, many teachers will just say, "Go back to the breath. That's not insight." It's unfortunate that people are not guided through the jhanas with teachers who can tell them how to use the jhanas for insight.

After we have experienced the first jhana, we have to do three things before we open our eyes. First is to recapitulate how we got there, because people have individual ways of doing it. Some get there through lovingkindness meditation, some through watching the breath, some through "sweeping" or other methods. The second thing we have to do before opening our eyes is to see that this pleasant state is impermanent. And the third thing is to ask, What am I learning? The jhanas are a means to an end, so we have to learn something from them. What we are learning from them initially is that the delight we are looking for in the world lives inside of us. Anybody who is able to meditate properly has this delight at their fingertips anytime they want it. Even in a dentist's waiting room... anytime.

So the experience of delight in the jhanic state is a very major breakthrough. The meditator will then understand that our senses—seeing, hearing, tasting, smelling, touching, and thinking—are only survival systems. They are not an amusement park. Everybody thinks their senses are an amusement park, and if they don't get the right kind of amusement from them, they get irate. But the senses are only our survival systems. And survival is a guaranteed failure. Nobody makes it. Birth is a guarantee for death.

IM: So the jhanas are the real amusement park, the place to go for a good time?

AK: Absolutely. A good time, and much more. In sutta sixty-six of the Middle Length Sayings (Majjhima Nikaya) the Buddha says:

> Here, Udayin, quite secluded from sensual pleasures, secluded from unwholesome states, a bhikkhu enters upon and abides in the first jhana.... With the stilling of applied and sustained thought, he enters upon and abides in the second jhana.... With the fading away as well of rapture... he enters upon and abides in the third jhana.... With the abandoning of pleasure and pain... he enters upon and abides in the fourth jhana.... This is called the bliss of renunciation, the bliss of seclusion, the bliss of peace, the bliss of enlightenment. I say of this kind of pleasure that it should be pursued, that it should be developed, that it should be cultivated, that it should not be feared.

My own teacher, the Venerable Nannarama Mahathera, who died in 1992 at the age of ninety-one, told me, "Go to the West and teach the jhanas. They are a lost art."

IM: Perhaps one reason why jhanas are not widely taught is because of a bias against the concept of "absorption," which has the connotation of being lost or spaced out or hypnotized.

AK: That might be the case. People often get scared at the beginning of the first jhana because they think they're losing control. As their teacher I tell them, "When you are swept away by feelings of ordinary unhappiness, you obviously have no control over yourself. A person who is in control would never voluntarily be unhappy. So in your ordinary life you must be lost, or out of control." By contrast, in absorption, we are no longer projecting our ego onto reality. We are experiencing a taste of the emptiness of self, and while it may feel as though we are losing control, we are actually, at last, arriving at truth.

Absorption means that we're within the feeling base of our inner being. We believe we're living on the thinking base of our being, but we're actually living on the feeling base. And the absorption brings us to that feeling base. The only way we can be enlightened is when we feel or experience that there's nobody home.

IM: Let's go back to that feeling base for a while. You left us in the first jhana. Tell us what happens next.

AK: The first jhana is characterized by delightful sensations. One of the most common of these is a feeling of losing gravity, a feeling of almost floating. Others include a feeling of warmth in the spiritual heart area, or a very pleasant movement in the body, such as tingling from top to toe. Another is a sense of losing the limits of the body.

In the first jhana there is also a feeling of joy. Now if we want to go to the second level of absorption, we can deliberately put the delightful sensations in the back of our consciousness and put the joy in the forefront, as the next meditation subject. The pleasant sensations don't totally disappear, but they are no longer predominant.

IM: So the joy was present in the first jhana, but it was in the back of the consciousness.

AK: Yes, and it is often quite difficult for Westerners to bring it to the forefront of their consciousness. They're not used to being joyful without any outside stimulation.

IM: Without being at the movies or being on a ferris wheel...

AK: Exactly. Or buying ice cream. But even though it may be difficult, we should never bypass any jhana when we are practicing them. They must be done step by step, and they must be learned in such a way that we know exactly which jhana we are in at any given moment.

IM: Do people have a hard time distinguishing between the delightful sensations and the joy?

AK: Usually not, at least when they are being guided by a teacher. The delightful sensations are more closely associated with the body, while joy is an emotional state, which appears in the area of what we call the spiritual heart. We will find that as we proceed on through the jhanic states, these meditation subjects become more and more subtle. For instance, the first four jhanas are called the fine material meditative absorptions, or rupa jhanas, and the last four are called immaterial or formless meditative absorptions, or arupa jhanas.

IM: Okay. And we are still only in the second jhana.

AK: But that means we are in joy. So what's the problem? (Laughs) What we are learning in the second jhana is that the joy we've been seeking through the senses has absolutely no comparison to the joy we're already carrying inside of us. That brings an enormous change in one's life, because what mankind is doing—and America is the great example of this—is looking for happiness through sense pleasures from the external world. It's not that we don't get pleasant sense contacts anymore. On the contrary. But we don't go looking for them, and when we get them we're grateful. The sense pleasures also become far more impactful because we're not trying to grasp them or hold on to them. They're just happening. And that's a result of the second jhana.

Now, to get to the third jhana we have to let go of the joy, and what happens then is a feeling of deep contentment. And when the contentment is dropped, that leads to the fourth jhana, which brings about utter stillness and peacefulness.

We can see how the jhanas are connected by cause and effect. Concentration leads to delightful sensation, delightful sensation leads to joy, joy leads to contentment, and contentment leads to utter peacefulness. It all proceeds through cause and effect, as is common in the Buddha's teaching.

By the time we are in the fourth jhana, the observing ego has receded far into the background. What we're learning from this jhana is that utter peacefulness can only come when the ego has been relegated far into the background. These realizations are all leading us toward the goal.

IM: In the Burmese satipatthana method people are taught that deep states of concentration are not vital to the attainment of wisdom.

AK: I would reply that it's like biting into the mango. If you've never eaten a mango and want to know what it tastes like, you won't find out by asking someone. You need to bite into the mango.

IM: Mmmm good! And we've still got four jhanas left to go.

AK: The last four are the formless jhanas. While the first four have a connection to the experiences we have with ordinary states of consciousness, the last four have no connection to our everyday reality.

Number five is called infinity of space, and we would never have any inkling of that unless we meditate. Number six is called infinity of consciousness. Seven is the base of nothingness. And the eighth and final jhana is called neither perception nor nonperception.

Five and six are particularly useful in experiencing that there's no limited person, no identity, because in the infinity of space and consciousness there is no personal form left. "Form is emptiness, emptiness is form." Not only is it unlimited, it's not ours. There's nobody having consciousness. It just is. From that we now realize also that there is universal consciousness. That's when we begin to take responsibility for the rest of humanity. We see the importance of not having any negative thought or emotion, which would have a detrimental effect on universal consciousness, because we are all intrinsically connected.

The seventh jhana can be called an extension of five and six because it shows us that there is absolutely nothing solid anywhere to be found, nothing to hang on to. There's nothing that we can put our finger on and say,

"That's what I'm going to have" or "That's what I'm going to keep" or "That's what I'm going to be." Nothing, nothing at all.

The eighth jhana is actually a refinement of the fourth, because the observer has receded to the point of almost disappearing altogether. There is neither perception nor nonperception. People who accidentally enter this jhana might think they've suddenly become enlightened, because the observer is so minimal. This experience brings enormous energy to the mind, making it clear and powerful. But this shouldn't be confused with enlightenment.

IM: Do you think it is possible to achieve enlightenment without doing the jhanas?

AK: I dare say it's possible. But it must be terribly difficult. This is such a smooth, well-oiled path.

Besides, I think that ignoring the jhanas leaves a kind of dryness in the Theravadan teaching. It takes a lot of the joy out of the path. Most of Theravadan teaching in the West is derived from the Burmese tradition, which is largely based on the Abhidhamma. The practices are therefore very analytical. The Abhidamma is concerned with taking reality apart, bit by bit, which is useful for people whose minds tend in that direction. While that practice certainly produces insight, it does not give access to elevated states of consciousness, which can enhance the quality of life and give us a taste of the end of dukkha. Furthermore, doing jhana practice does not prevent the meditator from an analytic observation of him- or herself. On the contrary, it facilitates the process, because the mind is unperturbed.

It is my fervent wish and hope that I can at least spread enough seeds so that people become interested and start practicing the jhanas. It changes their very being, and thereby the collective consciousness on this planet. It's the natural way for the meditative mind to go. These states are accessible to anyone. They are like a hidden jewel that we carry within.

IM: Once you've been through all eight jhanas, if you aren't enlightened, what is the result?

AK: There are two immediate and tangible results. One is that we have had a taste of freedom and will therefore continue to practice with vigor. The second one is an enhancement of our quality of life, based on a much deeper perspective.

However we don't actually have to go to the eighth jhana. The Buddha taught that after any of the jhanas we can attempt to have path and fruit. The path moment is the experience of being nothing and nobody; it is a universal experience, and everybody explains it in the same way, so the teacher has little trouble recognizing it. The experience is usually described with tears of joy. The meditator feels totally relieved, as if a burden has fallen off his or her shoulders. That's all one can say about the path moment. The fruit moment, which comes immediately afterward, is the moment when we realize what has happened. The fruit moment feels as though we have been turned inside out. After it happens, it is impossible ever again to believe that we are a separate person, or separate entity. We have to remember and relive the fruit moment over and over again in order to make that experience part of our everyday consciousness. That first path and fruit is only a knowing, but we can remember it whenever we put our mind on it again. When we don't put our mind on it, once again we become "me."

One other thing that happens after a path and fruit moment is that we have no doubt that the Buddha is our teacher. We couldn't possibly have anybody else because we have used the guidelines transmitted to us on the Buddha's path. Also, we can no longer break any of the five precepts, which is a lovely way of checking whether we have actually had this momentous experience. And finally, it is said, that after this path and fruit experience, we will only have seven more lives, maximum.

IM: Maybe if we had a few more lives, we could finish describing all the nuances of jhana practice. (Laughter)

From Volume 13, Number 1 (Fall 1996).

4

Passionate Dharma
Tantra Practice
An Interview with Miranda Shaw

Practitioners of Vajrayana Buddhism have a unique and, to some, shocking approach to the experience of desire, whether it be for sex, money, power—or even desire itself. No one explains this approach better than Miranda Shaw, Ph.D., author of the award-winning book Passionate Enlightenment: Women in Tantric Buddhism. *Shaw focuses her research on gender, sexuality, goddess worship, and sacred dance in Buddhism. Her latest book,* Buddhist Goddesses of India, *was released in the fall of 2006. We asked Miranda Shaw to explain the history and basic philosophy of Tantra.*

This interview was conducted by Barbara Gates and Wes Nisker in Muir Beach, California, in 1994 and updated by phone in 2007.

INQUIRING MIND: When people hear the word *tantra*, many will immediately think of exotic sexual practices. But as you explain in your books, tantra concerns itself with all of life.

MIRANDA SHAW: The word *tantra* comes from the verbal stem *tan*, meaning "to weave." Tantra is a spiritual path that weaves, or integrates, every aspect of life, including all daily activities, intimacy, and passion, into the path to enlightenment. According to tantra, there is one basic energy that courses through the universe and through our bodies. Thus, embodiment is understood as a dynamic, permeable mind-body continuum without fixed boundaries, the site of energies—inner winds and flames, meltings and flowings—that can bring about dramatic transformations on the path to enlightenment.

The tantric teachings originated in India and the Himalayas in the seventh through twelfth centuries C.E. They represent the pinnacle of a long path of discipline that begins with the basic Buddhist teachings on mindfulness, non-self, impermanence, and karma. It progresses through the bodhisattva path—compassionate motivation, altruistic activity, and the Mahayana philosophy of emptiness—and culminates in the tantric teachings.

IM: How does tantra understand the energy of desire?

MS: In tantra desire is honored. Of course, the tantric practitioner recognizes that there are negative expressions of desire, motivated by ego and selfishness—expressions that can lead to harm and suffering. But desire is not intrinsically bad or an impediment to spiritual realization. Tantra sees desire as an expression of the blissful relatedness that is the matrix of all existence. Desire is what calls different aspects of reality into relationship with one another. It's a movement toward the world and other beings, and as such is a positive expression of interconnection.

IM: Of course, when you work with the energy of desire you are playing with the proverbial fire. It is probably very easy to delude yourself and twist the practices to feed selfish hungers.

MS: Yes, there are many possible ways to fall off of the tantric path. That is why tantra begins only after lengthy practices of purification. What tantra adds to the mix of Buddhist practice is the ability to dissolve any emotion as it arises by seeing it as intrinsically empty. Tantra sees all the world as empty, as a pure, playful, illusory manifestation.

IM: What takes place in a tantric sexual relationship?

MS: A tantric relationship is a partnership that two people enter, voluntarily and consciously, as part of their path to enlightenment in this lifetime. People who enter into such a relationship will already have prepared for this path by learning mindfulness meditation practices, basic Buddhist teachings, and also a number of advanced philosophical teachings. They both agree that this relationship will be integral to their spiritual practice and is not set up to gratify the ego of either person involved. This is one of the overarching principles of the relationship.

IM: So the relationship is explicitly not for sensual pleasure?

MS: Sensual pleasure is a goal of secular life and ordinary relationships. In a tantric partnership, the intimacy and bliss of the physical union will be channeled toward yogic and meditative ends. The significant difference between tantra and other Buddhist paths is that tantra is a fully embodied path. That means that the sensuality, knowledge, and power of the body are interwoven into the path. They are not avoided. They are, in fact, cultivated and then channeled in very specific ways.

IM: So motivation is the key.

MS: The motivation is diametrically opposed to what normally propels people into personal relationships. The motivation is not security, and it is not emotional fulfillment of the ordinary kind. The motivation is to gain enlightenment for the sake of all sentient beings, and these practitioners will use every aspect of their embodied being to attain that goal.

IM: In the Theravada tradition, the way to do extreme practice is to close yourself off from all conventional sense pleasures. You go to a monastery where you don't listen to music, don't smell perfumes, don't eat rich foods. You don't look at the opposite sex or sleep under the same roof with a woman, if you are a monk, or with a man, if you are a nun. With tantra, instead of cutting yourself off from all of this, you enter right into the middle of it and work with it.

MS: But in tantra there are also periods of seclusion or retreat situations where the companions go together to a cave or retreat house and practice very intensively for many hours a day without interruption. But the energies that they cultivate then have to be integrated back into daily life.

IM: What happens on retreat? Are the partners engaged in coitus, working with these sexual energies for many hours a day?

MS: Practice with a consort is not synonymous with physical union. I prefer to use the word *intimacy* rather than *sexuality*, because sex is not the essence of the practice. That's our impoverished Western view of what intimacy entails. There are many other practices that tantric partners do together. One of these practices is gazing: long sessions where the partners cultivate pure

vision by gaining the ability to see one another as divine, as embodied manifestations of Buddhahood, and as enlightened in essence. There are other
exercises where they simply touch each other's fingertips or touch the palms
of their hands, or they eat and feast together as a practice of cultivating and
channeling their bliss.

IM: You have said that during their intimacy, the two partners make a deep
imprint on one another's karma.

MS: By combining their energies and then channeling that energy through
their bodies into the subtle yogic anatomy, they are absorbing the quality
of their partner's consciousness and, in fact, absorbing their partner's karma.
Together they generate the energy that enables them to blast through some
of the knots created by that karma. They are sharing karma because they are
then both working with the same set of pooled karma. In ordinary relationships, you are also creating and sharing karma together. But it's like the difference between swimming in the ocean, in the case of an ordinary
relationship, and injecting salt water into your veins, in the case of a tantric
relationship. A very intimate communion takes place in a tantric partnership.
That is why the choice of tantric partner is such a delicate process.

IM: It is widely rumored that in the name of tantra some Buddhist teachers, especially in the West, have engaged in sexual relationships that have
been harmful to students, particularly women students. Could you talk about
that?

MS: In the West, we have gathered that tantra involves sexuality, so when we
hear about the sexual activities of a Buddhist teacher, we automatically think
that maybe it's tantra. Some teachers have hidden behind that label, and they
have been able to hide behind it because we Westerners don't know what
tantra means. But these liaisons, at least the ones that I have known about,
violate basic Mahayana Buddhist principles of compassionate motivation
and selfless, benevolent activity. It is a gross violation of bodhisattva motivation to express one's sexuality in a way that harms another person psy-
chologically or physically—and that includes any kind of coercive
relationship, or any relationship in which there is a disparity in the emotional
strength of the so-called "partners." Moreover, such a thing would be
unthinkable in the tantric context of a fully conscious, voluntary, and mutually enlightening relationship.

I'll give an example from my own experience of how such an abusive teacher might operate. I was once approached by a lama whom I believed to be a monk. I didn't know him well enough to have occasion to inquire as to which vows he had taken. After a very short acquaintance, he abruptly invited me to have sexual relations with him. He claimed that to do so would be of spiritual benefit to me. He was, in effect, attempting to sexually abuse me.

There was no relationship between us, so I was stunned by the unexpectedness of the approach. I was also astonished at the smoothness of his obviously well-rehearsed lines. He said, "I think it would be good for your meditation. I feel we have a karmic connection that should be expressed in this way." I was very taken aback: "I thought you were a monk." He said, "Oh no, no. I just wear these robes to please my mother and to enhance my teaching." That was a lot to assimilate, since he wears the full monastic regalia. Then I asked, "What do you mean by saying that it would help my meditation?" He said, "It will help you to relax." I said, "I never heard that meditation was relaxation. My lama never taught me that the essence of meditation is to relax." He said, "In general it will just help you." And I asked, "In that case, why doesn't anyone who has sexual relations become enlightened? Why isn't everyone enlightened?"

I decided to try to find out if, contrary to all appearances, he was a genuine tantric practitioner. I asked, "What tantric texts have you studied? What tantric methods were you proposing to employ?" He said, "What texts?" I replied, "Well, for example, the *Cakrasamvara Tantra*, is that what you've studied? Is that what you practice?" He said, "Oh, no, I haven't done any of that practice. I'm not talking about tantra. I'm not qualified to do tantra." He immediately backed down, his bravado just evaporated, and he slunk off.

After my encounter with this practiced predator, I found out that he has left a body count of ruined lives. I feel it is important that we become knowledgeable about tantra in part so that we have some handle with which to evaluate the behavior of such teachers.

IM: Is there a practice for those not totally committed to this path, perhaps a "beginner's tantra," teachings that are relevant for ordinary practitioners in their intimate relationships?

MS: First of all, I would say that anyone can do this practice, if the primary understanding is that your relationship is a sacred bond and exists for the purpose of the liberation of both partners. Keep in the foreground the fact that you are both spiritual seekers.

You could also begin to view your partner as divine. See the purity and Buddha-essence of this other being, and make those qualities the conscious focus of your interaction. Behave toward your partner as you would toward a deity, literally. Make offerings. Treat your partner as the divine.

At the same time, you have to remember that the bliss and completion that you seek is not to be found in another person. In other words, you aren't placing the responsibility for satisfaction in the hands of your partner. What you are working on is your own capacity to experience the inherent blissfulness of reality.

From Volume 23, Number 2 (Spring 2007).

5 Buddhist Humor Practice: It Hurts So I Laugh

By Rev. Heng Sure

In my training as a monk, I made a pilgrimage that involved making a full prostration to the ground every three steps. I bowed 800 miles along the California Coast Highway from Los Angeles to Ukiah, in Mendocino County. The journey took nearly three years, and I traveled about one mile a day. During the pilgrimage, and for three years after, I kept a vow of total silence, speaking only to my teacher, the late Ch'an master Hsüan Hua. My bowing companion, Heng Ch'au, and I ate one vegetarian meal a day, and except for the wild roadside greens we gathered, our survival depended entirely on goodwill offerings by kind-hearted donors along the way.

One foggy morning in Santa Cruz, where Highway One becomes a residential street in the middle of town, I came up from a bow to see a young schoolgirl, perhaps nine years old, on her bicycle. She had stopped to stare at the bowing monk and ponder what in the world I was doing on the sidewalk. She silently watched me make three steps and slowly bow to the ground, then stand, step, and bow again. I looked ahead and bowed past her. Several houses later, I heard her bicycle approach from the rear. She came around front, and when I came up from a bow she opened her lunch box and held out a wax-paper package: "Here, Mister, you better take this sandwich. The way you're going, you'll need it before you get to the corner."

What do Buddhists laugh at? Often Buddhist humor comes from suddenly awakening to the transient, unsatisfying, and impersonal nature of reality. The glossy surface of the events of our lives is illusory, offering a promise of satisfaction that so rarely delivers. When life hurts, one way to begin healing is to laugh at how much it aches.

How is Buddhist humor different from slapstick, from Punch and Judy cruelly beating each other with clubs, from cynicism? Buddhist humor heals the hurt because the jokes and stories lift the banana peel after the hero slips and falls, to hint at the nature of living beings: that we are "born drunk and dying in a dream." If the dream is a nightmare, waking up can be a jarring but blessed relief; it was only a dream after all.

Sometimes it hurts so bad you laugh. During the pilgrimage, one evening near Santa Cruz, Heng Ch'au and I parked in a cul-de-sac behind the fence of a housing unit. I lit the kerosene lamp and we meditated. The next morning after chanting, Heng Ch'au boiled a pot of water for tea. He handed me a scalding bowl. I was still in meditation mode, sitting in full lotus, my feet bare and upturned. Careless of the steaming bowl, in the confined space I upended the tea onto my lap. The tea scalded my upturned bare foot and ankle. Blisters formed within seconds. Oh, it hurt! How was I going to bow on a burned foot? Heng Ch'au poked his head through the door curtains and joked, "Wow! That's pretty good tea, eh? It could really wake a guy up, huh? Did you get enlightened?" I laughed so hard I couldn't feel the pain—for at least a minute.

There are other aspects to Buddhist humor. Sometimes the bodhisattva, or awakened being, in Mahayana Buddhism serves as a trickster figure, like Coyote or Br'er Rabbit. The trickster bodhisattva has an eye open to reality beyond the reach of ordinary people. In the past, Guan Shi Yin Bodhisattva or Manjushri has appeared as an enigmatic figure, a powerful and all-wise teacher who uses mischief or harsher measures to wake up students.

Once a hermit cultivated the Way in the mountains. He saw his practice of the spiritual life as essentially complete. He was particularly pleased with his strength of concentration, his "samadhi power." He felt that he was patient before all states of mind, pleasant or unpleasant, and that his mind never moved, regardless of the circumstances. Near his meditation hut, he nailed together two boards and on them inked three words: "Mind like ashes." He tied the boards to a pointed stick and hammered this sign into the ground. He dusted off his hands, sat down, and prepared to meditate.

At that point, Guan Yin Bodhisattva decided to test the cultivator's samadhi. In a moment, Guan Yin transformed into a young lad and knocked loudly at the cultivator's gate. He continued to knock for five minutes, and the sound echoed in the hills. Seeing nobody, he walked up to the hut and looked through the window to find the cultivator meditating unmoving on his cushion.

"Excuse me!" he said, "I'm sorry to interrupt but I saw your sign down by the trail and I'm really curious. What does it say?"

The cultivator slowly opened one eye, then the other. He seemed to make an inner decision and said quietly, "It says, 'Mind like ashes.'"

"Oh, what an agreeable sound. I can't read. Which word is *ashes*?"

The cultivator paused before answering, exhaled and said, "The last word says ashes."

"I'm not sure if I've got it right. It's such a lovely idea that I want to understand the meaning. Your mind likes ashes?"

"Like ashes, not likes!"

The questioning went on for thirty minutes until the cultivator, provoked beyond endurance, shouted, "You're an idiot, open your ears! How many times do I have to tell you, it's 'mind like ashes'!?"

The young boy suddenly leaped into space and transformed into Guan Yin Bodhisattva, appearing majestically in full lotus on a purple-golden cloud. "Well, it seems there are a few embers in the ashes yet. I'll come back in a year or two and visit you again. Be vigorous."

Buddhist humor presents suffering with principle. Dharma laughter comes as medicine to heal the universal human disease of mortality; the suffering involved in birth, death, and rebirth are no joke. Because the Buddha's project was ending suffering for good, leaving the cycle of birth and death completely, his parameters for humor tended to be earthy, broad, almost slapstick in illustrating our primal suffering. From the Buddha's perspective of wisdom, in our realm of desire, delusion reigns. Fundamental ignorance of how desire ties us down is the basic joke, and the laugh is on us. The Buddha describes us as upside down, running toward desire and away from liberation, dragging chains of ignorance that inevitably drop us back into suffering.

One rainy February week on our pilgrimage, Heng Ch'au and I bowed through the Golden Gate National Recreation Area, one of America's largest urban parks, making slow progress along the Great Highway just south of San Francisco. From the highway shoulder, movement was a constant assault: wind in the teeth, flying sand in the eyes, and restless thoughts haunting the mind. Thousands of cars passed by, with curious passengers staring, wondering and occasionally stopping to find out why we were bowing.

One such vehicle was a twelve-passenger van belonging to the park's rangers. A red-haired, cheery Irish Catholic named Mickey hopped out and walked over.

"Hi, fellows. Guess you must be working for a spiritual cause. Buddhists? I'm with the rangers here at the National Recreation Area, and I drive up and down this coast all day long. Must have seen you first down by Devil's Slide a month back. You guys sure stick with it. I'm kind of a lapsed Catholic myself, but I sure like the way you just keep moving up the coast. So, hey, I stopped to tell you to be careful up ahead, they're patching the Great Highway, and you'll want to stay over on the grass by the ocean side, all right?"

Mickey kept watching out for us across the Golden Gate Bridge and down to Fort Baker, giving us advice on road conditions, even bringing us hot soup from his kitchen. One Monday, he stopped by at lunch with a story.

"What a joke! You guys seem to be having some kind of an effect. I've got a coworker in administration who doesn't like you two, not a bit. He says he would just as soon roll his truck up the curb and run over the both of you. He thinks you're the devil himself. He's a decent enough guy. It must be something about religion that pushes his button. He came in last week and said, 'Look at those two jerks. What losers! They can't come up with anything better to do than bow on the road in public? Who are they trying to impress? Why not go do that in a closet?'

"So the guy shows up for work this morning with a black eye, a missing tooth, and a hangover. 'I went on a date to Tahoe to ski and play the slots,' he told us. 'The trouble started when we were driving to the Interstate and passed by those two freaks bowing. You know me, I let them have it. When I said the world would be better without those guys, my girlfriend piped up and told me to lay off. She said they're probably bowing for world peace and weren't hurting anybody. They were actually doing something meaningful instead of complaining about things all the time.

"'I told her, "No way! They're total losers, zombies, they're probably cursing the cars driving by." We argued all the way to Sacramento and then she stopped talking to me. Bad start. When we arrived at the hotel, I lost my car keys and we couldn't open the trunk to get to our liquor stash. We wound up having to buy premium stuff and I got drunk. I took a swing at my girlfriend, fell over the railing, broke a tooth, and lost my wallet in the snow.

"'She left with the car and I had to take the bus to Sacramento, where my brother picked me up. I went looking for a good time this weekend but came back miserable, without my wallet, my keys, my car, or my girlfriend.

"'But the strangest part of the trip was what happened when I got back. It was late Sunday afternoon, and when I reached Highway One, there were those two monks, bowing like it was Friday, or Monday, or last month, except now they were three miles farther north than when I went to Tahoe.

They were still doing that same bowing thing, wearing the same expression on their faces and...I couldn't believe what had happened to me since Friday. I had my life turned upside down; they suddenly seemed kind of peaceful. I wonder if they've figured something out. Funny how it made me think, you know.'"

Mickey summed up, "Well, I guess 'losers and winners' is just a state of mind. Here's a loaf of bread I baked on Sunday. You guys take care."

We continued to bob up and down in the gutter, demons or devas, depending on how close to the pain you can stand it. Sometimes you look through the windshield and all you can do is laugh.

⋮ From Volume 21, Number 2 (Spring 2005).

6
Undiluted Dharma Practice
An Interview with Joseph Goldstein

In the introduction to our earlier interview of Joseph Goldstein, we mentioned that many senior meditation teachers go to him for guidance in their practice. When we learned that Goldstein was teaching a special class for the staff of the Insight Meditation Society called "The Undiluted Dhamma," we asked him what exactly he was teaching.

This interview was conducted by Jack Kornfield together with Barbara Gates and Wes Nisker in Berkeley, California, in the summer of 1989.

JOSEPH GOLDSTEIN: I am trying to include ideas that don't get talked about at length in the normal meditation retreats, such as the Buddhist cosmology, the planes of existence, the rounds of rebirth, the thirty-seven principles of enlightenment, and the possible kinds of happiness and suffering that are attendant on this vastness of vision. These teachings of the Buddha have greatly enhanced my practice, and I wanted to share them with others. They provide a large context for the meditation practice and can give a very powerful sense of urgency, meaning, and direction to our lives, deepening the sense of path and of what is possible for us to achieve.

IM: Can you elaborate on how the Buddhist cosmology informs your own practice and vision of the Dhamma?

JG: The Buddhist cosmology gives a sense of how brief our life is and how quickly it passes. Sometimes it feels just like a long weekend. The cosmology offers a long-range vision of things, a vision of our journey unfolding over lifetimes. This provides a special sense of both spaciousness and purpose, because there's not the same compulsion or frenetic need to experience everything in this one lifetime. It becomes easier to prioritize what is of most value, and to give a focused energy to these areas.

The Buddhist cosmology also has tremendous implications for understanding what is meant by suffering—the endlessness of our wandering through rounds of rebirths, without ever coming to a place of rest or peace. In this context, the Buddha talked about the Dhamma as an uplifting support, something that becomes a condition for our happiness and for our wellbeing. I think that because of the emphasis placed on understanding the truth of suffering, we often forget that what the Buddha actually taught was a path of happiness.

IM: After the Buddha's enlightenment, he exclaimed that he would never have to be born again. Is that the bottom line for you?

JG: I do think that's the bottom line, but I also think that this position can be easily misunderstood. Basically, I think the question is not rightly put. The Buddha went beyond the concept of life to the direct experience of what life actually is. In many of the suttas he talks about the five skandas, the five "heaps" of psychic and physical events. We may make up all kinds of images, concepts, and stories of what life is about, but when it comes right down to experience, it's just these five *skandas* arising and passing, arising and passing. From that perspective, we begin to understand that the process itself is unsatisfying. To reach the place where these processes—which are empty of substance, empty of self—come to an end is to open to an unconditioned reality, to nibbana. The profound realization is that there is no one who has taken birth, and therefore no one who will cease to take birth—just suffering and its end. This is the teaching of the Buddha.

IM: Does that mean that life is a mistake, something to get out of?

JG: (Laughs) Well, I don't think it's a mistake, in that it happens because of causes. The causes are desire and craving and ignorance. If we think of life as a mistake, then we lose sight of the actual way it all unfolds. The other question is whether it's wise to get out of it or not. I think the more skillful way of framing the question would be: Isn't it better to come out of ignorance and then to see with the eye of wisdom what follows?

IM: You've stated that a primary motivation for your teaching is to help people achieve at least stream entry, the first stage of enlightenment, so that they won't risk being reborn in lower realms. How does this work?

JG: According to the traditional teachings, one takes rebirth according to the process of karma that is operative at the time of death. It's said that what completely assures a rebirth in one of the happy kinds of existence—as a human or higher being—is the experience of nibbana, this opening to the unconditioned, which uproots the identification with the concept of self. Because of the potential for rebirth into so many different realms of existence and the immensity of suffering that exists in some of these realms, I feel the greatest gift I can offer is to help create a situation where people can walk on a path that frees them completely from this danger.

Meanwhile, in our society and culture there's often an avoidance of the shadow side of things. Just as we've avoided acknowledging the madness of nuclear armaments, the danger of toxic wastes and acid rain, people often don't want to learn about the dangers of existence and the possible dangers of rebirth. They want to think of life's journey as being unidirectional, going inexorably to more love and light. This is not at all my understanding of what the Buddha taught, nor is it my experience. Just as in the psychology of the mind, where there's a light side and a shadow side, in the spiritual world, there are tremendously beneficent forces as well as real dangers and potentials for suffering.

IM: How do you understand stream entry, and why is it given such an important place on the path?

JG: What's important in the experience of stream entry is the fact that it uproots the belief in "I" in the concept of some unchanging self to whom experience happens. Therefore, this uprooting of the belief in self becomes the measure of the experience. The Buddha emphasized again and again that the idea of some permanent unchanging self who is the owner of experience is "wrong view" and the cause of much suffering. So the uprooting of that concept of self, through training, is a tremendously liberating force in the mind.

IM: You say that the goal of practice is to become fully enlightened. Have you ever met anyone whom you felt was fully enlightened?

JG: There's really no way of knowing from the outside. There's no sign that people wear, and so, at best, it's an intuition or a hope. But I have met people who seemed pretty free of craving and desire, empty of self. There are also some people who will acknowledge that they're not fully enlightened arahants, but who may be at various stages of enlightenment, and some of their qualities are very extraordinary—qualities of love and compassion and emptiness.

IM: With all the people in the world, why do you think there are so few who are fully enlightened?

JG: There may not be multitudes of fully enlightened beings because it takes such an extraordinary effort. We know how much of a struggle it is just to watch a few breaths. To actually come to the end of the journey takes an extremely courageous effort. Another possible reason we may not see many enlightened people around is that as people purify themselves in practice, there's a very strong likelihood of rebirth in one of the higher realms, in the deva or the brahma realms. So people at the first stages of enlightenment, or even just well established in the practice, may take rebirth in a higher realm of existence and actually continue with the process from there. It is said there are brahma realms that are populated only by *anagamis* (nonreturners) and arahants.

IM: You put a lot of emphasis on people sitting at meditation retreats. Do you see these intensive retreats as the best way for most people to progress on the path?

JG: I do. Strong concentration is needed for the development of deep wisdom. This is hard to accomplish in our fast-paced lifestyle. I think the form of intensive retreats is very well suited to Western culture because it gives us the chance to slow down, to live in the great beauty of silence, to realistically begin training the mind.

IM: Why are those other periods necessary? Why wouldn't you suggest to somebody who was bent on enlightenment just to sit and to not stop until they got full enlightenment?

JG: If I felt the person were right for it and mature enough to do it, I would. I have a great love of that intensive retreat form, and I've experienced tremendous benefit from it and the power that comes from it. So I'm not at all hesitant to encourage people to do that if the conditions are right and if they're ready for it.

I also think that there are cycles. There comes a time when the energy for intensive sitting practice may be dissipated, and it really is time to get more involved in some kind of work or study, and again, at some later date, to go back to intensive meditation. These are the cycles that I'm experimenting with in my own life—integration of periods of long intensive practice with periods of active engagement with others in teaching.

There are also great feelings of compassion and awe that come from the sense of the immensity of these rounds of rebirths and the vastness of the Buddha's vision. Feeling this and seeing that there is a path out of the suffering brings a strong desire to share that path with others. This feeling is so well expressed by the Zen poet-monk Ryokan:

> O, that my monk's robe were wide enough
> to gather up all the suffering people
> in this floating world.

The practice is never for ourselves alone. Wisdom and compassion are the two great wings of the Dhamma.

From Volume 6, Number 1 (Summer 1989).

7 Compressing Eons of Lifetimes into One
Vajrayana Impermanence Practice

By Robert Thurman

Recognizing impermanence is a crucial first step in breaking down the substantialization habit of the ego, which thinks that you are a fixed entity who is going to live forever. To erode this illusion, you must viscerally know about impermanence (anicca) before you can understand the suffering inherent in all experience (dukkha), or before you can begin to comprehend selflessness (anatta).

You begin by witnessing the impermanence of objects, seeing their dissolution and instability, then moving on to the impermanence of mindstates, seeing the same conditions there. Then you move on to death and the impermanence of life.

Meditation on death is a core practice in all Buddhist traditions and focuses on what are called the "three roots." The first root is the certainty that you will die and includes meditating on yourself as dead. You imagine your body as a bloated corpse going through different stages of decay, in the process deglamorizing the physical body and loosening your attachment to it. You also reflect on your inability to maintain your identity: the inevitable loss of your memory, your relationships, and all the other things you think you own. In other words, during meditation on the first root you imaginably subtract yourself from the universe.

Meditation on the second root is recognizing the uncertainty of when you are going to die and the fact that it could take place at any minute—possibly while you are reading these words. You see that young people sometimes die before old people, that healthy people die before sick people, or that those who live in a supposed safe situation can die before those who live in danger. When you recognize that death is totally unpredictable, you must confront what is called the "immediacy of death," which you then attempt to embrace. Once you can embrace the immediacy of death, then all sorts of time-wasting, energy-wasting attachments begin to drop away: attachments to possessions, status, or identity.

The third root is the idea that at the moment of death the only thing that will be of benefit to you is the Dharma you have integrated, the wisdom and perspective you hold in the marrow of your being. The Dharma referred to here has nothing to do with doctrines, because you won't be able to remember words at the moment of death; you won't know the English language, the Sanskrit language, or the Tibetan language. All of that will vanish with the coarse mind. What will be with you is the mental stability you have developed through meditation—the wisdom you have gained, meaning acceptance of the nature of reality; the openness of mind and heart you have acquired through the generosity of having given gifts; the sensitivity to others you have developed by focusing on their interests rather than your own; and the resilience of mind you have achieved by cultivating patience and tolerance.

These meditations on the three roots are essential Tibetan Buddhist practices, which come, of course, right out of the Pali Canon. It is interesting to note that in the Tibetan analysis of the Pali Canon, the most fundamental theme is considered to be the preciousness of human life. Before you start looking at the impermanence of your life, you must first appreciate the embodiment that you have, with your critical human abilities to be self-reflective, self-transcending, and compassionate. These incredible human faculties do not exist among the gods, animals, or hell beings. You begin to reflect on what an immensely valuable embodiment you have as a human, and furthermore, as a human with access to the Dharma. In this way, you develop some self-esteem and self-confidence before you start looking at impermanence and death. Those who start out meditating on impermanence and death have a tendency to get depressed and nihilistic. But if you can link the moment-to-moment awareness that comes from meditating on impermanence with a simultaneous sense of the extreme preciousness of any single moment of human awareness, then the intensity is channeled in a positive and creative direction.

The Buddha was very sensitive to the possibility of people getting depressed by their insights into impermanence or the suffering of existence. In the *Sarvastivada Vinaya*, the Buddha warns his followers against meditating exclusively on these characteristics. He did this after a group of monks hired a bandit to kill them, one by one. They had gotten deep into meditations on impermanence and the hell realms and become very depressed. Instead of committing suicide—there was a proscription against killing themselves, and they were also a little scared to do it—they hired a hit man to sneak up and do them in, a kind of mad Jack Kevorkian scheme. The Buddha expelled those monks from the order posthumously for having committed suicide, which is breaking the vow against taking life. This incident caused a big debate: first, since they were dead already, why bother kicking them out of the Sangha; and second, did they really commit suicide when another person killed them? But the Buddha said that the monks had to accept the karma for their own deaths. He also said that the monks' error was in not fully realizing the value of their human incarnation.

So the Tibetans first emphasize the preciousness of human life and follow with the theme of impermanence. For the same reason, it is important to meditate on impermanence before jumping into the theme of suffering. First you begin to melt the inner feeling of durable solidity, which is the coarsest level of the self-habit. If you plunge right into the ocean of suffering, it is too overwhelming to the core feeling of self, and there might be some sort of backlash.

In the Vajrayana tradition there are some wonderful ways not only to practice but to celebrate impermanence. For instance, during a ritual, when you rattle the little drum called a *damaru*, on one level you are reminding yourself of impermanence, and at the same time you are summoning the dakinis to come and celebrate it. You are beating the drum of Dharma. Preferably, it is made from a skull, so you are embracing the immediacy of death as you celebrate impermanence. Of course, everything you do in tantra, or Vajrayana practice, has multiple meanings, multivalence.

There's another quite fascinating way to look at impermanence from a Vajrayana perspective. In the Mahayana, you must live three incalculable eons of lifetimes accumulating merit and interacting beneficially with trillions of living beings in order to create the Buddha Land for all. The Vajrayana, on the other hand, says, "I can't stand to wait billions of lifetimes to liberate everyone, including my billions of mothers." But since you can't simply cancel your karma or the evolving you have left to do, the only solution becomes compressing all those lifetimes into just seven or sixteen lifetimes, or even a single lifetime. Therefore, in the Vajrayana, when you enter the bardo, that state between death and birth, you can die many, many times. For instance, Milarepa would die maybe a thousand times in one night in a cave, in one samadhi. During each of the lifetimes he went through during that one meditation session, he would perform the ultimate self-sacrifice, giving away his life and body, his eyes, whatever was necessary. He would go through the karmic equivalent of a thousand lifetimes in one meditation session.

In some sense, therefore, impermanence is the very bloodstream of the Vajrayana. Impermanence is what makes possible the collapsing of a life into a moment or thousands of lifetimes into a single meditation session, so that you can experience death and rebirth in every single moment.

For these practices, the Vajrayana works with the subtle mind-stream. You can have a dream tonight in which you are flying over Vietnam during the war in a big spaceship, swallowing up all the B-52s before they drop their bombs, swallowing up the pilots without hurting them, and saving all the villages. But then you reach a point where you have to reveal yourself, maybe to show the pilots that you are not some aggressive superpower, so you surrender your own life in some way. Then you wake up and realize that you died in that dream. Even though you were just dreaming, you gained the merit in your subtlest mind-stream.

You can practice that kind of sacrifice in your dreams, and as you develop more sophisticated samadhi, you can do such things in millions of different circumstances and millions of different ways. Imagine that you've become a buddha. Suddenly, you come face-to-face with a mad gorilla, a tiger, a man-eating tarantula, and a tyrannosaurus rex one after the other. They are all beings who live by the rule of eat or be eaten, and they want to pounce on you. Instead of being frightened or aggressive, you smile and offer to feed yourself to them, causing something to dawn in their minds at the subliminal level. As a buddha, you have to be able to do that with every being you meet. You rehearse through the subtle mind practices of Vajrayana, which are based on a belief in the ultimate impermanence and transformability of every life form.

Finally, one of the deepest practices of impermanence in the Vajrayana is to enter your own subtle body, the subtle nervous system of tantra, where each moment contains the universe and all of evolutionary causality. It is to unravel the 72,000 knots of the energy channels and open up to the pure flow of bliss. It is like the satipatthana body scan of the Theravada tradition, where you melt the sense of a rigid structure in the body. As you feel it dissolve, you begin to realize great relief and even bliss. That is why monks and yogis in the forests and retreat caves are having such a great time. They are opening up the neural, Reichian armoring and feeling the bliss of the flowing energies. In the deepest practices, we find that impermanence becomes bliss and freedom. In the end, impermanence means that we are transformable, and that is central to all of the Buddha's teaching.

◇
◇ From Volume 17, Number 1 (Fall 2000).
◇

VII

ARTISTS & JESTERS
OF THE DHARMA

In Sri Lankan carvings of Gautama Buddha cut into a mountain of stone, in Japanese Zen gardens and the quirky epiphanies of haiku, in the Tibetan thangkas and spontaneous poems in praise of consciousness—in every culture the Buddha Way comes alive with art, poetry, and humor used both as teaching tools and as expressions of realization. So it is in our land, in our time. In this section, Steven Goodman sets the tone with his discussion of Buddhist tricksters. Former *Inquiring Mind* poetry editor Judith Stronach turns Pablo Neruda's couplets into koans. Patrick McMahon reflects on the teachings of Jack Kerouac, whose suffering heart reaches out to the back-alley bums and winos. Andrew Cooper imagines the Buddha as a film-noir hero, his story told by a Raymond Chandler–style character named Sam Sara. Poet Allen Ginsberg suggests that Westerners, by example, might be able to revive Buddhist meditation in China. Sitting with Allen Ginsberg's corpse, poet Anne Waldman eulogizes her friend and his large and generous life. Finally, John Cage, one of the great philosopher/artists of the twentieth century and deeply influenced by Zen, teaches us how paying attention can turn all sound into music.

1 Wisdom Crazy
An Interview with Steven Goodman

As a core faculty member and codirector of the Program in Asian and Comparative Studies at the California Institute of Integral Studies (CIIS) in San Francisco, Professor Steven Goodman teaches classes on a wide variety of Buddhist themes and their counterparts in Western philosophy and psychology. In 1994, Goodman was awarded a Rockefeller Fellowship at Rice University Center for Cultural Studies for the study of Tibetan mystical poetry. He is the coeditor of a source book for the study of Tibetan philosophical and visionary literature, Tibetan Buddhism: Reason and Revelation *and author of "Transforming the Causes of Suffering" in* Mindfulness in Meaningful Work. *For the last twenty-five years he has lectured widely on Buddhist psychology and meditation in Asia, Europe, and the United States. In addition to his regular classes, he conducts workshops at CIIS on trauma, the "shadow," the trickster, and creativity in relation to Buddhism.*

Wes Nisker interviewed Steven Goodman in Oakland, California, in 2005.

STEVEN GOODMAN: In my "Tibetan Buddhist Practices and the Trickster" workshop at CIIS, I introduce the notion of crazy wisdom, a phrase that got on the map thanks largely to Chögyam Trungpa Rinpoche. In Tibetan, the words are *yeshe cholwa*, with *yeshe* meaning "wisdom that's always been there," and *cholwa* meaning "wild or uncontainable." Trungpa Rinpoche said you might as well just say "wisdom crazy." It refers to someone who seems to be intoxicated with an unbounded, luminous, loving energy. What we call crazy is only crazy from the viewpoint of ego, custom, habit. The craziness is actually higher frequency enjoyment. Besides, the great spiritual adepts, the mahasiddhas, don't decide to be crazy. Crazy wisdom is natural, effortless, not driven by the hope and fear machine of the ego.

IM: When you teach about crazy wisdom, are you essentially drawing on the tantrika or the Vajrayana school of Buddhism?

SG: I start at the core of the Mahayana tradition, which is wisdom and compassion. Wisdom is the living energy that comes from the insight that there are no fixed points in reality, an insight that is sometimes called emptiness. We go searching for fixed reference points like a "you" and a "me," and we don't find anything, so it's said that the not finding is the great finding. It's liberating; it's openness. And with the loss of any fixed reference point, including the loss of self, then one can more easily be present with other living beings, hence empathy or compassion. So compassion is the living proof that one is in the process of embodying the wisdom insights.

Those twin energies of wisdom and compassion are the operating system or the lubricant that makes possible all of Vajrayana, which can be seen as dancing with the apparent display that arises in one's mind. It proclaims that everything can be worked with, or even played with. So it's sometimes called the *upayayana*, the vehicle of many methods, each applied according to an individual's temperament—calm, domesticated, wild, feral, you name it.

What also makes this Vajrayana dance possible is the Mahayana insight of a basic indwelling clarity and goodness, Buddha-nature. Inside of us are these already enlightened qualities that are temporarily covered over, and Vajrayana gives us many ways to unleash, rediscover, and live in the light of that which has always been there.

IM: Where do all the wild-looking deities enter into the picture?

SG: In fact, all of the wild depictions that you find in Vajrayana—of devas and devis and extra-ordinary beings doing extraordinary things—are all tropes, sort of archetypal outtakes that represent how things can be when you're living beyond yes and no, when you're no longer hiding behind the barricade of hope and fear. From that space you can use contradiction, trick of the eye, double entendre, parody, ridicule, and jokes all as ways of alchemically transforming the lingering resistance to waking up into pristine play.

IM: So all those stories we hear about the yogis flying through the air and appearing in two places at once are just that, stories, used to crack one's ordinary frame of reality?

SG: Yes, on one level. But there's this phrase in Tibetan, *gangla gangdul*, which means "to each according to his or her capacity." So a teacher will teach dance steps according to the capacities of the disciple. For many, their whole life might be a practice of lovingkindness, or reflecting on the impermanence of all conditioned things. A whole lifetime devoted to the simplest of insights.

But if someone is sufficiently awake and not afraid, he or she may engage in a bit more of a dance. One of the things that Vajrayana emphasizes, not unlike Western therapy, is the need to provide a really safe container. This is not just a walk on the wild side. And therefore, even though the ego might say, "Crazy wisdom, great! Trickster, great!" we are actually rather delicate and sensitive beings, so it's always good to establish a boundary, a ritual sacred space, invoking transmission and the wisdom of the elders, and then within that space, which works largely at an unconscious level, engage in these orchestral dance movements.

IM: Tell us one of your favorite stories of a tantric master pulling the rug out from under a seeker.

SG: The Buddha himself was a great trickster and a master of methods, and he always worked with people according to their capabilities. For instance, there's the famous story of Angulimala, a killer who was making a rosary (*mala*) out of his victim's fingers (*anguli*). Having killed 999 victims, he thought, "Oh, only one last finger. Then I will get power, fame, happiness." As he was about to slay his own mother, he became distracted by the presence of the Buddha, who tricked him by walking very slowly and yet eluding Angulimala's hot pursuit. Intrigued, Angulimala wondered, "Who is this being?" Already his consciousness was changing, and eventually he became a disciple of the Buddha. The Buddha worked with Angulimala by using his desire for power. The Buddha didn't say, "Power is not the way." He said, in essence, "You want to be powerful? I'll show you how to be powerful. Know your own mind."

Another great trickster story concerns Padmasambhava, sometimes called the "second Buddha," who was invited to visit Tibet from India in the eighth century. When he arrived, the king who invited him, Tisong Detsan, waited for this "mere religious man" to bow down before him, and there was a kind of king-versus-yogi standoff. The king was wearing royal silk garb, and finally Padmasambhava sent a shot of energy toward the king that shredded his garment or, you might say, shredded his royal defenses. In that moment the king recognized the real locus of power in the room and took a fragment of his shredded white silken garment, bowed down, and offered it to Padmasambhava. That's said to be the origin of the Tibetan custom of offering a white silk scarf whenever you meet another being. You are acknowledging that person's Buddha-nature and inherent greatness.

IM: You've led several trips to Bhutan, a nation that pays homage to a rascal figure, Drukpa Kunley, who is considered to have been enlightened. Yet he drank and fornicated a lot and seems to have paid no attention at all to the moral precepts. Explain how Kunley fits into Bhutanese Buddhism.

SG: There are many stories, both of Drukpa Kunley and Akhu Tonpa, or Uncle Tonpa, who are archetypal trickster figures. They teach liberation, usually by challenging holiness as a form of spiritual pride. If people are holding on too tightly to chastity, then they need a little prodding, they need some tickling, some humor. Remember, if a teaching is not threatening to the ego, the armored archetype within us, then it's not doing its job. So if people are fixated on chastity, a display of licentiousness will be useful. If someone thinks licentiousness is the path, then emphasize chastity. Sobriety, drunkenness. Logical thought, crazy thought.

The mixture of the sacred and profane is common in Himalayan Buddhism. At festival time in Bhutan, people perform these sacred dances of enlightenment, and shadowing these very wonderful dances are trickster figures called *atsaras*. They're slightly dangerous, untrustworthy jokers, and their role is to ape and mock the sacred dances at the same time the dances are going on. Often they will go into the audience and do rude things, such as dance around with a wooden phallus with a ceremonial scarf draped over it. The lesson is that it's healthy to invite all of us into the dance, and every part of us as well. And it's very healthy to laugh. The holy comes with a sense of humor.

IM: Can you give us a story of a modern crazy wisdom master at work?

SG: I was recently at a teaching in San Rafael with Lama Tharchin Rinpoche, and after everyone was settled he said, "You know that we all have Buddha-nature. And that means that at some point we'll all become fully awakened."

There was a big pause, and then he said, "Are you ready? Maybe in the middle of the talk tonight, you will become fully enlightened. Are you ready? It could be very inconvenient. What about all of the plans that you've made about where you'll go after the teaching? You're depending on not waking up, aren't you? Maybe you shouldn't have made so many plans."

From Volume 21, Number 2 (Spring 2005).

2 Poems & Not Poems
Neruda's *Book of Questions*

By Judith Stronach

A child asks, "Why is the sky blue?" and I realize I have no idea. In the space of experiencing "no idea" wonder opens: at sky, at blue, at blue sky, at the horizon, at what lies on this side of it and beyond. Koans are devised to take us from our ordinary mind to this "Don't-Know Mind" and the joy of being a mystery within a mystery.

Western practitioners of Buddhism usually turn to traditional Asian sources for their koans. Cultures closer to home can also help to free us from clinging to what is known. One such source is the *Book of Questions* (*El Libro de Las Preguntas*) that the Chilean poet Pablo Neruda completed only months before his death. The book contains seventy-four short poems made up of couplets that pose 316 questions. Like koans, they release us from the seduction of reasoned solutions. Our rational minds cannot penetrate the surface of these questions, but if we surrender to the imagery, we can move below to an unseen place.

Lemons and pomegranates, doves and condors refer to something beyond themselves, and Neruda looks at them with a heart/mind poised on the exquisite coincidence of form and empty. Balanced here, he distills his imagination into questions that invite us to see not only infinity in a grain of sand, but also the grain of sand in infinity.

Tell me, is the rose naked
or is that her only dress?

Is the sun the same as yesterday's
or is this fire different from that fire?

How do the oranges divide up
sunlight in the orange tree?

Where is the center of the sea?
Why do waves never go there?

How many weeks are in a day
and how many years in a month?

How long does a rhinoceros last
after he's moved to compassion?

What did the tree learn from the earth
to be able to talk with the sky?

And what is the name of the month
that falls between December and January?

Why do the waves ask me
the same questions I ask them?

When does the butterfly read
what flies written on its wings?

If all rivers are sweet
where does the sea get its salt?

Many of Neruda's questions have the maddening unanswerability of a child's questions: "Where does shadow withdraw to?" "And why should leaves be green?"

Why are a child's questions maddening? I think because they reveal to us that we don't know, and we like to pretend that we do. A child's questions remind us of the time when we looked on the world with wonder, and the wonder made up for the insolubility of our questions. Neruda says, "What we know is so little, / and what we presume so much."

After reading Neruda's questions, it occurred to me that children might provide another source of koans from within our own culture. So I interviewed Iris, the five-year-old daughter of a friend. It was an odd interview, since the answers I sought were questions. Here are a few:

How did there get to be seeds?
Why does it grow cold?
How did glass become breakable?
Why do worms bite into apples?
Why did grand-daddy die?
How did darkness get made?
How do tears come when you're sad?

On another visit, I sat up with this child during the difficult period of trying to fall asleep. Questions about existence and God had her stirred up that
night. Each question offered less and less satisfaction. Her anxiety peaked,
and she folded her arms across her chest to think in silence. Then she said,
"Who made the world? How did there get to be a first person? That's a really
hard question. But not the hardest." More silence. "Now I have it! How did
there get to be the first thing? See, now I have the question." And promptly
she fell asleep, not with a final answer but with a final riddle. Her question
took her one step closer to the very ground of being, where no answers are
possible and the mind must accept its own incapacity to know. The mind
that accepts this not-knowing is at peace.

From Volume 10, Number 2 (Spring 1994).

3 Illuminating the Sky of One Mind
Jack Kerouac as Dharma Ancestor

By Patrick McMahon

The photograph propped in my window shows a man seated next to his mother, cat on her lap. His elbow leans on the back of her chair, his chin propped against his hand, half his face in shadow, the other half pensive. Or perhaps I read *pensive* into it: knowing he's Jack Kerouac, knowing that at this point in his life he's nearly written out, exhausted at forty-four from a prolific and turbulent writing career. Or maybe the melancholy is in my own disposition, preparing to write about a man so close to my own spirit, so disturbing to my own heart. Then again perhaps the mood is in the atmosphere of this late winter afternoon. Outside, the brown leaves of the oaks hang motionless on their branches. Time of day, season, and mood put me in mind of the closing passage of *On the Road*:

> [T]he evening star must be drooping and shedding her sparkler dims on the prairie, which is just before the coming of complete night that blesses the earth, darkens all rivers, cups the peaks and folds the final shore in, and nobody, nobody knows what's going to happen to anybody besides the forlorn rags of growing old, I think of Dean Moriarty...I think of Dean Moriarty.

Moriarty (Neal Cassady in the flesh) was to Kerouac as Kerouac, I reflect, is to me: traveling companion, literary muse, and spiritual guide. Kerouac's was a mind that reflected and expressed the 10,000 things he met on the road: junkies, harvest hands, truck drivers, waitresses, salesmen, hobos, drunks, "a moody whitefaced cow in the sage."

In a winter frame of mind, then, I think of Jack Kerouac...I think of Jack Kerouac.

He died in 1969, just three years after the photograph in my window was taken. It was also the year I first read him. At the time I hardly noticed his passing, preoccupied as I was hitchhiking my own routes, pursuing the Dharma in my own fashion. *On the Road* was a signpost, *The Dharma Bums* a hint scrawled on a boxcar.

Without such roadmarks, however, finding my own way would have been even more solitary than it was. Just out of college, facing the Vietnam War on one horizon and the nine-to-five routine on the other, I welcomed the example of one who'd followed the crooked bent of his own genius at any cost. It was a crooked course indeed, and Kerouac has instructed me as much by negative example as by positive. Inspired as I was by his dedication to awareness and art, I was also sobered by his self-destructive history with alcohol and drugs.

In particular, Kerouac's early explorations of the Dharma were a light on the path for me as well as for many of my peers of the '60s as we wandered onto the Buddha Way. In 1956, influenced by Gary Snyder and Philip Whalen, Kerouac read Dwight Goddard's *The Buddhist Bible*, a collection of sutras in translation. He shared his discovery with Allen Ginsberg, crooning to him in Frank Sinatra–style the three refuges: *Buddham Sarranam Gochami, Dhammam Sarranam Gochami, Sangham Sarranam Gochami*. In the works (*The Dharma Bums, Some of the Dharma, The Scripture of the Golden Eternity, San Francisco Blues, Mexico City Blues, Satori in Paris*) that followed Kerouac's reading of the sutras, he cast Buddhism into the terms of his time and, in particular, into the thinking of the Beat generation. If anyone ranks as our American Dharma ancestor, it's he.

Forty years after the publication of *On the Road*, the novel that first brought Kerouac to the public eye, there's been a renewal of interest in him and the Beats in general. I recently took in an exhibit of "Beat Culture in a New America" at the de Young Museum of Art in San Francisco. Here were the photographs: a crew of by-now legendary poets lined up in front of Lawrence Ferlinghetti's City Lights Bookstore; Allen Ginsberg pointing to the Metropolitan Life Insurance Building that inspired his generation-defining poem "Howl"; William Burroughs flopped out in his underwear on a hot night in Tangiers; Kerouac and Neal Cassady, traveling companions of *On the Road* and *Visions of Cody*, arms around each other's shoulders. Here were the videos: Kerouac, accompanied by jazz musician Steve Allen, reading from *On the Road*; "Pull My Daisy," narrated by Kerouac, with a full cast of Beats, playing over and over as museum-goers came and went. Here were the matching coffee mugs and appointment books with cartoon caricatures and catchy quotes.

I came away from the exhibit with the disappointment I've often felt at much of the recent Kerouac revival, with its *People* magazine focus on the details of his life: the drugs, the drink, the sex, the sad end at forty-seven years. Where, in the midst of the images and icons, were the words that first inspired me? "Live your life? No, love your life!" he'd declared. I couldn't find those words in the superficial interest around the man.

Granted, he was a guy whose dynamic personality and Hollywood good looks commanded attention. Granted , particularly once he was famous, he helped fabricate his own legend. But the confusion of the personality and the art was no good for him, and the quality of both his work and life took a dive following fame. The confusion has been equally misleading to his readers, the legend distracting from the literature. As he railed at an interviewer, "Don't ask me, read me!"

Reading Kerouac, however, turns out not to be so easy, not because he's complicated but because he cuts so keenly to the core of phenomena. That core can be hard, in the sense that Shakyamuni's insight into suffering is hard. Kerouac's vision, Shakyamuni's vision, aren't beautiful. Beauty, in fact, is precisely not the point when the intent is going to the core, the brute fact. *Beauty* implies ugly, setting the stage for an art that pursues one and ignores the other. Kerouac's vision and art, in contrast, ignore nothing and nobody, however down and out.

The poems of *San Francisco Blues*, for example, feature characters that an eye intent on beauty wouldn't even see: "fat girls in red coats with flap white out shoes," "guys with big pockets in heavy topcoats and slit scar," "the furtive whore looking over her shoulder," "the bony character in plaid workcoat and glasses carrying lunch stalking and bouncing slowly to his job."

We find in the 10th Chorus to *San Francisco Blues* one of the downest of these nobodies, the drunk we've all seen on the downtown back streets of every major city of America. "Dig the sad old bum," Kerouac instructs us and then, through a series of images, one darker than another, has us follow our man into a flophouse we'd rather not imagine, to listen to him cough and groan in a white tile sink at 3 A.M.

As poet rather than religious thinker, Kerouac pictures suffering rather than explain it, cutting through ideas about misery to misery itself. Cutting to the core, ironically, liberates one from suffering in its fundamental sense: the unease of separating oneself from anything or anybody. To dig the sad old bum is to be no longer afraid of him and all he represents, is to keep kind company with him in that long night all of us know or will inevitably come to know.

Easier said than done. Easier to ignore him. Easier, even, to "help." Years ago, coming into San Francisco for a meditation retreat, I got off the Greyhound Bus at 3rd and Market Streets. (Later I'd realize that that very area had been a haunt of Kerouac's.) Taking a short cut down a back alley I encountered a man reeling from one wall to another. Steadying him, I got a closeup of a face I'd up to this point managed to keep at a safe distance: stubbled, no older than mine, bloodied, bad teeth, chapped lips, matted hair. His clothes were as gray-grimed as the redbrick walls. Through the tears and hiccups I made out that he'd been rolled. His "If I ever catch that goddamned son-of-a-bitch..." trailed off into futility.

As I supported him, I wanted the world in which this kind of thing happened to be different from what it was, and I wanted him to be different from who he was. I wanted, in short, to help. He was hungry: Did I have a buck for food? I bought him a hamburger he barely touched. He hadn't slept all night: Did I have five bucks for a bed? I took him to a hotel, paid the clerk for a room, and, with a sense of returning from a detour to the course of my own purposes, walked on. At the street corner I looked back, only to see my man leaving the hotel, en route again to such comforts as he knew, comforts not to be had in hamburgers or clean sheets. So much for helping.

Kerouac shows a compassionate alternative to helping the bum: dig him, delve into him. Getting the Good Samaritan out of the way might be the ultimate act of compassion. At 3 A.M., in the darkest hour, we stand beside him as he coughs and groans in the tiled sink. If compassion means "to suffer with," then with Kerouac, with the bum, because compassion requires it, we wake up out of our daytime dream of spiritual and material well-being to stagger "In the reel of wake up / Middle of the night /" smack into "Flophouse Nightmares."

Allen Ginsberg names the first vow of the bodhisattva, that of liberating all beings, as key to Kerouac's motive as a writer: "I vow to illuminate all is the purpose of Kerouac's writing, and the ultimate ethic of his writing." "All" isn't a matter of numbers. As the vow in its entirety reads, "Though the many beings are numberless, I vow to liberate them." "All" might be better stated as "leaving no one out." We tend to leave out, ignore, those closest to us, those of our own Market Streets. It's too painful to let them in, easier to exhaust our sympathies on television images of a distant famine. Not so for Kerouac. He insists on seeing what's commonly ignored and devotes his imagination to giving voice to what's commonly dumb.

In doing so he follows the well-worn path of the poet-pilgrim, noting what others, in their helpfulness as well as their callousness, might overlook. The Ch'an and Taoist poets of China, crossing mountains and rivers without end, followed that path, as did the Zen poets of Japan, such as Basho, taking their narrow roads into the interior. These pilgrims made inroads, through vision and expression, into ignorance, into the human tendency to overlook what is so often painful.

Kerouac follows also in the footsteps of Shakyamuni Buddha, in particular pursuing Shakyamuni's insight into the universality of suffering, formulated as the first noble truth. It's a bleak vision: "[N]obody, nobody knows what's going to happen to anybody besides the forlorn rags of growing old." Shakyamuni's words, or Kerouac's, tasted on the meditation cushion or in a poem, can be bitter indeed. In the 211th Chorus of *Mexico City Blues* he borrows Buddhism's Wheel of Samsara, or the round of birth and death, to follow through to where his own wish to jump off the wheel ends up:

> The wheel of the quivering meat conception / Turns in the void expelling human beings,... / All the endless conception of living beings / Gnashing everywhere in Consciousness... / Illuminating the sky of one Mind— / Poor! I wish I was free / of that slaving meat wheel / and safe in heaven dead.

Having thought and thought about Jack Kerouac, having followed the sad old bum into his flophouse nightmare, having recalled the futility of being a Good Samaritan to my own sad young bum, having seen that the wish to be free of birth and death ends up in a dead heaven, I end up, as this short winter day comes to a close, a little more at ease. I suspect it's possible to relax from the strain of both saving and ignoring living beings, be they groaning in agony or groaning with pleasure. After all, they, altogether, nobody left out, illuminate nothing less than the sky of one Mind! Kerouac suggests the possibility of illuminating all beings. Nothing could be easier: my hand finds the soft belly of my cat, my bare feet touch the cold floor. Outside the window, dead leaves hang from the oaks, the sun goes down behind the hill, and night comes on.

—And now a frog croaks with just the sound a drunk might make at 3:30 A.M. as he hangs on for dear life over a white tile sink.

From Volume 13, Number 2 (Spring 1997).

4

Beat Poetry Returns the Dharma to China
An Interview with Allen Ginsberg

Poet, activist, and Dharma student Allen Ginsberg spent two and a half months in China in the winter of 1984–85 teaching American Beat-era poetry to Chinese university students. Ginsberg had been at the center of the Beat writer's circle, a group that made Buddhism visible and hip in America and the West in the 1950s and '60s. In the 1970s Ginsberg became a student of Chögyam Trungpa Rinpoche and at Rinpoche's request cofounded the Jack Kerouac School of Disembodied Poetics at Naropa University.

The following conversation took place in North Beach, San Francisco, in late March, two weeks after Ginsberg had returned from China. Jack Kornfield, Lee Chenoweth, and Wes Nisker took part.

ALLEN GINSBERG: My big ambition was to go and meditate in China. I hardly sat at all.

INQUIRING MIND: Is anybody practicing sitting meditation in China?

AG: There are some. There is a temple in Beijing that I went to with Gary Snyder when he was there. It was closed and then I went back myself later. It's the headquarters of the Chinese Buddhist Association and also a practicing, teaching Ch'an school. There are branches in Nanjing and other places where they have some preliminary schools in sitting meditation.

IM: And the government allows them to continue?

AG: Yes, but controls it. I heard that the guys who were running it were government functionaries who didn't meditate and weren't interested. It was just a job. And that the old survivors, whoever they were, were very quiet and were in the back. You could get to talk to them if you had some way of introducing yourself. But they were sort of retiring and didn't want to get into trouble. I talked to some of the directors who were quite learned and seemed to know what they were doing in meditation. At least there is a Chinese Buddhist Association, and they've reconstructed a lot of temples that were destroyed or vandalized in the tourist cities. But going into Baoding, which is a non-tourist city where I spent almost a month, there wasn't one single temple or one single visible Buddhist meditator in any direction in a province of 50 million people, a province that at one time had been somewhat of a center of meditation before 1949.

IM: So the reconstruction of the temples was for the tourists?

AG: Yes, build tourist temples up to save face. Because they have realized that they did the wrong thing. It wasn't just Buddhist temples: it was the Taoist, Confucian, and Buddhist temples. Almost all of them were vandalized throughout China. The week I left I saw in *China Daily*, which is the official English language newspaper, an announcement that 200 tons of damaged statues were returned to a delegation of Tibetans. Wherever we went, except for the giant Tibetan temple compound in Beijing, which was left alone and protected by the army for some political reason at the time, all the other temples we went to were bare walls. The Tibetan temple, and maybe one or two others I saw, hadn't been disturbed, and they were crowded with dust, antiques, and artifacts of a thousand years, with statues intact, painting on the walls, trinkets and doodads, gods and goddesses. Whereas, in almost all the other temples, the walls were bare, because everything had been taken out and burned or vandalized or thrown into warehouses.

IM: Did you sense that there has been any new flowering of literature or poetry in the last few years?

AG: Yes. There's a whole new literature of the scar. It's allowable now to write literature of the scar, the wounds, like the Russian Solzhenitsyn literature. It's allowable to write, within limits—a limit being that you cannot question the territorial integrity of China or the basic rightness of socialism or the basic integrity of the Communist Party or the basic integrity of the present leadership. But you can question the basic integrity of the past leadership up to thirty percent. Or maybe forty percent, depending on the month or the year. Maybe sooner or later it will be Mao is seventy percent bad and thirty percent good. But at present it is seventy percent good and thirty percent bad.

IM: How do you know when you've crossed the line?

AG: That's exactly the point. As an example of what has happened, this young pretty girl in Shanghai said to us, "When I was growing up I saw a few movies and fell in love with Gregory Peck, and I would see all of his movies. But then the Cultural Revolution came and we couldn't see any more movies, and I always dreamed during the Cultural Revolution that someday I'd be able to see Gregory Peck movies again. And so I want to read you a poem I have written to Gregory Peck." (Laughs)

See, that would be wild for these older people because what that meant was the acceptability of romantic ideas and the frivolity of pleasure in Western culture. That was so forbidden during the Cultural Revolution; you could be kicked to death in the street for saying that you like Gregory Peck, a bourgeois stinker. But now all the students want to study English and absorb Western culture from Gregory Peck to Kerouac. Kerouac is considered a big hero. The official American literature textbook, edited in Chinese with the English text, includes fifty pages of *On the Road*. Every Chinese junior, senior, and graduate student will study that and a piece of Mailer's *The Executioner's Song*. "Howl" is translated. Gary Snyder and I are the most famous Western poets to the younger Chinese; we're the ones that they know about.

IM: Do they recognize you as antiestablishment, revolutionary voices in America?

AG: Oh, yes. They see us as the opponents of American materialism, opponents of the Vietnam war, and opponents of capitalist excesses. But still working within the high-tech capitalistic society and, so, intelligent people who know our way around in the difficulties of the twentieth century's hyper-industrialized landscape. For them we are very valuable.

IM: How do they relate to the spiritual dimensions in your writing?

AG: They were puzzled by the Buddhist references. They think that may be some naive thing. So what I did, finally, as part of my teaching of Gary Snyder's writing, I taught my class how to sit. I think the historical role of the American generation will be to bring Sowa Ch'an Dharma back to China. (Laughs) Actually.

IM: Wasn't it Joyce who said, "The West will shake the East awake, and ye shall have night for morn." That's what's happening now with Theravada Buddhist meditation in some parts of Southeast Asia. It's being reintroduced by Westerners.

AG: Yes, that's very interesting. What Mao did was to introduce Western Marxist religion to replace Buddhism, Taoism, and Confucianism. It covered as much territory mentally as a religion and as a social organization. Now that has collapsed, and there's total disillusionment with both the old and new religion. So maybe the role of Westerners will be to reintroduce the essential, active, muscular form of meditation to China.

IM: Hopefully the Chinese won't blindly replace their socialist materialism with our capitalist materialism...

AG: Yes. The one thing that would possibly have made their socialism work was the thing that they attempted to exterminate, which was the bodhisattva practice, the Buddhist practice of awareness and mindfulness, care, consideration, and sympathy. The one thing that actually could have made their communism possible was precisely the nerve center that, in their blindness, they destroyed.

From Volume 2, Number 1 (Spring 1985).

5

Notes on Sitting Beside a Noble Corpse—
Light Breeze Stirring the Curtains, Blue—
Faint Tremor of His Blue Shroud

By Anne Waldman

Allen Ginsberg will never raise this body up, go out board a shiny
      airplane travel
  a thousand miles—Denver?—thousands—Milano?
  to pump the harmonium—how ecstatically he does this!—chant
    OM NAMO SHIVAYA
  "all ashes, all ashes again"

Allen Ginsberg will never sit across the street hunched over Chinese
      noodle bowl,
  the old professor stayed up late reading the young poet's poems

Allen Ginsberg will never meditate this body, spine straight to heaven,
      holding up the roof
  of the world on the bright orange cushion

Allen Ginsberg's eyes will never water again—of tear gas, Bell's palsy, or
      flow on the
  death of a guru, read Blake Shelley lines to freeze your soul & you
      weep you weep
  & the whole Naropa Disembodied Kerouac tent is weeping

Allen Ginsberg will never tell awkward teen boy he's known since birth
      he's sexy again
  from hospital bed, the boy stood at the window while his mother
      sobbed
  because Allen Ginsberg said he's dying today

Allen Ginsberg will never brush this corpse's thin hair, get groomed, oil
    feet, brush teeth
(he's so conscientious!) mix mushroom leeks & winter squash
    breakfast again

The telephone rings, Allen Ginsberg will never answer it again

Allen Ginsberg will never embarrass China, Russia, the White House, dead
    corrupt
    presidents, Cuba, the C.I.A. Universe again

But Allen Ginsberg will ever ease the pain of living with human song & story
    that's borne on wings of perpetual prophecy—life & death's a spiral!
    He's mounting the stairs now with Vajra Yogini

Full Century's brilliant Allen's gone, in other myriad forms live on
See through this palpable skull's tender eye, kind mind kind mind don't die!

(Written by the poet's bed, at home in his own loft,
body in repose after death,
Gelek Rinpoche & monks chanting
Chakrasamvara sadhana
April 5, 1997, New York City)

From Volume 14, Number 1 (Fall 1997).

6

The Big Awakening

By Andrew Cooper

Almost all we know about Shakyamuni Buddha is drawn from the accounts in the sutras, and Ananda, being the Tathagata's attendant, disciple, cousin, and friend, is always the narrator. One might well ask: If all the sutras are told by Ananda, might not our picture of the Buddha's life and times and teachings be very different had somebody else done the telling? What would the sutras be like if, instead of Ananda, they were recounted by someone like Sam Spade or Philip Marlowe—the kind of hard-boiled private eye portrayed in the stories of writers like Dashiell Hammett and Raymond Chandler and brought to life by Humphrey Bogart in great films like *The Maltese Falcon* and *The Big Sleep*?

The following article was written in answer to that very question.

Paranasi. A dirty little burg on the Indian plains. Sometimes it rains so hard you'd think it was time to put a rudder on your house. Sometimes a hot, dry wind comes barreling across the parched grasslands, curling the hair on your neck and making your skin crawl. It was a day like that, when even Vedic chanting parties end up in fights and the most devout Brahmins eye their cattle and lick their lips.

Sara's the name, Sam Sara. I'd been traveling with my boss, the Great Shamus Shakyamuni Buddha, for twenty years, and I'd seen a lot of tough towns before. I'm not one to complain: preaching the Dharma's what I do and it's what I like. But on days like this, in towns like this, it's best just to make your pitch quick and pretty, grab some Z's, and get out real quiet-like the next morning.

When we arrived in the Paranasi environs, it was just getting dark. We decided to hole up overnight in a little mango grove on the outskirts and rest our bones. Even this far out of town, we could hear the racket. I didn't wonder what all the commotion was about. I didn't want to know.

We got up early the next morning, went into town and grabbed some alms, chased it down with some sour rice milk we copped at an all-night tea joint, and were back at the grove before most townsfolk had finished sleeping off the last night's festivities. She was waiting for us when we got there.

She wasn't too beautiful; she just made any other dame I've ever seen look like a monkey with its nose cut off. Her deep brown eyes were moist, her full lips quivered, and she held her long slender body erect despite the fact that she was shaking. The Boss indicated that she take a seat and then took one himself.

"Now what can I do for you Miss…uh…"

"Vasanti, Shanti Vasanti," she murmured.

"Suppose we start at the beginning, Miss Vasanti." He spoke politely, without emotion.

"Well, it's…I hoped…Can you…?" She bit her lower lip; her dark eyes looked up at the Boss pleadingly. A smile crossed his face, playful but serene.

"It's my brother Chandra. Two years ago he left home saying he was going to join your order. My parents had hoped he would take over the family business, but we're a good Buddhist family—we really are—and we were all so very proud of him." Her eyes lowered, gazing down at the floor: "We haven't heard from him since he left." She paused, her lips trembling, her fingers playing nervously with the mala beads in her lap.

She went on: "Then, maybe two weeks ago, a friend of Daddy's said that Chandra had not joined the Sangha after all. He said Chandra was keeping company with a most unsavory bunch of hooligans who preach strange doctrines and slander your teaching in public and whose guru says your meditation methods are foolish and…and…" Her body heaved as she put her head in her hands and sobbed.

The Boss spoke to her soft and even and real mellifluous-like. Pretty soon she had regained her composure and seemed in pretty good spirits, all things considered. The Boss sat still in deep samadhi for a few minutes. Then, looking over at Shanti Vasanti, he said, "Not to worry, Miss Vasanti. We'll take your case. We'll get on it right away."

We didn't have much to go on, and by now the kid could be anywhere in the subcontinent. We decided to go into Paranasi and see if we could dig up any leads. As we were passing the doorway of some seedy little temple, we heard a noise from the shadows.

"Psssst!" A figure appeared in the darkness and motioned us inside. It was Yogi Bhuktananda, or Yogi Bugs as he was known in the rackets, a small-time fixer, alibi provider, and epidemic chaser who'd been running his grift out of backwater temples for years. "Hey Tathagata, I got some news for ya if the price is right."

If there was a caper rigged in this burg, you could bet that Yogi Bugs knew all about it. The Boss said, "All right, Bugs, spill."

"You can say 'spill' all you want, but if I don't see some dough..."

The Boss gazed evenly straight at the ferret-faced little yogi and spoke gently, almost in a whisper: "Bugs, two years ago in Sarnath, the bulls put the crush on that alms kickback racket of yours. Two of my boys were framed for the scam and took the rap. The word is that you set 'em up, put the finger on 'em, and took it on the lam. I'd say you owe me one, my friend."

Yogi Bugs, his eyes darting back and forth, shifted his weight uneasily. Then the Boss stepped right up to the yogi and whispered low and hard as a diamond, "I don't have time for the runaround, Bugs." As though contemplating his next move, the Boss paused, but you could feel the power of his merit accumulating into a force that could've brought the Ganges to a standstill. Then he shrugged and with a lazy grin said, "Besides, you know I don't handle money."

"Okay, Tathagata, okay!" said Yogi Bugs, his scheming mind stopped cold for the moment. The Boss stepped back. The little yogi ran his bony fingers through his greasy matted hair, then he said, "The word is that some of your organization has been seen keeping company with a big shot guru who blew in from the coast. Calls himself the Kishmeer N'Tuchos."

"Yeah, so what's the big deal," said the Boss. "They're grown up; if they want to study another teaching, that's their business."

"That ain't the half of it, O World Honored One." A smile played on the yogi's thin lips. He was trying to get a rise out of the Boss, and he thought he had him. "This Kishmeer, he goes in real big for trances, miraculous powers, ecstatic states—the works. Nothin' new, but they say he's good, real good. He works with a dolly goes by the moniker Loka Deva. I hear she's no bimbo; a real high-class knockout, this one is."

Yogi Bugs waited for the Boss to respond. He got nothing. So he continued: "Anyway, the word on the street is Kishmeer is sore at the way you've been bad-mouthin' trance states and miracles. Says your shtick that there ain't no fixed abiding self is the lamest song and dance he's ever heard and that you wouldn't know Reality if it came up and spit in your eye. They say he's looking to set you up to take a big fall, then move in on your turf. That's the straight dope, Tathagata."

Yogi Bugs's eyes gleamed with ridicule as they searched the Boss's face expectantly. "So what's the Great Shamus gonna do now?"

The Boss shrugged his shoulders casually, almost carelessly, as though someone had just asked him for the time. "Beats me, Bugsy," he said. "Sure beats me."

The gleam drained out of the yogi's eyes.

Turns out the Kishmeer N'Tuchos had set up shop right off of Paranasi's main drag and wasn't hard to find. There was a crowd gathered in front listening excitedly to some guy on an overturned chapati crate telling them about the miraculous powers of the Great Kishmeer. People sure go goofy for a good miracle.

The Boss tapped me on the arm and nodded toward a dimly lit alleyway. "Be mindful and attentive," he said. "Someone might be expecting us."

We soft-footed it down and around to the back door. I took a piece of dried bamboo I keep for special occasions out of a fold in my robe. I inserted it between the lock and the jamb and, with a slight click, the lock gave. Slowly, I pushed the door open.

"Well, well, well. If it isn't Sam Sara and...what did you say your name is, sir?" The speaker faced us from about ten yards away. He sat cross-legged on red, plush velvet pillows piled atop a raised platform. He was fat, real fat, with a puffy pink face and so many chins you'd need both hands to count them all. His small eyes gleamed, flat, cold, and grey. Sitting next to him was none other than Shanti Vasanti. "I trust you've met my friend Miss Deva," he chuckled. His fat shook.

"I heard you wanted to have a chat, Kishmeer." The Boss's voice was slightly mocking; so was his smile.

"By all means yes, Tathagata, by all means yes."

Just then, two thugs came up behind us, taking each one of us by the arms. The Kishmeer raised himself from his seat and lumbered forward, stopping a couple of feet in front of the Boss. I glanced over. I saw that the Boss had, on the sly, entered the samadhi which examines the dharmas, which in our thing is called Profound Illumination. I'd seen it before, up on Vulture Peak, together with a great gathering of monks, arhats, bodhisattvas, asuras, gandharvas, and all the usual suffering suspects in this mean old world. I knew that when the Boss got this way, he was about to cut through delusion like a hot sword through clarified butter.

The Kishmeer let out a laugh, but there was nothing funny about it. "So you don't think much of miracles?" he said, and as he spoke, he hauled off with his right fist. But it was too late. The Kishmeer's roundhouse caught nothing but air, which was exactly the same as what the goon behind the Boss was left holding. The Boss hadn't moved an inch, but it was like no one was there. And No One was.

As for me, I stomped my heel into the foot of the thug holding me and then drove my elbow into his gut. I knew I was going to catch a sermon from the Boss for the rock 'em sock 'em stuff. But like he always says, sometimes you just have to be a lamp unto yourself.

Then the Boss went into action. "Listen, Kishmeer, the only miracle that amounts to a hill of beans in this world is the miracle of a mind free of greed, hatred, and ignorance." When he gets it going like this, I can watch him for a kalpa.

The fat man's face flushed with anger. He charged at the Boss, shouting, "So you don't like bliss, huh? Well, then try this on for size." The Boss did nothing, or should I say Nothing, and the Kishmeer just careened past, landing with a gentle thump on his own stack of cushions.

"You want happiness, Kishmeer? Then cease clinging to conditioned mind-states, 'cause that's a happiness unlike any other."

The fat man stumbled as he turned; his eyes were glassy. He didn't have much left. The Boss stood poised for the Kishmeer's final charge. With his jaw clenched shut, the Boss spoke in a low guttural voice, quickly yet deliberately. "Cling to the pleasant and fear the unpleasant, you're just going to suffer. The Great Way's a snap; just lay off the picking and choosing."

The Kishmeer N'Tuchos swayed for a few seconds and then, with a thud that shook the room, collapsed on the floor, out cold. Loka Deva rushed toward the Boss. She threw her arms around him, her eyes moist and imploring. "Oh, darling, darling! It's over! At last the nightmare is over!" To me, she looked more beautiful than ever. But I'm a sucker for wounded birds.

The Boss was having none of it. He stared down at her; his eyes glowed as hard as a wish-fulfilling gem. "It's not over yet, not by a long shot." She stepped back from him, a look of confusion on her face. He continued. "You're good; you're real good. But it won't work, not this time. You set me up for this with that story about your brother. Figured to play me and the fat man off each other. If he won, you'd be sitting pretty by his side. And if I got the best of it, you thought you could play the wounded bird and I'd let you off easy with a light rap on the knuckles and a feel-good sermon." I winced when he called her on the wounded bird act. It felt like that one was aimed right at me.

The Boss's face shone fiercely. Holding Loka Deva firmly by the shoulders, he said, "I won't play the sap for you! I won't give you some watered-down teaching, some sugar-coated Dharma just to make you feel all warm and cozy. I won't do it 'cause every part of me wants to, wants to pat you on the head and dry your tears and tell you everything is just rosy, and because you've counted on that all along!"

"But," she whispered, "can't we be happy and deluded?"

"You want delusion, then you're going to pay for it. We're standing under the gallows, all of us, all the time." He paused and his lips stretched back, showing his teeth. "Listen," he continued. "If you haven't understood a word I've said, then forget it all and get this. All beings are intrinsically enlightened, but in their ignorance they think they exist as a separate ego-self. So they try to protect the self, gratify it, make it feel good, build it up nice and pretty and parade it down Main Street. But it's a sham!"

The Boss ground his teeth; his eyes blazed. Suddenly he shouted, "Clinging nowhere, raise the Mind!"

Loka Deva stepped back, dazed. Then a smile came to her face. She got the picture, the Big Picture. "Oh, Tathagata! I see now that there is no abiding self. I see that we are all intrinsically enlightened. But still there is something I don't understand. What is it that we delude ourselves with? What is it that causes us such grief and suffering?"

The Boss smiled and shook his head. "It's just the stuff that dreams are made of, sweetheart. Just the stuff that dreams are made of."

From Volume 21, Number 2 (Spring 2005).

7 Meditations on Laundry

By Barbara Gates

Wind, flag, mind move—
from *Case 29, The Gateless Barrier*

Crisscrossing the deck in our backyard, blouses, socks, and nightgowns shimmy in the wind. I stand here pinning the laundry on the line, and my thoughts, like disobedient sheets, swell and billow. Sixteen clothespins or they'll sail away. Three pins for Caitlin's soccer shorts, two for her lacy bra. (Our soccer girl betwixt and between, leaving us for college!) Four pins for my mother's dress. (Visiting from New York City for her birthday, she at eighty-seven with Marlene Dietrich legs). Two pins for my husband Patrick's boxers. Peekaboo. I see you. Now I don't. Now I do. Caught in the ballooning and collapsing, there's nothing to do but yield to the swirl of wet sheets. Hanging laundry gets me silly.

For many years our laundry had spun in a tangled wad, hidden in the dark, churning in artificial heat. In trips to the dryer, we hurried in and out of our dank cellar. Drying laundry fueled global warming and also bad moods.

Now, in the open space of our Berkeley garden, that sassy line of clothes, visible to all, flounces its colors. Blue, white, red, green, yellow. As the breeze winnows through, purifying the laundry, my occluded thoughts loosen and clear. Bending, stretching, breathing in the sweet scent, a face blind with sunlight, spirits brighten.

Recently I've been one of the editors of a Dalai Lama book. That mischievous monk can bring humor to the most unlikely places—even to the suffering of climate change or war—opening up the perspective. So it wasn't just hanging the laundry that restored playfulness to our family life. What a relief to be reminded, "It can be tremendously beneficial when dealing with difficulties to be lighthearted in one's engagement with life so that one will not take oneself too seriously." Easier said than done: whether taking instruction from HH the DL or from a dancing choir of mismatched socks.

A Daughter–Mother Tale

During my mother's visit, she and I got stuck one time in a daughter-mother knot. It was one of those difficult moments that daughters and mothers have. I stalked down to the laundry room, grabbed the wadded mess of wet clothes from the washer, shook out shirts, pants, dresses, and with ferocity pinned them to the line. As each piece unfurled, unaccountably, hidden feelings and memories unfolded too—old hurts, bitterness, guilt. All were newly felt—then released into the wind. A sadness opened up, so raw, so clean, and it too was felt, wept through, released, until I started to laugh, and all that was left was love for my mother, growing old and soon to be flying away from me across the continent.

I just can't take my "self" too seriously with all those blouses and pants flapping in the wind. As the breeze picks up, there it is, a loose-limbed dance, not exactly a dance of skeletons, but of bodiless clothes, a chorus line of jeans kicking up a no-self cancan.

A Mother–Daughter Tale

When Caitlin was little, at family photo shoots I would leap up behind Patrick as he was taking pictures, wriggle, jump, and jive, and make silly faces and sounds. Hey, let's relax and have fun! Let loose all those worries about whether to smile and which direction to look!

Last week, Caitlin and I got in a tangle over her plans for her trip to the Reggae Rising festival. (This time, I was in the mother role.) I was tight in there with her, worried and insistent; she was tight in there with me, angry and resistant. Stuck to each other and our own insistence and resistance, we were miserable. To her surprise (and mine) I suddenly found myself following the instructions of the Dalai Lama and the dancing laundry. I leapt up and started to clown, to jump, to hoot and caricature our angry faces. Hey, let's stop doing this. See how silly this fight is!

I've found myself increasingly entranced by these laundry-line images and the stories they've bought to mind. Recently, another angle came to me. It's not just that the laundry is playful and free in the wind; it's held to the line by clothespins. Indeed, the clothespins are the laundry's salvation, holding it fast so it can flutter in the sun and wind and not be blown away or tromped on. When the Dalai Lama was asked, "How do you avoid being blown around by the wind?" he said that one should stand firm according to one's own principles, and truly know one's mind and one's values. I see the clothespins as the discipline, keeping us still enough to get to know our minds and to hold to our principles.

Take my daughter-mother and mother-daughter tales. The essential principle I want to hold to, and the one I've found the most challenging, is nonviolence. That means nonviolence all the way around: with my mother and daughter, the rest of us silly, suffering, dancing clowns, and with the Earth itself. In the first tale, the clothespins did their job; as I put up the laundry, I kept steady until all the blames and resentments had blown away and something joyful and loving remained. In the second, the clothespins held me still enough to notice that I was taking myself very seriously in this mother-daughter tiff, secure enough to reassess and release into the breeze.

So throughout the summer and now as fall begins, we and our neighborhood family have been enjoying the colorful laundry spanning our deck. One evening, having dinner on the deck amid the laundry, our friend Amy hinted, "If there was a little more *atmosfera*, I'd think I was in Italy." So I leapt up from my soup and interlaced Patrick's boxers with some black lingerie.

The next morning, these flapped in the breeze by the table where my mother was having a rare reunion with her college friend Jane. Delighted by the fluttering decor, Jane mused, "This takes me back to Venice."

And it brought my mother back to a summer in the Michigan woods where she and my dad washed my diapers in a lake, boiled them on the stove, and hung them out to dry on a line between two trees. Laundry billowing, swirling, swaying—I could see it then—connecting our family with the generations of families around the world whose shirts, sheets, and diapers span alleyways and rooftops, loop through windows, beneath balconies, over canals, between trees, across moors and mountain passes. Laundry circling the Earth like ancient prayer flags.

Prayer flags in blue, white, red, green, yellow. When the wind—expressing the quality and nature of the mind—blows, the sacred flags flutter. For centuries, Tibetan Buddhists have planted or strung these flags imprinted with sacred mantras, prayers for the wellbeing of others, for the wind to catch and carry across the countryside. The Tibetan word for prayer flag is *dar cho: dar* meaning "to increase life—fortune, health, and wealth"—and *cho* meaning "all sentient beings." The wind horse, Lung-ta, the most prevalent symbol imprinted on the flags, represents the uplifting of life-force energies that make life go well. If the flags are strung with benevolent intention— may all beings everywhere receive happiness and peace—the virtue generated increases the power of the prayers.

Billowing laundry sends such blessings too, and the wind, like the mind, carries them across the world. I think of the mothers (it is mostly mothers) around the world who have washed their families' clothes and sheets. It's not as if we hang out our dirty laundry; this laundry has been baptized, scrubbed, loved, preserved by all those mothers sustaining their families, their villages, and their land. How they've scoured the detritus of cooking and celebrations, the rich stains of living and dying—sauces, wine, semen, blood, and shit. I picture the women carrying their baskets along creek beds, over hillocks, on rooftops, and down into courtyards, shaking out their sheets and diapers, bedclothes, bandages and death rags and hanging them to be bleached by the sun and dried by the breeze. And I imagine the breeze, carrying some spirit residue from the lives of those who wore the clothes, from the intentions of the mothers who washed them, sending renewed humor and hope trembling invisibly through the lives of strangers.

⋄ From Volume 24, Number 1 (Fall 2007).

8 John Cage and the Music of Sound

For over fifty years, John Cage (1912–92) worked in the field of music, trying to teach us how to listen. To accomplish this, he first attempted to break down the distinction we make between "music" and the ordinary sounds of the world around us. Cage wanted us to be able to hear it all as music, an ever-changing unfinished symphony. To train us, Cage wrote many unusual compositions for the classical music stage, some of which were the first so-called "happenings." These include a piece of music for "instruments" that can be found in an ordinary living room, and a piano piece in which the piano keys are never touched and there is no "intentional sound" made during the entire performance of the score. As Cage said, "My favorite piece of music is the one we hear all the time if we are quiet."

Zen Buddhism had a profound influence on Cage, affecting both his method of working and his philosophy of art. He used chance operations from the I Ching to help him write his compositions so that he could get rid of "the likes and dislikes of the ego" and learn to accept whatever arises. If art has any purpose, Cage said, it is to help us "become fluent with the life we are living."

I had the privilege of speaking with John Cage in 1986, when he was seventy-four years old. At the time he was working on an opera, using chance operations with the help of a computer. His enthusiasm and playfulness were infectious, and it was a pleasure to be in the presence of this artist whose stated business in life was "curiosity and awareness." The following article includes excerpts from our conversation and from Cage's exceptional book Silence, published first in 1971 by Wesleyan University Press.

—WES NISKER

The following conversation took place in Winter 1986 with Wes Nisker.

In the 1930s I went to see a Jungian psychiatrist who had me take a Rorschach test. He said it was clear from the Rorschach that I was in a state of confusion. He said that he could fix me so that I would write more music, but I was already writing so much music that the notion of writing more was alarming. So I didn't go to him as a psychiatrist.

In the mid-40s I worked with a musician from India who came to study in the West, and she was alarmed about the influence that Western music was having on Indian traditions. She told me that the traditional reason for making a piece of music in India was "to quiet the mind thus making it susceptible to divine influences." Meanwhile my friend Louis Harrison was reading a sixteenth-century English text and found the exact same reason given for writing a piece of music. Then I began to wonder: what is a quiet mind and what are divine influences?

In 1945 the great Buddhist scholar D.T. Suzuki came to Columbia to teach, and I went for two years to his classes. From Suzuki's teaching I began to understand that a sober and quiet mind is one in which the ego does not obstruct the fluency of the things that come in through our senses and up through our dreams.

I have never engaged in sitting meditation practice. My music involves me always in sitting so that any more sitting would be too much. Furthermore, by the time I came in contact with Zen I had already promised Arnold Schoenberg that I would devote my life to music, which is concerned with the sense perceptions. So my meditation has been through my music, where I am trying to get rid of my own likes and dislikes and open myself to the flow of experience.

There is a Zen text titled *The Huang-Po Doctrine of Universal Mind*, which has been extremely meaningful for me. It contains this magnificent statement: "Imitate the sands of the Ganges who are not pleased by perfume and who are not disgusted by filth." This could be the basis of any useful ethic we are going to need for a global village. We are going to have to get over the need for likes and dislikes.

In the early 1950s I began using chance operations to write my music, and after I became acquainted with the *I Ching* (The Book of Changes), I used it extensively. I apply chance operations to determine the frequency, amplitude, timbre, duration, and placement of different elements in my music. The chance operations allow me to get away from the likes and dislikes of my ego so that I can become attentive to what is outside of my own psychology and memory. By using chance operations I am accepting what I obtain. Instead of expressing myself, I change myself. You might say I use chance operations instead of sitting meditation practice.

If you develop an ear for sounds that are musical, it is like developing an ego. You begin to refuse sounds that are not musical and that way cut yourself off from a good deal of experience.

The most recent change in my attitude toward sound has been in relation to loud sustained sounds such as car alarms or burglar alarms, which used to annoy me but which I now accept and even enjoy. I think the transformation came through a statement of Marcel Duchamp, who said that sounds that stay in one location and don't change can produce a sonorous sculpture, a sound sculpture that lasts in time. Isn't that beautiful?

If I liked Muzak, which I don't, the world would be more open to me. I intend to work on it.

I think that life is marvelously complex and that no matter what we do there's room to be irritated. I don't think we ever arrive at the stillness that we imagine. I love the story of the Zen monk who said, "Now that I'm enlightened, I'm just as miserable as ever."

I have always tried to move away from music as an object, moving toward music as a process that is without beginning, middle, or end. So that instead of being like a table or chair, the music becomes like the weather.

I gave a performance of my piece called "Empty Words Part IV" for the students of Chögyam Trungpa at Naropa Institute in Boulder, Colorado. The piece goes on for two and a half hours and contains long silences of four and five minutes' duration, and then out of that silence I just say a few letters of the alphabet, following a score which was written through chance operations from the journal of Henry David Thoreau. Meanwhile there are these very faint images of Thoreau's drawings being projected on a screen behind me, but they are very dim and hardly change at all—perhaps once every twenty minutes. I thought it was an ideal piece for a

Buddhist audience, but they became absolutely furious and yelled at me and tried to get me to stop the performance. The next morning I had a meeting with Chögyam Trungpa, and he asked me to join the faculty at Naropa.

Theater takes place all the time, wherever one is, and art simply facilitates persuading one that this is the case.

In Zen they say: If something is boring after two minutes, try it for four. If it's still boring, try it for eight, sixteen, thirty-two, and so on. Eventually one discovers that it's not boring at all but very interesting.

There's a beautiful statement by Wittgenstein, the philosopher, who said that the word *beauty* has no meaning. It simply means that something "clicks" for us. Then he said that people should put a clicker in their pocket so that when something doesn't appear to be beautiful to them, they can just take it out and click it.

I am trying to check my habits of seeing, to counter them for the sake of greater freshness. I am trying to be unfamiliar with what I'm doing.

All I know about method is that when I am not working I sometimes think I know something, but when I am working, it is quite clear that I know nothing.

There is no such thing as an empty space or an empty time. There is always something to see, something to hear. In fact, try as we may to make a silence, we cannot. For certain engineering purposes, it is desirable to have as silent a situation as possible. Such a room is called an anechoic chamber, its six walls made of special material, a room without echoes. I entered one at Harvard University several years ago and heard two sounds, one high and one low. When I described them to the engineer in charge, he informed me that the high one was my nervous system in operation, the low one my blood in circulation. Until I die there will be sounds. And they will continue following my death. One need not fear about the future of music.

Our intention is to affirm this life, not to bring order out of chaos or to suggest improvements in creation, but simply to wake up to the very life we're living, which is so excellent once one gets one's mind and one's desires out of its way and lets it act of its own accord.

The highest purpose is to have no purpose at all. This puts one in accord with nature in her manner of operation.

⋄
⋄ From Volume 2, Number 2 (Winter 1986).
⋄

VIII

TENDING TO THE WORLD

The spread of Buddhism westward in the middle of the last century helped to inaugurate a radical new approach to our world—to politics, the environment, and living in society. (Do no harm. Hatred begets hatred. Drive all blames into one. All things are interrelated.) Activists and philosophers influenced by the Dharma as well as other ancient sources of wisdom are addressing our modern dilemmas in unique ways. In this final section of the book, our interviews with Joanna Macy and Gary Snyder reveal the metaphysical shift now taking place, what Macy calls the "third turning of the wheel of Dharma." The wheel turns in Thailand, where Ajahn Pasanno ordains trees in order to save them, and later it turns in California when he chants blessings for Julia Butterfly Hill sitting in her redwood tree, Luna. It turns in the garden where Zen teacher and gardener Wendy Johnson finds the very ground we live on teeming with life, all interrelated in "nothingness." It turns in the soil of our North American continent, where Native American teachers Eduardo Duran and Loraine Fox Davis, Tibetan Buddhist teacher Tsultrim Allione, and Zen teacher Susan Murphy reflect on the interface of indigenous Earth-based ceremonies with Buddhist practice. The wheel turns in an innercity high school, where math teacher Naomi Baer begins her classes with one minute of silence, and in the prisons of India and America, where prison administrators Kiran Bedi and Lucia Meijer set up ten-day vipassana retreats. Meanwhile, Jarvis Masters does his Tibetan Buddhist practice every day in his cell on San Quentin State Prison's death row and risks his life to protect a scapegoat in the prison yard. Lucky for us, as China Galland writes, the Goddesses are still around, protecting the Earth.

Our anthology ends with these inspiring stories from followers of the Buddha Way who commit their lives—from the rainforest and the redwoods to the high schools and the prisons—to serving others, realizing the universal Buddhist blessing: may all beings be free from suffering, may all beings be liberated.

1 The Third Turning of the Wheel
An Interview with Joanna Macy

When we arrived at her home, Joanna Macy was on the phone trying to raise money for a full-page ad in the New York Times *urging women to get out to vote for Dukakis for president. "The polls say it's hopeless, but I've just got to do something. Then I've got to let go, knowing I've done what I could.... That's really the hard part."*

As teacher, feminist, ecologist, and social activist, Joanna Macy's path is to combine her work on herself with her work in the world. Macy's interests have led her to Sri Lanka, where she worked with Sarvodaya Shramadana, a Buddhist-inspired village self-help movement, which she documents in her book Dharma and Development. *In the United States, her involvement in the antinuclear movement awakened Macy to the psychological obstacles that prevent effective social action, and as a result she began to develop what is now called "Despair and Empowerment Work," which she describes in her book* Despair and Personal Power in the Nuclear Age. *Macy has also been a seminal figure in the Deep Ecology movement and is coauthor of* Thinking Like a Mountain: Toward a Council of All Beings.

Macy serves as an adjunct professor at the California Institute of Integral Studies as well as several other schools. She is an inspiring teacher. At one point, when we were talking about the Dharma, her eyes lit up and she exclaimed, "Its so beautiful...just pick it up anywhere!" We might say the same thing about Joanna Macy's work, which shines through in the following conversation with her.

Joanna Macy was interviewed by Wes Nisker and Barbara Gates in 1989.

INQUIRING MIND: How has your meditation practice and your study of Buddhism been a basis for your action in the world?

JOANNA MACY: The real philosophical grounding of my work comes from the Buddha's central teaching of *paticca samuppada,* or dependent co-arising, the understanding that everything is intrinsically interrelated. The Buddha said, "He who sees the Dharma sees dependent co-arising, and he who sees dependent co-arising sees the Dharma." When I first encountered Buddhism, the teaching of causality was the farthest thing from my interest or inclination, but after I explored it a little I began to see what the Buddha meant by dependent co-arising and how radical and profound that insight really was. With it—with his "turning of the wheel of the Dharma"—he turned the thinking of his time on its head. And that teaching is central now to our enterprise of living and to our liberation.

In the "second turning of the wheel" the idea of dependent co-arising comes to the fore in the literature called the Perfection of Wisdom. That's when the bodhisattva ideal is born: vowing to save all beings, knowing that there are no separate beings. Now let me just say that what we're having now in our time, I'm convinced, is a third turning of the wheel. We circle back to the original teachings, with an expanded understanding of the implications of pattica samuppada. Note the emphasis now, in our time, on moving beyond separateness into interconnectedness and interbeing. That is the central thrust of Thich Nhat Hanh's teaching.

IM: It is also the approach of the Deep Ecology movement and seems to fit in with the whole concept of *gaia,* the Earth as one living organism. These new progressive philosophical movements seem to have that same understanding of conditioned co-arising. It's the Buddha's wisdom come around in different form.

JM: Right. So in the third turning of the wheel we've got the earliest teachings of the Buddha picked up again as the wheel just—whoosh!—spins again. And the ecologists are on it and the feminists are on it.

It is the old teaching and it's new again at the same time. We can imagine ourselves released from the squirrel cage of ego, released from the terrible trips we play on and lay on ourselves, released from our own addictions and from the behaviors that devastate the world. For centuries we have focused on the fetters and suffering that we seek release from. Now, with this third turning of the wheel, our eyes are turning to what we're released into. We're released into interbeing, into the dance of the holographic universe, where the part contains the whole. We suddenly find that we live and act on behalf of all beings and by virtue of all beings.

And it's not a moral trip. It's not some kind of righteous burden that says, "On top of everything else I've gotta do I've gotta go stand at the polls." Rather it springs naturally from the ground of being. It is not something more we ask of our self, but rather the release from that self—release *through* action and *into* action.

IM: What role does meditation practice have to play in this third turning of the wheel?

JM: In this third turning there will be no split between meditation and action in the world. These two dimensions of experience seem to have become polarized. For example, when I was in graduate school in the early 1970s, I wanted to do a tutorial on meditation and revolution, and my department advisor said, "Well, that's a contradiction in terms; those are polar opposites." Now that view is beginning to change. You don't want to lose the distinctions between the two but instead to see how they are mutually reinforcing—like our friends who are doing meditation out on the railroad tracks at the Concord Naval Weapons Station.

IM: There are some who would say that going and sitting in a cave and meditating is also social action. Purification of your own "self" also helps purify the web. You might say, "They also serve, who only sit."

JM: I agree and would add that the reach of their practice extends farther than one would think, because the part contains the whole. We're so interconnected that someone who, let's say, is on retreat or working alone to restore a tract of wilderness is actually affecting us all, not just because it's arithmetically true that one-billionth of the world is getting cleaner but because there's a co-arising dynamic there. The whole is intrinsically altered, and each of us with it.

IM: That's the one-hundredth monkey business.

JM: (Laughs) Yes. That's it. With the third turning of the wheel we see that everything we do impinges on all beings. The way you are with your kid is a political act, and the products you buy and your efforts to recycle are part of it too. So is meditation. Just trying to stay awake and aware is a tremendous task and of ultimate importance. We're trying to be present—to ourselves and to each other—in a way that can save our planet.

IM: Saving the planet implies taking responsibility for the future as well.

JM: Well, lately I have been practicing co-dependent arising with beings who aren't born yet. I evoke them, I see them; they become very real to me. You see, I have been working on the issue of radioactive waste. The reality of it is so overwhelming that it's easy to give in and think there's nothing we can do. That is when I feel the presence of the beings who are not born yet. It's like they say to me, This is a really important time, and we're with you. We know you're working for our sake. In the Dharma we are here for each other, and to sustain each other, over great distances of space and time.

IM: Do you think it is possible to have that vital insight of dependent co-arising without meditating? Can that understanding be taught or realized in other ways?

JM: I really don't know. I don't see how, personally, you can sustain that insight without meditating. But that doesn't mean that in order for our world to heal we've got to get 5.2 billion people sitting on zafus.

IM: Whew!

JM: We will heal by what Robinson Jeffers called "falling in love outward." That's our mission, to fall in love with our world. We are made for that, you see, because we are dependently co-arising. It is in the dance with each other that we discover ourselves and lose ourselves over and over.

IM: In this third turning of the wheel we go from personal salvation to planetary salvation, back to the community of all.

JM: Yes! And it all comes back to co-arising, to reciprocal action. The motto of the Sarvodaya movement was, "We build the road and the road builds us." Through that which we seek to heal will we be healed.

From Volume 5, Number 2 (Winter 1989).

2 Chan on Turtle Island
An Interview with Gary Snyder

For many years, Gary Snyder has lived near Grass Valley, California, in the Sierra Nevada foothills, where he and a group of friends established the Ring of Bone Zendo. As poet, Dharma teacher, social critic, and conservationist, Snyder has forged a unique vision of how to live on this planet for both individuals and society, and as near as possible, he seems to live that vision. When former California governor Jerry Brown once asked him why he was always going against the grain of things, Snyder replied, "It's only a temporary turbulence I'm setting myself against. I'm in line with the big flow."

Gary Snyder combines a vast knowledge of anthropology and history with the wisdom of a Zen meditation practice, all grounded in his deep love and understanding of the natural world. Author of many books and winner of the Pulitzer Prize for poetry, he has been one of the most important interpreters of Asian wisdom for the West.

Catherine Ingram, Barbara Gates, and Wes Nisker participated in the following conversation with Gary Snyder in Oakland, California, in October 1987.

INQUIRING MIND: We want to explore the emerging nature of American Buddhism with you: what it might look like, what elements of the Asian cultures it might retain, and what might be uniquely Western about it. As a starting place, describe some of your own experience in establishing a Buddhist community here in California.

GARY SNYDER: When I moved back to the Western hemisphere in 1969 after living in Japan for most of ten years, I knew that I was going to move up to the Sierra Nevada mountains. We started building up there in 1970 and have been there since. Some of the neighbors and young people who volunteered to help us work on the house were interested in joining my wife, Masa, and me in our meditation practice. We did zazen every morning in a little clump of pine trees on the edge of the meadow. So the zendo evolved from that nucleus of people who sat together. It has grown over the years as an open and very democratic lay Buddhist group.

I knew from the beginning that I didn't want to replicate a priestly or hierarchical kind of Zen organization, and when we finally became formally organized it was with a board of directors elected from the group at large. We view ourselves as a sort of mountain peasant Buddhist temple with a community approach.

IM: To what extent does the Ring of Bone Zendo have a Japanese flavor? What elements of the Japanese Buddhist culture and style of practice have you transplanted there in the Sierra foothills?

GS: The essence is certainly zazen. We run the hall like you run a zendo anywhere. My background is Lin-ji [Rinzai] with a little bit of Soto influence. So we walk the stick in the hall, and we chant the traditional chants. We translate as much as we can into English and learn it in English. We try to maintain those all-important things like the tone, the rigor, the clarity, the freshness, the timeliness (everybody on time!); that's very much a part of what Zen is all about. Serving the meals and cleaning up, everybody contributing when it's time to work, everybody working silently. Then when the silence is over, everybody having a good time together.

IM: So you don't let the precepts get in the way of having a good party together.

GS: Westerners tend to approach the whole idea of precepts in a Judeo-Christian way. My sense of it from many years of living in Asia is that Far Easterners do not look on the precepts as some kind of black-and-white, win-or-lose code, a set of rules against which you must always harshly measure yourself, but instead as a set of creative challenges that you try to live up to in different ways and on different occasions.

In Japan the most commonly broken precept is the one about not drinking, not becoming intoxicated. Monks and priests don't fret themselves a whole lot about that precept. They look at it as a question of how do you move in the world convivially and make your Buddhism work under all conditions. So when the local village is having a harvest festival and you do take part, then the question becomes, "What is the nature of being a slightly drunk good Zen Buddhist?" (Laughs) They treat all of the precepts in a creative and open way that always drove the early Christians crazy. They said, "These Orientals aren't serious."

So the Japanese way is an example of Buddhism becoming creatively comfortable with folk culture and folk religion.

IM: What could that mean here in America? It is difficult to even identify a folk culture or religion in the West today.

GS: That is very true. The condition of Buddhism in this country right now is the condition, say, of Buddhism very early in China when it was studied as an exotic new topic by a small highly privileged aristocratic elite. In the third and fourth century C.E. when it first started coming in to China, there were aristocratic circles that were completely captivated by Buddhism and formed Buddhist study circles and read and translated and started little early monastic or meditation groups. But it was way above the level of what was going on with the people, so it took some centuries to begin to work its way down and out. And even at the very beginning, those aristocratic people were Confucianists basically, so they were measuring Buddhism against their Confucianism and their Taoism. It was the Taoism that softened Buddhism and began to make it distinctly Chinese.

Now, theoretically, you could say the folk religion of the United States would be a kind of combination of Native American spiritual vision and seeing our national parks and wilderness areas as temples. That would be part of what North America is. The other part of it would be the Constitution and the Declaration of Independence as the folk philosophy of all of America. There's almost nothing Americans agree on except for the Constitution.

IM: They may agree on it, but they will certainly interpret it differently.

GS: But essentially, I think that the appreciation of nature in America and that willingness to borrow some of the imagery and metaphor and myth from Native Americans is probably the direction of our future folk religion in this country. So it's a kind of emergent "Turtle Island Shinto."

IM: Recently you said that after many years of being in nature you were just now learning how to be in nature.

GS: There are many ways to be in nature, and it's fascinating to me to see how many levels there are. The most common way that people approach it is to become to some degree "nature literate," which is to say, to become amateur naturalists. So you begin to try to learn some plant names and some bird names. There are some wonderful areas of information that take you into more and more refined levels of understanding of the actual ecological processes that are going on, better and better seeing.

IM: It sounds like a meditation practice.

GS: Yes. But so far we are still all on the level of an assumed distinction between the seer and the seen. We have some understanding, but nature is still being seen as an object. However there's a very interesting shift that takes place when you understand yourself—and feel yourself—as an animal. People know from high school texts or teachers that theoretically, in Darwinian organic evolution, we are animals, but most people don't really feel it as an actual fact in themselves. And if they do, they feel it's kind of a transitory thing: "Well, that was the animal in me."

I think the next layer of feeling for me at some point was when it just hit me that I really am an animal and that all of the things that we call "human" are simply part of that, including our spiritual capacities. It's just another thing that animals can do. When I began to feel myself in that way, I saw many new things. I saw my mammalness, my mammality, and I saw that reflected throughout all mammals. I started looking at little mice that I live-trapped, and I saw them as mammals. I could see their genitals, I could see their teets, and I could understand this was a female and that she nursed her infants.

And then when you butcher animals, you see the absolute parallel of anatomy in the vertebrae. We all have the same parts, arranged in almost an identical way. You watch animals mate and you understand that they are experiencing an ecstatic state of release in their relationship with each other too, and that their fear and pain is as intense as human fear and pain.

So I've begun to feel more connected to mammals and vertebrates, and that sense of connection can spread into broader and broader appreciations of cellular life, all the energies that are at work.

IM: So it's not a matter of learning how to be *in* nature, but understanding that you *are* nature.

GS: Yes. And all of what I said is theoretically comprehensible by a biology class, but internalizing it, feeling it as your reality, is another step.

IM: It sounds like you are describing a Taoist perspective: not only being in harmony with nature but feeling the interconnectedness, the nonduality.

GS: It's the Taoist view of organic process and the understanding that we can never be in a struggle with it because we are too much a part of it. You might be able to do an extraordinary amount of damage, but the damage would heal itself eventually, and it would just be another thing that happened. Taoism is a kind of folk religion. What we just described is actually postscience, postbiology Taoism, internalizing the complete sense and actual fact of interrelatedness and interconnectedness of the universe and certainly of our planet.

IM: Maybe your analogy about Buddhism in fourth century China continues to work here, if we think of the American folk religion as being a kind of Native American Taoism, manifesting once again in our ecological-spiritual movements.

GS: I've been reading and teaching a lot of Muir and Thoreau in the last couple of years, and right there in our American tradition is a very interesting spiritual ecological line that is entirely ours, and it will probably come to be understood more and more so as ours. It's truly American. You would never find an Emerson or a Thoreau on the European Continent. They would never have evolved on the Continent. Even though the transcendentalists were educated initially in the European Occidental tradition, they made another step, and I think the step they made in part was a deep psychic response to the vast wilderness of this continent. There's a big space opening up.

I'm just thinking this stuff out. It hadn't really occurred to me that this really is our American folk religion. Even though they didn't call it a religion. Shinto didn't even call it a religion. It's called "the way normal people see things." Everybody normal, all the way through human prehistory, assumes that everything is alive. It's not a theory.

IM: In an interview a few years back in *East West Journal* you said that of the three treasures of Buddha, Dharma, and Sangha, here in the West we pay least attention to, and have least understanding of, Sangha. Could you elaborate on that part of the triple gem and how we find it.

GS: Okay. In America, our social and cultural experience just does not prepare us to have appreciation for the community. That's the first problem. We're out looking for teachers. We're out looking for teachings. Many people would just as soon skip the Sangha part of it. "I want the teachers and the teaching. I don't want to have to hang out with these other turkeys." (Laughs) That translates into an unconscious resistance, on many levels, to appreciating the history, the sociology, the humanity, the responsibility, the dish washing, and the floor wiping that must, from the Buddhist side, be considered every bit as important. The triple gem is not hierarchical. These three treasures are presented as equal. The Sangha is every bit as important as the Buddha, every bit as important as the Dharma.

Also, there is a difference between the Theravadan and the Mahayana approach to this question of Sangha. The Mahayana has been quite explicit for many centuries now that the Sangha is "all beings." But there are many levels of Sangha. The Sangha in one sense is fellow practitioners and the priesthood. In another sense, it's the whole community, it's the watershed, it's the farmers over here, and it's the merchants over there. Then, in a larger sense, it's all of humanity, and in an even larger sense, it's all of nature. So Thich Nhat Hanh's meditation on "Where does this wheat come from?" is really a Sangha meditation. Nature-literacy and the Taoist view of nature's organic process is a Sangha meditation. It's a meditation on interdependence and interrelationship and interconnection and how we serve each other.

IM: And it applies on a local level as well as on the cosmic level.

GS: Yes, of course. The local-cultural-political approach is expressed in something like bioregionalism, which deliberately says, Let's look around and see what forces and processes are at work here, and see if we can tune ourselves in to them. Who are the other human beings here? Where does the water come from? Are the fish getting better water upstream? When do the ducks come back? We ought to learn Spanish because there are a lot of Chicanos joining us in this watershed. That's also the bioregional way of saying, Let's ground ourselves. Or the even more fundamental bioregional perspective: Let's not move around anymore. Let's not be mobile. What does that mean? How does that change our lives? It means that we take responsibility for where we are and for the people who are there, and that the community comes to include the blue jays and the raccoons.

IM: One last question: As a poet, activist, Dharma student, and teacher, how would you describe your primary work in the world?

GS: For me, the most effective way of being in the world is to move in the direction of the stream of the Dharma. But one is not automatically "in the stream of the Dharma." That's where practice comes in. Meditation, devotion, Dharma studies, cause-and-effect studies, chopping wood and carrying water, and more meditation yet are the ancient and modern and future paths of entrance into the timeless truths of Buddha, Dharma, Sangha. My role in part is to try to marry (like in marrying big hawser lines from ship to shore, a language of making knots) the strengths of American openness, nature-love, humor and vigor, independence and energy, egalitarian spirit and commitment to democratic values, to the traditional forms of Asian Buddhism with their refinement, diffidence, precision, and nonjudgmental humorous firmness. In my own field of endeavor, what I look forward to is not "Zen in America," which to me means the replication of robes and temple procedures, married priests with station wagons, Japanese business contributions, expensive downtown centers, and some sort of hybrid Japanese-Protestant etiquette with its own kind of dourness. I'm working toward a "Ch'an on Turtle Island," which for me means an earlier and more open and more T'ang Chinese sort of spirit: old women trading insults and teacakes with wandering monks, really chopping literal wood and carrying actual water, a Chan for ordinary people and a few ghosts and spirits thrown in, on a real continent of mountains and streams on which we ask how to include in our zendos the sagebrush and the rabbits, the farm workers and the growers of Manteca and Turlock, as well as the highly educated, slightly troubled professionals. All of that will be more fun, but it will take a while.

⋄ From Volume 4, Number 2 (Spring 1988).

3 In the Language of Love
A Conversation between Ajahn Pasanno
and Julia Butterfly Hill

A monk in the Thai forest tradition, Ajahn Pasanno ordained trees in Thailand as a way of saving them. Activist Julia Butterfly Hill climbed into one of the grand old redwoods of Humboldt County, California, in order to save it, creating news that inspired millions. Inquiring Mind *editors Barbara Gates, Wes Nisker, and Dennis Crean brought the two of them together in 2005 for a conversation about activism, trees, and love.*

AJAHN PASANNO: Soon after I arrived at Abhayagiri Monastery in Mendocino County, people began to tell me about this woman, Julia Butterfly, sitting in a tree. After speaking to her on the phone a couple of times, I decided to take some of our community to visit her. We brought some offerings and did some chanting for her.

INQUIRING MIND: As a Buddhist monk in what's commonly referred to as the Thai forest tradition, you too must feel a deep connection to the forest.

AP: Well, I live in the forest and it helps form the ethos of my tradition of Buddhism. The Buddha was born in the forest, he was enlightened in the forest, he gave his first teaching in the forest, and he died in the forest. Thai forest monks repeat that truth almost as a mantra, and we are constantly referring to how much the forest plays a part in our lives. My teacher Ajahn Chah would place a big emphasis on how nature teaches us all the time—if only we are aware enough. The basic truths of existence are there for us to see in nature. So when I heard about Julia's commitment to protecting and saving forests and her role in being a catalyst for others in this work, I wanted to support her.

IM: Julia, did you have any connection to Buddhism when you began sitting in your tree?

JULIA BUTTERFLY HILL: Not much. I was raised with a traveling preacher for a father, and we lived in a thirty-one-foot camping trailer that we pulled behind our car, going from church to church throughout the Midwest and South. In my early teens I became disgusted with what I saw as profound hypocrisies in Christianity and with a tradition that really didn't allow me to be honored as a woman, other than the role I might play for a man.

For a while I thought I didn't believe in God, and then I realized I was angry at God. But how can you be angry at something you don't believe in? (Laughs) Eventually I began to study different religious traditions, including Buddhism, and I started taking little pieces from many of them. But I didn't really embrace any spirituality until I was up in the tree, when everything—my mind, my body, my heart, my spirit—was completely broken. At that point I started asking myself, How can I make every moment an act of meditation? That was the only thing that was going to allow me to survive. And now that's the way I try to live my whole life.

One of my practices now is to get up in the morning and sit. In my meditation space I have different sacred objects that people have given me, including a little amber bracelet from Ajahn Pasanno. While I'm sitting, I pick an intention for the day based on where I am feeling some weakness or need. So on days when my heart is hurting, I'll choose to be focused on love. On days when I'm feeling shy and withdrawn, I'll meditate on connecting with people. I set the intention and then try to live that day with that intention as my meditative practice.

IM: Did you make that practice up or did you read about it somewhere?

JBH: I think it came partly from my reading, partly from my life experiences, and partly from my experiences in nature. I've found that all faith-based traditions have a way to tap into sacred wisdom and interconnection, and one fairly common path is through nature. So after I came down from the tree, people were telling me that my spiritual practices were just like tai chi, or just like tonglen, and I thought to myself, Wow! My tree taught me all that.

AP: Julia, you are now out on the road a lot, trying to encourage people to focus on protecting the life of the planet. But I live in a monastery in Northern California, which is to some degree in a cultural and political bubble. From what I read and sense about the current social climate in America, people are caught up in a lot of fear. Is that your experience?

JBH: Yes, the common language being spoken is often one of fear. So I am trying to be a holistic practitioner, and my medicine is the language of love, which creates a space where all people can sit down together. Our world is literally dying for us to become emissaries of love, and that love has to be based in every thought, every word, every action. I've been blessed to see real miracles happen in that space. But when I fall out of my center and begin thinking of a lot of four-letter words—none of them *love*—you can bet I don't have nearly as much success.

AP: At the monastery we get your newsletter, and I have noticed that you always try to go underneath the individual issues to the place where human beings can be with each other as human beings. It reminds me of one of the practices of monks in Thailand who traditionally begin discourses or sermons by greeting people as "brothers and sisters in old age, sickness, and death," as if saying, Here we are together in this human condition. So what are we going to do?

JBH: My whole approach to the people I meet is to communicate the language of love, so I make it a point not to have conversations based on issues. I learned in the tree that "issues" are just symptoms of a disease.

IM: But Julia, how do you talk about the environmental crisis without talking about individual issues, without talking about the species die-offs or the need to transform our oil-based economy? Where do you go?

JBH: In my organization, Circle of Life, every time we approach an issue or problem, we approach it from the place of the solution versus the place of the problem. We focus our intention and awareness on what it is we want: peace, love, justice.

When I climbed up in that tree I was new to activism, but I soon realized that we had become so good at defining what we were against that what we were against was beginning to define us. I saw the problem in meetings where activists were "clear-cutting" each other with their words and their anger. As people were talking, I could literally hear the chain saws in their words, cutting each other apart. I saw that the peace rallies had become anti-war rallies, places where I couldn't even walk up close to the rally because of the way people were speaking through the megaphone; it sounded like they were dropping bombs.

This all became clear to me about halfway through my time in the tree, when I was experiencing a lot of pain and really felt like I was falling apart. That's when I went deeper and realized I had climbed up in the tree not because I was angry at corporations and governments—although I was angry at them—but because I loved the forest and I loved the planet and I loved this sacred life that we're all a part of. And so I began to approach all the issues from that place of love.

When we are committed to approaching issues from the perspective of what we want—rather than what everyone else is doing wrong—it's important to look into our own daily practice to see all the ways we are out of integrity with the world we want to live in.

IM: So on a concrete level, how can we live our daily practice with integrity?

JBH: I am committed to raising awareness about what I call "disposability consciousness." I went up in the tree with this disposability consciousness, and I came down without it. Now I see forests in every paper cup, every paper plate, every paper napkin, and every paper bag. In every plastic cup and plastic lid and plastic bag I see the oil fields of Ecuador that I've walked through and the people whom I've worked with in Africa. I now see the Earth being destroyed by our disposability consciousness.

So now I am a fierce communicator about this. I've been in meetings where we were getting ready to do a direct action, and when I saw disposables in the room, I said out loud that we hadn't earned the right to do that action. How can we tell a company to stop logging when we're throwing away paper cups that support that logging? Saying such things doesn't make me very popular in the moment. But I am passionate about this because our work has to be about creating what we are for. Such work, truly based in love, can only happen if we do what we do with integrity. I want us to become what I call the "resolutionaries."

IM: How did the tree teach you to see the world through love? Can you describe any specific events or moments?

JBH: I compare it to when I was little and learned how to take a magnifying glass and turn it in the sun to just the right angle so that it concentrated the rays and started a fire. I feel like my time leading up to the tree was the forming of the magnifying glass, but the tree really focused it until it ignited my passion. Then, when I was completely broken, the fire turned into love. I was literally in the fetal position, sobbing, rocking back and forth, saying, "I can't take this anymore!" All around me I heard the saws whining and saw the trees falling. And I'd breathe through a wet rag while they lit the clear-cuts on fire with diesel fuel or with napalm from helicopters. It felt like the pain and grief were killing me.

One day I was praying and begging for help, and the answer that came was, Julia, you must simply love. I thought, That's a funny answer, and I kept praying, but the same answer came again: Julia, you must simply love.

I am grateful when the universe has given an image to me when I needed it. What came into my mind was a tree. Big surprise. As I was focusing on this tree in my mind, hearing, Julia you must simply love, the branches of the tree began to move—out and back in, out and back in; it looked almost like arms that were gathering in the air. I started seeing all of this dense-looking smoke and grit being absorbed into the tree. As the branches moved back out, I saw little prisms of light coming out of the tree. At that moment I had an epiphany: trees actually grow by transforming our toxins into healthy air. That is what love is all about.

Previously, in my life and in my mind, love was either associated with lust or somehow conditional. Suddenly I saw it as a transformational tool. Every time I can take something that's hurting, something that's toxic, something that's out of balance, and actively participate in its transformation, that act will help me to grow. And then I will be able to take on the next challenge, which may be even bigger. One day when I was sharing all of that, someone told me about the practice of tonglen. Once again, I realized that the trees had taught me a spiritual practice.

AP: It occurs to me as I'm listening that the Thai word for nature, *dhammachat*, could be roughly translated as "the birthplace of truth." Embedded in the language is the idea that nature is where we can see the Dhamma, both in terms of how the teachings display themselves in the world as well as in the natural truths the Buddha pointed to. In Buddhism we look at the cycles of nature that are outside of ourselves, but also inside. That's what meditation practice is all about, looking at how we experience our own nature—the ways we live and breathe, experience emotions, create suffering, or live in harmony. We can only really understand this within ourselves. That's why your theme of love is so important, Julia. When we're in conflict with something, we're pushing it away and making it "other." It's only when we rely on love, or have a very caring attitude, that we bring the outside into ourselves. Only then do we understand it, do we see its truth.

IM: Ajahn, the forests of Thailand where you lived and studied for so many years have also been decimated. Can you tell us about your practice of ordaining the trees to protect them?

AP: Yes, I've done that on many occasions. It's quite a skillful means for drawing people together and then being able to talk to them. I actually started a couple of organizations that worked with villagers in northeast Thailand to protect areas of forest. Sometimes the dynamics that go into cutting a forest are very complex. Often it's outside interests that are paying to cut down the trees, so it's important to get the local people involved to truly make it their forest.

We found that one good way of protecting the trees was to ordain them. We put robes around trees and held traditional ceremonies, and then we chanted for the protection of the forest. We would always pick the largest tree in a particular grove for ordination, because the people believe that guardian devas live in those trees. We wanted to get people to reflect on that.

In northeast Thailand, people's lives are completely intertwined with the forest. Traditionally, they plant rice and keep a little garden patch of garlic, chilies, and spices, but all other nurturance comes from the forest—bamboo shoots, mushrooms, edible leaves, the creatures who live there, and the water, which disappears as soon as the trees are gone. But the villagers are very poor and easily enticed by the promise of money. Our ordination ceremonies offer a tangible way to remind people of their sincere wish to protect the forest and make it sacred rather than seeing it as a resource to be exploited.

The protection of the forest is delicate work. There are some areas where people have marched in to do tree ordinations without doing the groundwork and have literally been shot. I know one particular monk who ended up in prison trying to protect the forest. There were just too many forces against him. But generally the ordination ceremonies offer an opportunity to draw people from different factions together and create a base of communication.

IM: Maybe you should take some monks and hold an ordination ceremony for Luna, Julia's teacher tree. How is Luna doing, Julia?

JBH: About a year after I came down from Luna, someone attacked her with a chain saw and tried to kill the tree. All the best scientists and tree experts said that two-thirds of the tree would die back and become a snag while the other third would continue to grow. They said we would begin to see significant dieback within two years. It's been four years now and there is no dieback at all. In fact, every spring the tree is covered in new growth. This is largely due to the work of amazing scientists, structural engineers, tree biologists, activists, and even workers from the Pacific Lumber Company, who all came together to save the tree.

I was in the tree for more than just trees. It was my commitment to create a space of healing for all of us. What really moved me was that some Pacific Lumber employees put their metal shop to work building what are basically metal bandages to hold the tree's cuts together while the wounds heal. I talked to some of these Pacific Lumber workers, and they said, "Julia, we didn't necessarily agree with what you did, but you were always respectful, you never called us names, and you came to a respectful agreement with the company. Whoever attacked this tree does not represent all of us." When I was thanking them, one of them even said, "Anything for Luna." He even called the tree *Luna*! This is what our collective work is about—healing our planet, our world, and ourselves as one—peace on Earth and peace with the Earth.

From Volume 22, Number 1 (Fall 2005).

4 The Nothingness of the Ground

By Wendy Johnson

Not long ago a friend of mine and a teacher at San Francisco Zen Center gave me an old, unpublished teaching from Suzuki Roshi. This piece of writing has been working on me ever since I received it.

> I think most of us study Buddhism like something that was already given to us. We think what we should do is preserve the Buddha's teaching, like putting food into the refrigerator, and that to study Buddhism is to take the food out of the refrigerator; whenever we want it—it is already there. Instead, Zen students should be interested in how to produce food from the field, from the garden, should put the emphasis on the ground. The joy of Buddhism is the joy of taking care of the garden, and our effort is to see something come out of the ground, out of the nothingness of the ground.

As a gardener I know this "nothingness of the ground" when I work the soil that is the pulsing web of life and death under my feet. Within a single teaspoonful of fertile garden soil, up to three billion microscopic bacteria live and die. Under the best conditions they double their populations every hour, feeding the soil and plant community with their sloughed-off debris. All around the bacteria a thriving Sangha of soil micro and macro organisms fills the ground. Fungi, actinomycetes, algae, nematodes, rotifers, mites, springtails, sowbugs, millipedes, spiders, ants, beetles, centipedes, slugs, snails, and earthworms are all working the ground. Like the nothingness of the ground of being, this nothingness seethes with relationship, and in the dirt beneath my fingernails vast communities of beings live and die.

When I am confused or upset it helps me to sit still on the bare ground, to come back to the fundamental. In Buddhist practice, the ground is fundamental. The ground is where we walk and sit, where we stand and lie down. It is the living support of our life.

Ground means "bottom." The word has its roots in Old English *grund*, which means "foundation" or "earth." It is also a cognate of *grynde*, meaning "abyss," and thus is linked with death and mystery. A grounding was originally a fish living on the bottom of ponds. And meditation is all about getting to the bottom of life, about grounding ourselves in the nothingness of the Earth and not turning away from what is fundamental.

At Green Gulch Farm early every spring we welcome a new group of farm and garden apprentices who come to live and work and meditate with us. After the niceties of introduction and orientation are complete, our first meditation assignment is to fan out over the bottomland fields of the farm and find a spot of earth that calls to each of us. Then, forgetting all the elaborate details of zazen instruction—how to hold the spine and thumb tips while meditating—we sink down and sit still on the ground.

"Buddha tried to save us by destroying our common sense," said Suzuki Roshi. "Usually, as human beings, we are not interested in the nothingness of the ground, not in the bare soil itself. But the Buddha's teaching is not about the food itself but about how it is grown. He was interested in the ground from which various gardens appear."

It is fundamental that we forget what we know and see, stop fussing with crops and credos, and sink down onto the Earth and sit still. Our real work is to face the abyss. We are joined by our common love for the nothingness of the ground, bound together by the invisible hyphae of the fungal net that pervades the bottomland soil where we sit.

◇
◇ From Volume 14, Number 1 (Fall 1997).
◇

5 Indigenous Dharma
Native American and Buddhist Voices
Eduardo Duran, Lorain Fox Davis, and Tsultrim Allione

"When you know the place where you are, practice begins," says Dogen. One could say that every stage of Buddhist practice, including realization itself, forms and deepens a covenant with the Earth. We bear witness to the Earth by learning to really be here, and when reality breaks through and shakes us to the core, it is the Earth reciprocating that intimate gesture of custodianship. It is one elemental act of kindness being met by another. The testimonies that follow from Native American and Buddhist teachers bring to light some of the affinities of Buddhist practice with the old, native Earth-based traditions and their protocols for creating and tending good relations with the Earth, the source of life.

In my own practice as a Zen teacher in Australia, it has felt increasingly important to me to begin consciously to walk the song lines of the Way, to seek out Aboriginal Law holders. I actively explore the affinities and resonance between Aboriginal and Zen spiritualities as they meet in the place where I am. It will not be the first time that Buddhism has been received, enlarged, and refined by the more ancient Earth-based spirituality that awaits it in a particular place. The Dharma is wanting to learn to stand up here in olive-gray saltbush and red earth, gray kangaroos and satin bowerbirds. It is never complete, and it is the Earth that constantly completes it.

Our human conversation with the Earth has a chance to resume when we grow quiet and still and do some listening, some asking, and a bit of thanking. Meditation itself is a ritual action of respect, literally, "looking again," with patience and forbearance. Respect structures the spiritual authority through which both Native American and Buddhist teachings are offered and transmitted; and respect—a kind of nameless gratitude—marks every mindful gesture and breath, gradually maturing into a conscious minding of the universe.

—SUSAN MURPHY

EDUARDO DURAN

There is some troublesome karma connected to the land of my ancestors. The trouble is this: the land that we were promised in perpetuity by President Teddy Roosevelt is where you now find Los Alamos, New Mexico, the hometown of the atomic bomb. We were supposed to have claim to that land forever; but one day in the mid 1930s my grandfather came home and all the cattle had been shot, there were Army people swarming everywhere, and my family was escorted off the land at gunpoint. It is interesting that the area chosen by the government to build the atomic bomb is known as Sipapu, which is understood by the original people of that land to be a place of energy.

I understand that a few years ago the Dalai Lama sent some lamas to place packets of incense in and around Los Alamos to try to neutralize the energy in that area. I was very excited to hear that because it resonates with the Indian way of purification. It's a shamanistic approach to dealing with evil forces that are the result of negative mind-states. I think the Buddha understood that kind of energetic power, which led him to advise his monks to use lovingkindness, metta, as a way to cope with the fear of ghosts and vicious animals that were troubling them in the forest.

I see the Buddha as a tribal person. I find that revealed in his deliberate action just before he became enlightened, when he reached down and touched the Earth, saying, "The Earth is my witness." The Buddha was keenly aware that the Earth has consciousness and can even bear witness to karma.

My sense is that Westerners somehow stay separated from a deep connection to the Earth. I've been going to Buddhist meditation retreats for twenty years now, listening to talks, and I think there is profound wisdom being taught and wonderful benefit happening for people. But I sense that the Western psyche, with its grounding in the Cartesian worldview, somehow stays separated from nature. People go inside themselves and dissolve themselves, but they don't connect with natural processes.

Native people use ritual and offerings to bring themselves into relationship with the Earth. I went on a backpacking meditation retreat with vipassana teacher Eric Kolvig on the Rainbow Trail on Navajo land, and along the way we engaged in some ceremonies for the Earth. One participant asked, "How do we acknowledge the Earth?" Since it was almost Mother's Day, I asked, "What are you going to do for your mom on Mother's Day?" The answer was, "I'm going to give her a present and send her lovingkindness." I said, "Just so, you can do the same for the Earth. Give her a gift and send her lovingkindness, and those acts will bring you into relationship with the Earth."

When I go to meditation retreats I always do some Native ceremonies on my own. I usually take the pipe and make tobacco offerings, asking the land's permission for us to be there for this purpose of meditation. Often I do this in secret because I don't want to disturb anyone. Meanwhile, I've brought Buddha's mindfulness into my Native rituals and ceremonies, which themselves are skillful means to focus the mind. When you add mindfulness to a four-day fasting ceremony, you've got a powerful tool for liberation. When I'm doing ceremonial dances I try to maintain mindfulness by repeating the mantra, "Dancing, he knows he's dancing."

Lately I've been practicing in the Tibetan Buddhist tradition, which I feel is closer to the Native way. The Tibetans hold a lot of ceremonies that are similar to ours, relating to Earth, the elements, and different energetic conditions. I think the Tibetans are basically Natives, just from a different tribe. They even have similar beliefs and customs. Padmasambhava's prophecy is that the teachings of the Buddha would someday be revealed in the land of the red face, and here they are.

I recently attended a special retreat for Native Americans, taught by vipassana teacher Joseph Goldstein. Most of the Natives were doing meditation for the first time, and afterward Joseph said he was astounded at how steady and still the people were when they sat. We have ceremonies where we are required to sit still for long periods, so we don't seem to have a problem with sitting, at least not physically. Native ceremonies foster profound levels of concentration, and many of them are practices of generating metta for all beings, including the Earth. We would be willing to teach some of these practices to Westerners if they want to learn them.

I like to think of the Buddha as my great-grandpa. This way of thinking helps to remove the perception of separateness that usually occurs with those who have become spiritual icons. If I imagine him as one of us, then I can believe that liberation is possible for me as well. The Native relationship to nature is revealed in Native hunting and food-growing practices. It is believed that the animals we hunt, whom we view as our relatives, offer themselves to us as an act of metta. In return, the hunter has to do something for the animal, for instance a deer dance or buffalo dance, to thank the animal and pray for regeneration of the animal's family. When it comes to the food that we grow, we have dances and seasonal fertility rituals, which are ceremonies that bring us into direct relationship with the spirit of plants and Earth consciousness.

I see the whole Native way as realizing our relationship to everything and ourselves as an integral part of all things, which in turn causes us to treat the Earth and other forms of life with respect, as part of our family. Western civilization is finally recognizing that relationship. Suddenly people are saying that the Earth is alive and talking about Gaia and holistic worldviews and systems theory. Native people are basically saying, "Yes, welcome home." *Aho!* All are my relatives.

LORAIN FOX DAVIS & TSULTRIM ALLIONE

TSULTRIM ALLIONE: I've always felt it's crucial for American Buddhists to relate to the spirits of this new homeland of Dharma. It was not until Padmasambhava had connected with the local spirits of Tibet that Buddhism was able to take root there. For us, the Native Americans are the people who hold this relationship with the spirits of the land and the elementals.

My connection with Native American people goes back to my childhood in New Hampshire. My family lived in a house that had been previously owned by a Lakota man, Charles Eastman, who was educated at Dartmouth College and was the doctor at the battle of Wounded Knee. He was a mythic presence in my childhood. Years later, while I was living on the East Coast, I began participating in many Native American sweats and vision quests.

Tara Mandala, the Tibetan Buddhist retreat center I started in Colorado, adjoins Ute land. When we first arrived in 1994, Bertha Grove, a Ute medicine grandmother, came to conduct ceremonies. Over the years Grove and other Ute elders—as well as Lakota teachers like Arvol Looking Horse, Nineteenth-Generation Holder of the White Buffalo Calf Pipe—have continued to do ceremonies connecting to energies of our land. The Tibetan lamas who have come to Tara Mandala have been very interested in meeting the Native American elders. I've led retreats with teachers of Native American spirituality, including Lorain Fox Davis, who also practices Tibetan Buddhism and teaches Native studies in the environmental department at Naropa University.

LORAIN FOX DAVIS: My path spans both Native American and Tibetan spirituality. On my mother's side, I'm Cree and Blackfeet—Cree from Canada and Blackfeet from Montana. I studied for many years with a traditional Lakota teacher, Irma Bear Stops. While it is rare for women to sun dance, Irma was a very respected sun dancer. Although I wasn't Lakota, she introduced me to Lakota spirituality, and I was honored to dance by her side for seven years at Pine Ridge, South Dakota. My husband and our oldest son danced there also. My son and one of our daughters have returned to our Blackfeet ways, and they sun dance in Montana. It is a challenging and humbling, yet deeply harmonious, way of life to follow these traditions based in nature and the elements. We all need to come back in balance with our ancient connections with Mother Earth.

I was introduced to Tibetan Buddhism over thirty years ago, and my primary Tibetan Buddhist teacher is Tulku Urgyen Rinpoche, who married my husband and me when he came to Crestone, Colorado, in 1981. We were living in Santa Fe at the time and were invited to join his traveling entourage. He was a great teacher of gentle compassion and wisdom. Since that time we have lived here in Crestone, where several Buddhist centers have been founded in the past few years.

There is a great similarity between Native American spirituality and the Tibetan Buddhist teachings of compassion and respect for every living creature. This respect for all life is what I learned from my Cree grandmother when I was a child. There are many Tibetan teachers who come through here, and I try to attend their sessions. They are grounded in the environment, and they have ceremonies similar to ours of burning cedar to invite and honor the spirits—the spirits of the mountains and of the water, the Elemental Beings and the great Thunderbird who brings the rains of purification and regeneration. The spiritual power of thunder and lightning is central to both Native and Buddhist traditions. These ancient traditions hold that Thunder Beings are the spiritual and physical manifestations of Spirit.

TA: Some of the Tibetan Buddhist practices and most of the Native American ones are grounded in relationship to the elements and all beings. The Tibetans have a smoke-offering ceremony called Sang in which you make a fire and then put in juniper branches and other offerings like grains, honey, and milk products to make smoke. You see the smoke from that fire turning into offerings for all beings. The Native Americans also use smoke from cedar and sage for purification.

For me, the sweat lodge, or Stone People's lodge, is a bit like the Tibetan Buddhist mandala. The mandala is a template of the enlightened mind based on the center and the four directions. In the lodge there are four directions and four rounds (sessions of prayer), and each round has a different meaning. During the sweat, you go through a process of death and rebirth. When you enter the lodge, you shed everything, and then during the four rounds in your praying you touch in on every aspect of your being. When you come out, you are symbolically reborn. Both the mandala and the sweat lodge ceremony are centered in a physical mandala of the universe; both are deeply transformative architectures for the psyche.

The Stone People's lodge and Tibetan Buddhism both include teachings of the integration of masculine and feminine. The sweat lodge symbolizes the feminine womb of rebirth, and the fire outside the masculine. Rocks are heated in the fire and then brought into a pit in the center of the lodge. In Tantric Buddhism, one of the primary symbols is the union of the masculine, representing skillful means, and the feminine, representing wisdom. Their sexual union represents the nondual state, like the union of the fire and the womb in the lodge.

LFD: The underlying theme in Native American spirituality, as well as most indigenous spirituality, is to honor the sacredness of the great circle of life. Sacred circles, medicine wheels, and mandalas are images that direct us to the center of our being, to the truth of who we are. Within the sacred circle of "everything that is" we begin to remember our relationship with all life. We recognize our relationship with Father Sun and Mother Earth and the Great Spirit, Creator. It becomes obvious that we are all related brothers and sisters in one great family, not just our human family. The Indian elders say, "We must remember also the four-footed, those who swim and those who fly, those who crawl and those who move very slowly like the stone people, and all the green and growing things." Within this sacred circle we are one. What we do affects everyone, everything. These great teachings remind us of our responsibility to care for all life. In our pursuit of progress and comfort we have separated ourselves from our place in this great circle. Earth traditions bring us back into harmony and balance within the circle.

The sun dance of the Plains Indians is the center of our spiritual traditions. It is a ceremony of sacrifice and thanksgiving honoring the sacredness of the circle of life. From sunup to sundown each day for four days the participants dance and fast, without food or water. Each day the four major races of people are prayed for—children, adolescents, adults, and elders—along with beings who swim, fly, and crawl; the green and growing things and the stone people; each of the four sacred directions and the powers of those directions; and the elements. Everything is brought together in the circle; all living things are danced and sung for. In the center of the circle is the Tree of Life, the axis mundi, that which connects the Heavens and Earth. The people dance around her. They dance and sing and focus on "all our relations and our humble place in the circle of life." For four days the dancers pray for all of creation first, before they include themselves. The Lakota end all prayers with "*O Mitakuye Oyasin*," meaning "I do this for all my relations (or all sentient beings)."

TA: Like the ceremonies of Tibetan Buddhism, the Native American ceremonies open to an experience of nonduality, but the methods for accessing this experience are different. The Indians get there through a direct relationship with Earth, sun, moon, and the Great Spirit. Dualism happens when egocentricity develops, creating a split with nature, each other, and all life. When I was departing for a year-long retreat in the Tibetan Buddhist tradition, I told the medicine woman Bertha Grove, "I'll be alone for a long time." She replied, "You're not going to be alone. When you go outside and look around, you won't feel alone at all. You'll be completely accompanied by the trees, the plants, the birds, and the animals." For many years, I had learned about nonduality and the teachings of integration, but Grove's way of saying it was like a direct transmission.

In both the Tibetan and Native American traditions, inside and outside are ultimately not experienced as separate. You form a truly interactive relationship with the environment. For example, you're walking outside and you have a question in your mind. Then a raven flies over and crows three times. For most Americans that event would have no meaning; but for a Native American person that would be understood as a direct answer to the question because of his or her experience of the interconnected world. In other words, there's no "out there" out there.

The Tibetans also have an interpretive relationship with the phenomenal world that stems from insight into the interdependence of all phenomena, called *tendrel*. When the world is perceived in this way, things that happen are seen as "signs." Take the example of the raven flying and crowing three times. In Tibet, there's a whole divination system based on the calls of the ravens, how many times they call, and from which direction they're flying. You're actually living in a world that is responding to you and to which you are constantly responding, rather than one in which there's a "you" who is alive and then everything else which is more or less irrelevant and unresponsive. One aspect of awakening in Buddhism is an experience of this dynamic interdependence.

From Volume 22, Number 1 (Fall 2005).

6 Just One Minute

By Naomi Baer

In a big inner-city public high school, in a Midwestern city, in my classroom, I start every class period with one minute of stillness. I am a mathematics teacher.

This began in the fall of 1997 with one particularly disruptive class. Not knowing how else to quiet things down, I started class one day talking about how we react to what goes on around us. We react to our friends, to the teachers, to each other. We react to the loud speakers, the classes next door, the commotion in the halls. We are bombarded by outside events. So I invited them to breathe in, straighten up the spine with feet flat on the floor, and be still for sixty seconds. Not to react to anything. I rang a bell, closed my eyes, and breathed. When one minute passed I rang the bell again, breathed slowly, thanked them for the minute in which they gave their best, and invited them to thank those nearby. From this spontaneous response to one difficult class, I have continued to start all my classes in the same way. This is the fifth year.

In the beginning, it was questionable as to whether the practice had much of an impact on that disruptive class. Some students humored me and others ignored me, but for that one minute the noise level reduced at least a notch, so I continued. Over time, more students started thanking each other. First in jest, they playfully said to each other they would try better next time, and so it went.

I maintained the process, yet I never once made reference to meditation. I could do with my own minute what I chose without imposing anything on the students, and many days I practiced metta (lovingkindness meditation). About a month into the practice, in the middle of a lesson, there was a particular outburst from a student whom I had to escort out of the classroom.

When we returned to the lesson, another loud student commanded, "Ms. Baer, I think we need to do that minute thang again!" Vulnerable as I was, I closed my eyes in that class.

One day when I was delayed, a student spoke out, "Let's marinate," and rang the bells. Everyone did the one minute with him! From then on others wanted their turn to ring the bells. The noise and disturbances were reducing for the minute. The practice, however imperfect, gave even the most boisterous students a tool to use to settle the mind and body. I was convinced that it served not only me but the students as well.

In some of my advanced math classes, where discipline was not such an issue, there were mixed reactions. Most participated willingly in the minute of stillness, but a few were visibly uncomfortable and overtly resistant. I always thanked them especially for their minute of cooperation. Over time even these resistant ones became relaxed without having to work so hard at their resistance. It just was. A minute to do nothing.

This year one of my classes, mostly tenth graders, repeatedly requested to extend the minute of stillness even longer. So one day, with consent from everyone in the class, we did five minutes. When I rang the bell at the end, the stillness continued to linger. Wow! It was "awesome." They said they liked it when it was so quiet. They have continued to ask for more time, so we agreed to extend the minute on Fridays.

Our one minute has produced all sorts of responses. Once a parent complained to the principal, who assured the parent it was appropriately secular if it came from me. Last spring as a student handed in his final exam before leaving for the summer, with tears of appreciation in his eyes, he thanked me for the daily minute. He said it meant a lot to him. This year three students from a class next door come daily to join my class for the minute, afterward thanking their buddies before returning to their own classroom. Parents of former students have come up to me in the grocery store to tell me how much their son or daughter appreciated that minute. They thanked me.

If nothing else, our sixty seconds has given me a degree of equanimity at the start of each class. That has been reason enough to continue. It was a huge challenge to accept the chaos in that first loud and disruptive class. But for just that one minute I told myself to let go of all my judgment—I am the responsible teacher, I have to keep order, it is my right and duty to judge and correct. I learned to accept just what is in that one minute.

Over time the minute has softened me to my students. I have feelings of compassion for their being exactly who they are. The effect is evident when I see little respectful responses, some thoughtfulness, or a smile I would not have expected from them or from me. I continue to gain from our minute: to close my eyes and open my heart, to see the kindness that seeks an invitation to express itself from under the harsh exterior that circumstances have somehow created in my students. They show me myself.

⋮ From Volume 20, Number 1 (Fall 2003).

Author's Note: Ten years later—in 2007—I am still teaching at the same high school, and many of my classes now request one minute on Mondays, two on Tuesdays, and so on up to five-minute Fridays.

7 Living Time, Not Doing Time
An Interview with Kiran Bedi and Lucia Meijer

A transformational tide is rippling through the prisons of the world, spreading out from the Tihar Central Jail in New Delhi and the revolutionary experimentation of Dr. Kiran Bedi. In 1993, as inspector general of Tihar, Dr. Bedi invited teachers from one of S.N. Goenka's meditation centers to conduct a ten-day vipassana course inside the prison. The program was so successful that there is now a special wing of Tihar to house prisoners who meditate, while similar vipassana programs are being initiated in jails and prisons throughout the world. Dr. Bedi has since been given many honors, including the 1994 Ramon Magsaysay Award, also known as the Asian Nobel Prize. A documentary film about the Tihar program, Doing Time, Doing Vipassana, *has been inspiring audiences and influencing prison authorities in the West.*

Inquiring Mind spoke with Dr. Bedi during her visit to the United States in September 1999. Joining in the conversation was Lucia Meijer, administrator of the North Rehabilitation Facility, an alternative detention site near Seattle, Washington. Ms. Meijer had started a vipassana program in that facility. She has been working in the field of addiction for many years, specifically with hard-to-reach populations that are not well served by traditional treatment programs. Also participating in the discussion were Harry and Vivian Snyder, teachers appointed by S.N. Goenka to conduct ten-day vipassana courses, working especially in prisons. The conversation took place at the KPFA radio studios in Berkeley, California.

INQUIRING MIND: Why did you introduce vipassana into the Tijar Central jail?

KIRAN BEDI: As a police officer and director general of Delhi prisons, I was responsible for creating security inside the jail, and I saw vipassana as a major measure of peace and harmony. Peace and harmony isn't created by the walls of a prison; it comes from the beings inside, and unless you address individuals, you cannot create a peaceful community. So I introduced programs that would enable individuals to be more peaceful. Vipassana addresses individuals.

As a prison administrator, you can create an enabling environment. If you have no library, you don't enable the individuals to read. When you introduce a library, some still may not read, but you are subtly sending out a message suggesting the value and availability of books. With the vipassana program, I was suggesting, "This is good. Try it."

It is my belief that prison per se is punishment, but if you don't work on reforms and if you don't work on corrections enabling the individuals to learn and change, then you actually are punishing doubly. When you punish a person doubly, you end up with an individual who, on release, is ready to hurt society; so you are hurting society in the end.

IM: So how did the idea to bring in vipassana first take shape?

KB: Actually, a guard suggested that we initiate this program inside Tijar; it wasn't me. I had talked about the importance of finding options for prisoners who are driven by revenge and violence and who can't handle these strong emotions. One of the guards suggested that I look into the vipassana program. When I said I didn't know what it was, he said, "Let's invite the vipassana teachers to make a presentation here at the prison."

So we contacted Mr. Goenka's Jabalpur office, which is his regional office for north India, and invited the teachers to visit the prison and speak with the prison population. They explained what vipassana stands for, what it means to voluntarily abstain from certain foods and "privileges," how the diet and lifestyle would be regulated, and how to practice meditation. All of this was shared in a lecture to a large congregation of one or two thousand people. After the talk, sixty volunteered.

IM: Tell us about the first course.

KB: During the first retreat at the prison, we experimented with a small group of inmates in a violent category—those who were incarcerated for life for crimes such as murder. So we started with the most difficult prisoners and came to the easier ones later. That's just how we did it; I'm not necessarily suggesting that it must be done in that order.

The teachers of the first course were Mr. Ram Singh, a former government official, and Professor Dar, who is a teacher in the Indian Institute of Technology. They stayed with the convicts inside the prison to do this program. In addition, these vipassana teachers required the prison guards to take the course and learn to meditate with the inmates.

On the third day of the course, the prisoners threatened the teachers and tried to get them to leave. But the teachers hung on because they had faith in the innate goodness of the prisoners. Of course, they were not without security guards, but the security guards were nowhere nearby because the teachers had insisted on this. The teachers kept their faith, and by the fifth day, the prisoners broke down and started to follow the teachings.

On the eleventh day of the meditation course when we broke silence, we didn't know what the participants would say. This was our first experiment. The media had been allowed inside the prison, and there we were sitting before their cameramen. The prisoners could have said anything: "To hell with the prison staff! Look what they did to us!" I was keeping my fingers crossed.

But when we broke the retreat silence, some of the men were in tears. I'd never seen these men cry. They only make others cry. As they were crying, they said things like, "I was planning to murder a magistrate or my witness or my victim's family when I got out, but now I realize the futility of that thought."

Then they urged me to make this program available for a larger group inside the prison. So we held a second course inside the prison for around 1,100 prisoners. I was dealing with a population of 9,700 people, and if I kept it small, I wouldn't be able to make a dent. The men who had taken the first course wanted to share their experience with the other prisoners. After completing the course, they urged the others, "Do it! You're doing time anyway, why don't you do vipassana?"

For this next large course of 1,100 students, Mr. Goenka came in to teach himself. He said that many decades earlier his teacher in Burma had predicted that one day he would be conducting a program with over a thousand prison inmates. He told us, "For me, it was my teacher's prophesy coming true."

IM: When they take their first vipassana course, what do you think happens inside of those prisoners so that by the time they break silence they are weeping? How has vipassana allowed them to open their hearts?

KB: I think that, most of all, they have realized that they can't tell lies to themselves anymore. They were always lying externally, but now when they looked inside, who was there to tell lies to? That's what *vipassana* means: looking within, looking at yourself. As they continued to look, their denial stopped. Acceptance began. They started to accept and take responsibility for their own conduct and misconduct. When the silence broke, the internal truth became an external statement.

They had committed crimes, but all along, to me, as a police officer, they would say, "We've been sent to prison wrongly." They were always denying their own crimes. It was not what I said, but meditation, this program, that made them acknowledge that they had, in fact, committed the crimes and that they would take responsibility for their own wrongdoing.

They also learn in vipassana to keep educating themselves. That daily practice of sitting, even for half an hour a day, keeps them looking at themselves, policing themselves.

IM: How about the guards? What do you think happens for them when they go through the course?

KB: The guard who introduced me to vipassana had been a very angry man. He had not been a good family man, but after the course he became a wonderful person with his family. His wife and children testified to that. Another guard who had been addicted to domestic violence and alcohol changed dramatically after taking the vipassana course.

IM: Did the authorities ever express reservations about offering a Buddhist-based program in an institution of a primarily Hindu nation?

KB: I'll answer that questions in two ways. First of all, India is dominated by people practicing Hinduism, but it is a strongly secular country that respects all faiths. Second, vipassana is not Buddhist. It was practiced by a man named Gautama who came to be called Buddha [Awakened One]. There's a very important distinction that we need to make. This program does not turn out Buddhists; it only makes more buddhas.

IM: The vipassana program at Tijar has launched a worldwide movement. There are now ten-day vipassana courses in jails in England, New Zealand, and Taiwan. In Seattle, there have been seven ten-day courses so far. Lucia Meijer, as the administrator of the North Rehabilitation Facility in Seattle, will you give us some sense of how your program got started and how it's going?

LUCIA MEIJER: Vipassana was proposed to me by one of our jail health staff who is a meditator and a teacher. At first, I thought that we didn't need it because we already had the stress reduction, the acupuncture, the tai chi, the this and the that. I thought to myself, We're doing the best that can be done as it is. Why go through all the effort to create a separate wing and to implement such a program?

But when I saw the film that featured Kiran Bedi's work at the Tihar prison, it occurred to me that we were missing something important, which was that elusive spiritual component. *Spiritual* is a word that I have always winced at because it really has only the content that you give it. Anybody can say it's anything, and I think it has been appropriated by some pretty fringe types. But after I saw the film, it occurred to me that this vipassana is something very old, very practical, and it has tremendous potential to reach that spiritual undercurrent in people.

Then we put out the word to the inmates. When we showed them *Doing Time, Doing Vipassana*, enough of them found it inspirational that we had sixteen men sign up for the first course. It was painful for them to make that commitment because in the culture of that facility, the sentiment was: "Are you crazy?" At least when you're in the general population, you can smoke, you can watch television, you can get visits, you can have mail.

At the end of the course, we had a reception, just as they do in India, so that the family members and other inmates could receive the guys who had sustained this commitment. Considering the climate under which they had gone into the course, they didn't know what kind of reception they were going to get when they came out. They didn't know if people were going to (figuratively) throw eggs at them or what.

We were all in the gymnasium, and the crowd, mostly consisting of inmates, settled down. The fellows walked in, all eleven of them, in single file. Spontaneously everybody stood up and cheered. It was a wonderful moment of solidarity. This is something that I see happening a lot with vipassana. It brings the staff together; it brings the inmates together behind a positive effort; it brings staff and inmates together with one another in making this effort.

KB: What did they say on breaking silence?

LM: Very similar things to what was said at the end of your program. First of all, they expressed their gratitude. This surprised me, because typically at these events the remarks seem self-aggrandizing. When we have a graduation from an educational program, the prisoners say, "I'm so proud of myself, and you can all be very proud of me." They tell long, sad stories about themselves and how much better they are now; then they cry. Everybody has a catharsis; there's lots of hugging; maybe the judge lets them go home early.

I bring a skepticism to these graduation events. As the administrator, it's my job to be more skeptical than anyone else. I've seen what happens a week later, a month later, a year later when they are sent back having committed more crimes. Tears do not move me. But when these guys came out saying, "Thank you," I have to tell you, I was close to tears myself. I had to leave the room. God forbid anybody should see me tearing up.

[Turning to Kiran Bedi] There is something you were saying that really rings true for me. At this event, following the experience with vipassana, I saw an authenticity that I had not seen before.

IM: How does that authenticity manifest?

LM: It is just what Kiran said. The prisoners are not lying to themselves anymore. After other programs, they would come out blaming themselves. There's a big difference between blaming yourself and taking responsibility. Coming out of the vipassana course, they were taking responsibility in an eyes-open way.

Now, old habits reassert themselves fairly quickly. You take people out of the environment, and even though they can continue to practice for several hours a day, those old habits are very deeply ingrained and they're going to reassert themselves sooner or later. So vipassana's not a magic bullet. But for our sixty-six inmates who have now completed courses in vipassana, something has become easier. It's like stretching a rubber band. There may be a lot of resistance the first time, but having had that experience, that sense of taking responsibility comes a bit more easily.

IM: What exactly do you mean when you describe prisoners as taking responsibility?

LM: I see them understanding cause and effect. If I do this, then such-and-such happens; so if I want things to happen differently, I need to do things differently. This is something that we call self-efficacy. It's hard to develop self-efficacy if you grow up in a world where you have no control over anything, where things just happen no matter what your intentions or actions. Many of our inmates have histories of prior physical and sexual abuse, of growing up in very chaotic, drug-infested, violent situations. They haven't developed that self-efficacy because they couldn't make the connection between what they did and what happened afterward. When they sit a vipassana course, that connection may become clear for the first time.

IM: Pretty soon you'll have people outside the prison picking a pocket so that they can get inside the prison and participate in these programs! (Laughs)

KB: Interestingly enough, something like that has been happening at our facility. When non-prisoners haven't been able to get seats in vipassana courses on the outside, they haven't minded coming into the prison and sitting with the prisoners.

LM: We've had a similar experience in Seattle. Because we're a jail, lots of people are incarcerated while awaiting trial. Many of the folks that go into the vipassana course call their attorney, or the judge, and say, "Don't release me until after I've completed this course, okay?"

IM: It's wonderful, what you are doing in these programs. This is truly a vipassana revolution in progress. Some day, you'll have monasteries right inside the prison.

KB: Our prison has almost become a monastery. It's a monastery that is full of joy and happiness, internal joy and internal peace. It's that kind of monastery that is silent and healthy.

IM: So when you walk from one side of the prison to the other where the inmates are doing vipassana, you truly notice a difference?

KB: You notice a difference written on the faces. In fact, you can tell if a person is a meditator. He's at peace with himself. He's got a natural smile already, because he's accepting the moment. The others are denying it and quarreling with it. That's the difference. One man is doing time doubly; the meditator is living time, not doing time.

From Volume 16, Number 2 (Spring 2000).

8

The Goddess Saves the Earth

By China Galland

This article was adapted from an interview with China Galland on her path exploring Buddhism, ecology, and the female deities who protect the Earth.

My life seems inevitably to lead me to love what's been excluded, rejected, and unacknowledged, whether it's a woman's body or the Earth on which we have wreaked so much havoc. It's become the path of reconciliation. I was drawn into it by stories and ancient myths, especially those of alchemical change where what's considered base is turned into gold. Like the stone rejected by the builders that becomes the cornerstone in the New Testament, the relationships I left out in my own life—with my body, the Earth's body, people of color—became precisely what I had to reconnect with and transform.

In 1981, when I began the path of recovery from addiction, I was catapulted into a spiritual crisis that ultimately reconnected me to my body as a woman as well as to the Earth's body. Though raised as a devout Catholic, I'd left the church by my early twenties. I missed the Church terribly but, as a woman, I found it impossibly oppressive. I longed for a spiritual home that was accessible, structured, and daily. In desperation by my thirties, I went to a Catholic retreat in New Mexico. I rediscovered Mary, but I could no longer relate to her. I knelt in front of Our Lady of Guadalupe and wept.

All the while, at home in my own backyard in Muir Beach, California, there were all these sweet bald people from San Francisco Zen Center's nearby Green Gulch Farm who hitchhiked over the hills between their farm and the nearest town. When I got back from Christ in the Desert, the next hitchhiker I picked up was the guest master at Green Gulch. Soon I was getting up every morning at 4:30 to sit zazen before it was time to get home and get my children up and off to school.

I studied there in the Soto Zen tradition for two years before I discovered that in traditional Buddhism, it's believed that you have to have a man's body in order to be enlightened. Though the Western teachers I was meeting dismissed the idea, it gave me pause to discover this deeply ingrained belief about the inferiority of women in Buddhism. It felt so Catholic! Some of the texts and prayers described the female body with great disgust. How could I continue?

Buddhism was my last resort; I didn't know where I could go from there. I loved Green Gulch and the people there, and I couldn't imagine having to give up that community. Still, I didn't see how I could embrace such a distorted view of women. After tea one morning at Green Gulch, someone who knew of my struggle took me aside and said, "In Tibetan Buddhism there is a female buddha, Tara, who vowed to be enlightened only in a woman's body."

Hearing this fragment of Tara's story was like tasting the sweetness of water after a long, hard thirst. Instinctively, I knew that a woman could be completely and fully enlightened, but this was the first time I heard that belief stated in the Buddhist tradition. That tiny sliver of Tara's story set me on fire and helped save my life. It also propelled me halfway around the world to India and Nepal to find this buddha Tara.

In India, I interviewed His Holiness the Dalai Lama about Tara. He assured me that of course women could be fully and completely enlightened, yes, yes. Almost every Tibetan monastery begins its day with praise to Tara, he explained, she is so central to their belief. One of his own teachers had been a great woman lama, he said, though he could not remember her name. For further Tara instruction he sent me to Locho Rinpoche, the head of Namgyal, His Holiness's monastery in Dharamsala. He would teach me about the traditional Twenty-One Taras, their different forms and colors—green, white, red, yellow, and black—but when I went to my appointment with the rinpoche he wasn't there.

My journey took me to Switzerland shortly thereafter. Other friends suggested that I visit Dora Kalff, a protégé of Carl Jung's and the originator of sandplay therapy. Dora was also a great friend of the Dalai Lama's and a devout Tibetan Buddhist practioner with a mind of her own. She was known to send her patients to the Black Madonna at the Benedictine monastery in Einseideln, outside of Zurich.

When I walked into Dora Kalff's house in Zollikon, I was promptly led upstairs and introduced to a Tibetan monk, Geshe Champa Lodro, who was sitting in a window wearing red and saffron robes that glowed with warmth. The bright winter sun streamed in around him. He sat there beaming, looking utterly familiar, and asked, "Do you want to know about the Twenty-One Taras?" My request for the Tara teachings was granted after all.

Geshe Champa Lodro Rinpoche told me that Tara had been an historical person once, much like the Buddha or Jesus Christ. Her name had originally been Yeshe Dawa, which means "Wisdom Moon." In ancient times, Yeshe Dawa developed her compassion, her generosity, and her wisdom so deeply that people came from all over to seek her counsel. Yet because of the belief that one had to have a man's body to be enlightened, people began to say to her, "Oh, Yeshe Dawa, the only difference between you and the Buddha is that you don't have the male form. Therefore we beg you to please magically transform yourself in this lifetime and take a man's body so that you will be a Buddha. If you can't do that in this lifetime," they pleaded, "please, please reincarnate in the male form. Then you will be a buddha the very moment that you're born!"

Yeshe Dawa knew these followers only meant well, and she replied, "I've thought about these matters for a long time, yet nowhere can I find what is male, nowhere can I find what is female. Worldly beings are always deluded about what is male and what is female. These are simply different forms of being, no more separate than a wave is from water. But, since most buddhas have chosen to come in the form of a man, perhaps it would be more helpful if I vowed to be fully and completely enlightened only in a woman's body."

And so she was. Once Yeshe Dawa was fully and completely enlightened, she became Tara, the Savioress.

I loved that story. It affirmed my experience and relieved me of all burdens about male and female genders. And how Buddhist is this? Tara relied completely upon her own experience against all the received traditions that said she had to have a man's body to be enlightened. Her vow has fortified me ever since.

Not only did Tara's vow affirm my own sense of possibility, but I discovered that the Green Tara, the main form from which all other forms of Tara emanate, is a forest goddess. The twenty-one traditional forms all arise out of the Green Tara of the Khadira Forest. This forest is described as Tara's heaven, the place where Tara has her palace amid the trees. Tigers and antelope play together, the texts say; all the animals are at peace, as in the mythical place where the lion and the lamb lie down together in peace. Tara's Khadira Forest gives us an image of the world transformed.

On a pilgrimage in India I discovered the Hindu Goddess Tara, who is also a form of the goddess Kali, Creatrix and Destroyer. Kali, in turn, emerges full blown from the forehead of Durga, the Hindu warrior goddess and queen who comes to save the world when it's on the verge of destruction. I made a pilgrimage to this Tara of Bengal and visited her shrine at Tarapith, where the stone in which she appeared is still venerated. The entire country of India is conceived of as the body of the goddess. Every locale has a story of the gods and goddesses who live there. Trees are venerated, stones revered, rivers are sacred, animals too—all, all is holy.

In Nepal in the village of Pharping outside of Kathmandu, I visited a shrine where Tara is reported to be growing miraculously out of a rock. Parallel stories of Mary appearing were coming in from around the globe too. Whether in Poland, the former Yugoslavia, Egypt, California, or Alabama, Mary was said to be growing in the barks of trees or emerging out of thin air. At Medjugorje in the former Yugoslavia, Mary was appearing daily to young visionaries. While I was there interviewing the visionaries, I remembered that Tara is famed for a compassion so great that she is said to come in whatever form someone needs to see her in—be it a bumblebee or a buddha—in order to provide immediate help. This loving divine female benevolence who manifests humbly wherever called, in whatever form helps, would appear in the West as Mary. I began to perceive the energies of Tara and Mary as the same phenomenon taking different forms for diverse cultures.

Though I speak of the "divine feminine," we have to remember we are all "male" and "female." Genetically we carry both within us. We become one gender or another by virtue of one or two x- and y-chromosomes. Nonetheless, there's been a deification of the behavior that we have agreed to describe as "male." So to say that now we have to include the "feminine" is to say that we need to include that part of ourselves which we've rejected, excluded, trivialized, considered inferior or Other.

Using the word *feminine* can be a way of acknowledging the emotional part of the self that feels, the part of us that knows, consciously or unconsciously, that life is sustained by the heart. It is almost impossible to have a child and not discover what it takes to keep life alive, how much love and attention is required to provide the enormous focus and nurturance that goes into supporting it. By honoring what we call "feminine," we're honoring the part of our humanity that is deeply wise about what it takes to nourish life, what makes it flourish and blossom with delight. The heart knows when the circle of relationship is broken. The pain of brokenness calls us together to be reconciled with one another, to make peace.

For me the feminine and the wild are related to darkness in its most beautiful, dynamic, and positive forms. There is an all-encompassing fecundity that girds the world, a generative power that seeds need to grow, that the womb encloses, that explodes with stars. The wilderness is an emanation of that positive, life-affirming darkness. Just as we've deified our ideas of the masculine, we've made a god of the concept of light and set up the dark in opposition. Can we speak of the wisdom of the dark?

In tradition after tradition, one finds stories of the divine feminine that link back to an earlier Earth goddess in the culture of indigenous peoples. The patron of Mexico and all the Americas is Guadalupe, who appeared at the shrine of the Aztec Earth goddess, Tonantzin. In Europe, it's inside mainstream Catholicism that we find these centuries-old dark and black Madonnas. Churches were often built over pre-Christian sacred sites to goddesses associated with the Earth who had been celebrated in communal and familial gatherings of dancing, feasting, and song. Can we take up the practice of rejoicing despite global warming?

In Catholicism, Mary's relationship with nature has often been disguised or met with hostility. Take Frassino, Italy: the Madonna kept appearing outdoors in the branches of a tree. Churchmen "captured" her to install her on an altar inside the church, but she kept escaping. Finally they chopped down the tree. You can see her at a side altar inside the church: a small dark Madonna on a piece of the tree that was cut down that now rests inside the tabernacle.

Tara's connection to the Earth as a forest goddess doesn't seem to have been obscured in the same way. On the other hand, it may not have been emphasized. Environmentalists and scholars have now delved into the world's religious traditions to find what moral frameworks they might provide for our relationship with the planet. The Forum on Religion and Ecology at Harvard Divinity School has translated and published several texts on ecology in the world's religions in the past decades. (www.religionandecology.org, environment.harvard.edu/religion).

In the meantime, to increase awareness and mindfulness of the Earth, I find it helpful always to invoke these heavenly Earth goddesses daily. I have an image of the Khadira Forest Green Tara that I've visually memorized so that I can "see" her no matter where I am. I continue to study Tara and the texts now being translated. I've taken Tara initiations with a small number of

Tibetan lamas and learned to visualize several of her forms. (Discernment is required, and qualified teachers of Tibetan practices need to be sought out.)

One practice that's been particularly helpful has been to visualize Tara outside myself, then to actually see her enter my body, and then to become her, become the deity herself. This has been supremely healing for me as a woman who was taught that being a woman was inferior. At the end of the meditation Tara goes back out into the void. In another practice I imagine that all sound is the sound of the deity's voice and all appearance is the appearance of the deity. It's been a great delight for me to extend my visualization of Tara in this way, to see everything as a form of her—divine, sacred, and alive—for the few moments that I can. When hiking on a mountain path in meditation, I visualize the path I'm walking as a tiny blood vessel inside Tara's body. I see myself walking inside this beautiful, living body of enlightened wisdom, of Tara. Over time, my sense of relatedness to the natural world is shifting, and when focused, I can experience more of the biological connections.

We seem to be living at the edge of time. We are not only at war, but we are in the sixth extinction this planet has known, the only one caused by humankind. It's not enough to only sit in meditative silence, and yet it is foolish to act without the silence. My actions need the wisdom of that still small voice heard only in the silence. Practice remains a joy when I do it, a battle to get to it or to remember to see all that I'm doing as practice and dedicate the merit. Lovingkindness and beauty are guides I can more easily find in the unbroken lineage of the Mother.

What gives me hope is the Hindu story of Durga, the warrior goddess queen. This ancient tale sounds as though it describes the world today if you remember that the demons in it are symbols for our worst human failings: greed, hatred, and delusion.

"Once before the world was on the brink of destruction," the story goes. "Once before" there was war everywhere, rivers dried up, plants wouldn't grow, people were starving. It was said that world was being destroyed by demons so powerful that the demons had defeated every one of the gods.

How could this be? Even the gods couldn't believe their fate. They abandoned the world to its destruction and withdrew to the heights of the Himalayas. There one of the gods remembered an ancient prophecy that demons would rise up who were so powerful and destructive that no one could defeat them but the Goddess. Only the feminine could save the world.

First they had to remember her, then they had to ask for her to come. They gathered in a circle and shot forth streams of divine fire. Out of those divine fires rose Durga riding her lion, her face blazing like a thousand suns; each of her ten hands holding a weapon of the gods, she rode out onto the battlefield and defeated the demons. Plants began to grow again, rivers returned to their courses, flowers bloomed, people could eat again, they sang, they danced; all the world rejoiced at Durga's victory. Even the gods appeared to crown her and begged her to stay and rule the world, but Durga would not. No, she said. However, they need not worry. She promised to feed her devotees with her own body, the Earth itself. And then she made one last promise: "If the world is ever in danger," she told them, "I will return."

I spoke with teacher of mine about this story of fierce compassion. She asked me if I knew how Durga defeated the demons. Yes, I told her. Durga pierced the heart of the king of the demons with her dagger. She said, "Yes, piercing the heart is opening the heart." Then I understood the story. Only by opening the heart can the world be saved, one more time.

From Volume 22, Number 1 (Fall 2005).

9 Stop! A Buddhist Is Here!

By Jarvis Masters

Jarvis Masters is a widely published African American Buddhist writer. He is the author of Finding Freedom: Writings from Death Row *and just recently completed his soon-to-be-published second book. He is a frequent contributor to* Turning Wheel *and has been published in several books and magazines, including* Shambhala Sun, Tricycle, Men's Studies Review, Recovering, Men's Council Newsletter, Wingspan, The Sun, Utne Reader, Paths of Learning, *and other publications. He is the recipient of the 1991 PEN Award for Poetry for his poem "Recipe for Prison Pruno."*

Jarvis Masters has been incarcerated in San Quentin State Prison for twenty-five years and on death row for seventeen years after being wrongfully convicted of participating in the murder of a prison guard. His appeal is currently before the California Supreme Court. Jarvis Masters, his attorneys, and his supporters believe that his conviction will be overturned and he will be exonerated.

In 1989 Masters took his vows in prison as a Tibetan Buddhist from the Tibetan teacher Chagdud Tulku Rinpoche. He is now a student of Pema Chödrön, whom he calls his "Dharma mom." Masters has described his empowerment ceremony with Chagdud in the San Quentin maximum security visiting office. By phone, through a glass window, the rinpoche gave him his second vow: "From this day forward I will try to end suffering of all human beings and other beings." On hearing this, Masters asked, "In here, helping others could cost me my life. Can I qualify my vow by common sense? Can I use my intelligence not to cause my own death?"

We had only been out on the San Quentin maximum-security exercise yard for an hour when I noticed a new prisoner entering the yard gate, looking as though he were a woman. I couldn't believe it. No San Quentin exercise yard hated homosexuals more than this yard. Gays came in second only to informants to be stabbed and killed. My mind instantly said this was some kind of mistake, or a dirty ploy by the prison administration to get someone killed. Wondering which of these two evils it could be, I peeked up at the tower gunmen. I asked myself what a Buddhist teacher would do at this point.

I'd personally never held anything against homosexuals, but I knew that the prisoners on this particular yard hated them. Some hated them just for hate's sake. Others hated them out of fear: especially those who had arrived at San Quentin in the early '80s with life sentences or those who were waiting on death row to die and had long ago been taken in by the very first media reports of how AIDS was just a homosexual disease. Later, prison officials told us that other diseases like tuberculosis were something else that homosexuals were spreading throughout the prisons. The men on this yard had come to believe all this. They were scared of homosexuals and hated them all.

I stared with disbelief at this gay person waiting at the entrance of the yard gate. I thought, This guy isn't going to last one full hour out here! I didn't have to turn around to know that there were other prisoners behind me, looking on coldly. Everyone was watching. I could just feel it. There was silence all over the yard. I didn't have to see all the prison-made shanks being pulled out of waistbands to know what some of the men had begun doing. I wanted so badly to holler out and warn this stupid person who was still standing at the yard gate, "Man, this isn't your damn yard. Don't bring your ass out here." But I couldn't say this. I could not say anything. It would've been considered snitching. And I am not a snitch. So I swallowed, kept my mouth shut, and prayed.

Then came the loud clinking and whining sound of the motorized gate letting this person onto the yard. When the gate slammed shut, my heart dropped. He had just become another walking dead man. I had seen a few others like this in my eleven years of incarceration.

The entire yard, from everyone on the basketball and handball courts to the scattered groups of others over by the pull-up bar, all watched in total silence as this fragile-looking man with tiny breasts, his hair in a pony tail, Vaseline on his lips, dressed in really tight state jeans, began swishing along the yard fence.

My blood pressure boiled with anger and frustration at the prison administration's negligence for letting something like this happen. It made absolutely no sense to put a "he-she," who looked more like a woman than a man, out here on this high-security exercise yard. This is totally insane, I thought, trying to not show any facial anger.

According to the laws of prison life, none of this was supposed to be any business of mine. But secretly, it was. This time it had to be. For all the life in me, I wasn't able to look at this gay person, who was now sitting alone against the back wall of the exercise yard, and not see an innocent human being there. Yet I did not want to have to summon up the courage to become a snitch and risk my own life for his to warn him off this yard. Why me, anyway? I felt crossed up.

I looked up again at the two gunmen hovering over the exercise yard and saw they had already gotten in position. They both had their semi-automatic rifles hanging over the gun rail, readying themselves to fire down on the north wall of the exercise yard. Obviously, they already knew what everybody else knew.

I had to do something. Not later, but now. I began walking alongside the wall of the exercise yard. What could I possibly do? Violence was just waiting to happen. Dammit. I asked myself, why are things like this happening even more since I took my vows? What would all the thousands of people outside these walls who call themselves Buddhists tell me to do? Would they say, "Let's all be Buddhists and everybody just put their knives up and smile?"

I made my way around to where the homosexual was sitting against the wall. Not stopping, I passed him several times, wanting to give myself a really good look at him. I wanted to find out if he was aware of what was going on, that someone was about to stab and kill him. The fool was not! He sat there like a tiny fish in a shark tank. Now I needed to get away from this guy, quick. I needed to think, because I felt time was running out—even for me.

I spotted Crazy Dan on the opposite side of the exercise yard. He was squatting down, and secretly cuffing a long prison-made shank in the sleeve of his coat. "Damn!" I mumbled, "No! Not Crazy Dan." My heart began to pound as I watched Dan, a really good friend of mine, preparing himself to kill this innocent person, whose only offense was that he was gay.

Dan and I had known each other for more than eight years in San Quentin, and it just figured that this good friend of mine wasn't feeling as I was about all this. I didn't want Dan to risk his own life, trying to take the life of another with these two ready gunmen watching.

Then, my mind went blank. Without thinking, I began walking down the wall, on the opposite side of the yard from Dan. It wasn't until we both suddenly turned the corners, coming toward each other, with the lone gay man squatting quietly against the back wall, that I saw the long shank slowly sliding down from Dan's coat sleeve into his right hand. I quickened my pace to get there before Crazy Dan did. I didn't have time to be scared, or even to think. I knew I had to get there first.

Quickly, I knelt down in front of the gay man and asked if he had a spare cigarette. Dan was only six feet away. I glanced up and saw Dan stopped dead, standing there with his right hand hiding behind his leg, gripping the long shank. Dan was stunned. I could see all the adrenaline in his body freeze, as his eyes like those of a ferocious beast stared into mine. I'd never seen those eyes before. They were not those of the Dan I knew. For that split second I thought my friend was going to kill me instead.

Then something happened. Dan's eyes blinked hard several times as he suddenly began to realize my silent plea. I could see that he was remembering the time when I had once stood by him when he, too, had been marked for death. Dan turned and calmly walked away.

"Hey, Daddy, did you want this cigarette, or what?" the homosexual asked in a female voice, holding one out between his fingers. "No, I don't smoke." He looked around confused.

When I realized what I had just done, I almost choked on my fear. I was out of breath and felt like shitting. Why had I put my life on the line for somebody that I didn't know or hadn't even seen before? Am I crazy or just plain stupid? I wondered, looking in the face of this gay man who was still totally unaware of what I had just done.

I stood up and walked away, knowing that I was going to take a lot of heat later that day from everyone on the exercise yard. But I realized that I could make the case to the whole yard that all this had been one big setup. I would say that the prison authorities had been intent on shooting and killing some of us and that I wasn't about to let anybody that I knew, especially Crazy Dan, get killed by tiptoeing into their trap. The truth that I would purposely leave out in justifying what I did that day was that I honestly cared about the homosexual person too. He meant absolutely nothing to me—except that he was just as human as all of us. He never came back to our yard after that day, but he left me with a lot of questions.

Is what I did a Buddhist deed? Can't it just be a human deed? Can't everybody or anybody do this? Am I alone? Am I the only Buddhist out here? Does this mean I have to do this all the time? Am I, the Lone Buddhist Ranger, expected to be here to stop all this stuff? I imagine myself raising my hand and yelling, "Stop! A Buddhist is here!"

I'm not going to stop it all. It hasn't stopped at all. There are stabbings every day in this place. All I have is my practice. Every morning and night I fold my two bunk blankets and sit on them on the floor of my cell.

From Volume 9, Number 2 (Spring 1993).

Contributors

Tsultrim Allione was one of the first American women ordained as a Tibetan nun, in 1970. She later returned her monastic vows, married, and had three children. She founded Tara Mandala Retreat Center in 1993, where she is now resident teacher. She is author of *Women of Wisdom* on the lives of great female Tibetan Buddhist practitioners and *Feeding Your Demons* on Tibetan Chod practice.

Ajahn Amaro was born in England. Thai meditation master Ajahn Chah ordained him as a monk in 1979 in Thailand. He resided for many years at Amaravati Buddhist Centre near London. Since 1996 he has served as coabbot of Abhayagiri Monastery in Redwood Valley, California. He has written numerous books.

Guy Armstrong has practiced insight meditation for over thirty years, including training as a Buddhist monk in Thailand with Ajahn Buddhadasa. He began teaching in 1984 and has led retreats worldwide. He is a member of Spirit Rock Meditation Center's Teachers Council.

Naomi Baer teaches high school in St. Paul, Minnesota. She lived and worked in Tanzania for eight years, raised two children, and now enjoys her two grandchildren. She was introduced to vipassana in 1991 when her children were teenagers, and she continues to maintain a daily meditation practice.

Dipa Ma Barua(1911–1989) was born Nani Bala Barua in East Bengal. After her husband died in 1957, she took up vipassana and made swift progress.

In 1967, she moved to Calcutta, where she taught meditation to a wide range of students, including many who later became prominent teachers in America.

Stephen Batchelor is a teacher and writer best known for his secular approach to Buddhism. Born in Scotland in 1953, he trained as both a Tibetan and Zen monk. He disrobed and married in 1985. He cofounded Sharpham College for Buddhist Studies in England. He currently lives in France and teaches worldwide. His books include *Buddhism Without Beliefs* and *Living with the Devil*.

Kiran Bedi was the first woman to join the elite Indian Police Service, in 1972, and has developed innovative policing and prison reforms. Her many honors include the Ramon Magsaysay Award (the "Asian Nobel Prize"). She has also founded internationally recognized education, adult literacy, vocational training, drug abuse prevention, and counseling programs. She is the author and the subject of various books and films.

Lorraine Bonner. Page 97. *Internalized Perpetration*. 13" x 13" x 10". 2001. Clay. Lorraine Bonner is a physician who has turned to sculpture to enlarge the scope of her healing practice, both personal and planetary. She lives and works in Oakland, California.

Edward Espe Brown ordained as a disciple of Shunryu Suzuki Roshi in 1971, is author of the classic *Tassajara Bread Book* and *Tomato Blessings and Radish Teachings*, and editor of a book by his teacher called *Not Always So*. He also is the principal character in the critically acclaimed movie *How to Cook Your Life*.

John Cage (1912–1992) was a pioneer of chance music, electronic music, and non-standard use of musical instruments. He was one of the leading figures of the post-war avant-garde and is considered by many to be the most influential American composer of the twentieth century.

Margery Cantor is the designer of *Inquiring Mind*. In 1978, she began as an apprentice to Adrian Wilson at the Press in Tuscany Alley in San Francisco. Since that time, she has designed books for many presses, including University of California Press, Stanford University Press, Scribner's, Knopf, Shambhala Publications, and HarperSanFrancisco.

Lorraine Capparell. Page 199. *Mahapajapati*. 21" x 18" x 13". 2002. Bronze. Lorraine Capparell is a storyteller, gently enticing those who view her work to take a leap into an imaginative world of discovery. She is an accomplished artist, recognized for her work as a painter, sculptor, and photographer since 1975. She divides her time between creating visionary sculptural pieces and richly colorful paintings and watercolors that communicate her unique focus on life.

Andrew Cooper is an editor-at-large for *Tricycle: The Buddhist Review*. He lives with his wife, Liz, and daughter, Alana, in Olympia, Washington. He has been a friend, editing hand, and occasional contributor to *Inquiring Mind* since its inception.

Margaret Cullen is a therapist and Mindfulness-Based Stress Reduction teacher. She facilitates support groups for cancer patients and has taught and developed curriculae for several mindfulness-based research projects out of the University of California, San Francisco.

Ram Dass traveled to India in 1967, where he met his spiritual teacher, Neem Karoli Baba. His classic book *Be Here Now* brought him into the public eye in 1971. He has developed many service projects, including the Seva Foundation, dedicated to relieving suffering in the world. In 1997 Ram Dass suffered a severe stroke, yet he continues to teach, write, and lecture.

Eduardo Duran (Apache/Tewa) is a psychologist who has been working in Indian country for his entire professional career. He has been involved in Buddhist and traditional Native practices for many years. He is the author of *Buddha in Redface*.

Paul Ekman was a professor of psychology at the University of California, San Francisco, for thirty-two years. He has since applied his discoveries about emotion and expression to antiterrorism, law enforcement, and courses teaching emotional skills. He is the author or editor of fourteen books.

Jack Engler teaches and supervises psychotherapy trainees at Harvard Medical School and has a private psychotherapy practice in Cambridge, MA. He is coauthor of *Transformations of Consciousness*. He has been involved with the Insight Meditation Society and Barre Center for Buddhist Studies since their inception.

Mark Epstein has a psychotherapy practice in New York City and is a long-time vipassana practitioner. He is author of *Thoughts Without a Thinker, Going to Pieces without Falling Apart,* and *Psychotherapy without the Self.*

Rick Fields (1942–1999) was a prolific author and poet. His *How the Swans Came to the Lake* remains the standard reference work on the history of Buddhism in America. He was a founder of *Tricycle,* editor-in-chief of *Yoga Journal,* contributing editor for *New Age Journal,* and founding editor of *Loka Journal.* His last published work was *Fuck You, Cancer & Other Poems.*

Norman Fischer is a poet, author, and Zen Buddhist priest and abbot. He is the founder and teacher of the Everyday Zen Foundation. His most recent book is *Sailing Home: Using the Odyssey to Chart Your Life's Journey.*

Lorain Fox Davis (Cree/Blackfeet) is an adjunct faculty member for the American Indian Studies Program and on the advisory council for the environmental studies department at Naropa University. She is founder/director of Rediscovery Four Corners, which serves Native American youth and elders.

China Galland is author of *The Keepers of Love, Longing for Darkness, Tara and the Black Madonna,* and *The Bond Between Women.* She is a professor at the Center for the Arts, Religion, and Education at the Graduate Theological Union in Berkeley, California. She is founder and director of the Keepers of Love Project and Images of Divinity. She teaches and lectures internationally.

Barbara Gates is a cofounder and coeditor of *Inquiring Mind* and the author of *Already Home: A Topography of Spirit and Place.* She is also a freelance developmental editor.

Allen Ginsberg (1926 –1997) was a founding member of the Beat Generation literary movement, champion of human and civil rights, photographer and songwriter, political gadfly, and teacher.

S.N. Goenka was born in 1924 in Mandalay, Burma. He developed an interest in meditation to overcome his chronic migraines, becoming Burmese meditation master U Ba Khin's most prominent student. He founded an international network of vipassana teaching centers based at Dhammagiri in India. He is a prolific orator, writer, and poet, and he has lectured to audiences worldwide.

Joseph Goldstein is a cofounder of the Insight Meditation Society's Retreat Center and Forest Refuge programs and the Barre Center for Buddhist Studies. He has been teaching vipassana and metta retreats worldwide since 1974. His books include *A Heart Full of Peace, One Dharma, The Experience of Insight* and *Insight Meditation*.

Steven D. Goodman is codirector of Asian and comparative studies at the California Institute of Integral Studies. In 1994, he was awarded a Rockefeller Fellowship at Rice University Center for Cultural Studies for the study of Tibetan mystical poetry. He is coeditor of *Tibetan Buddhism: Reason and Revelation*.

Rev. Heng Sure, Ph.D., just released his first CD of Buddhist songs: *Paramita: American Buddhist Folk Music*. A celibate monastic and a vegan, Heng Sure is looking forward to life as a musical Dharma storyteller. Monks increase in value as they age. His mom will settle for that, even without grandchildren.

Julia Butterfly Hill spent over two years living high in the canopy of an ancient redwood tree to help make the world aware of the plight of ancient forests. She tells this story in the book *The Legacy of Luna*. She later founded the Circle of Life Foundation and has traveled extensively, speaking on the environment and social justice.

Jitindriya was a Buddhist nun in the Forest Tradition of Ajahn Chah and Ajahn Sumedho for over 16 years. In late 2004 she took leave of the monastic community and training and continues to practice and teach internationally as a lay practitioner. She has completed an M.A. in Buddhist psychotherapy practice with the Karuna Institute in the U.K. and now resides and practices in Australia.

Charlie Johnson was introduced to yoga and meditation in the early 1970s while a student. Throughout the nearly thirty years he worked as a chemical engineer in the petroleum industry, he continued to practice. In 2000 he retired from industry so that he could pursue his long-time spiritual interests.

Wendy Johnson is a thirty-five-year practitioner of Zen meditation. As a lay-ordained Dharma teacher, she has trained at the San Francisco Zen Center and in the tradition of Thich Nhat Hanh. She writes a column, "On Gardening," for *Tricycle*. She is the author of *Gardening at the Dragon's Gate*.

Jon Kabat-Zinn is a scientist, writer, and meditation teacher. He is a professor of medicine emeritus at the University of Massachusetts Medical School, where he founded the Center for Mindfulness in Medicine, Health Care, and Society and the world-renowned Stress Reduction Clinic. His many books include *Full Catastrophe Living*; *Wherever You Go, There You Are*; *Everyday Blessings*; and *Coming to Our Senses*.

Ronna Kabatznick, Ph.D., is an assistant clinical professor in the department of psychiatry at the University of California, San Francisco. She is a social psychologist in private practice and works with people dealing with weight, depression, and relationship issues. Dr. Kabatznick also teaches vipassana meditation at centers throughout the San Francisco Bay Area.

Ayya Khema (1923–1997) was born in Germany and later emigrated to the U.S., where she married and had a son and daughter. She was ordained a Buddhist nun in Sri Lanka in 1979 and established Wat Buddha Dhamma in Australia, the International Buddhist Women's Center and Parappuduwa Nuns' Island in Sri Lanka, and Buddha-Haus in Germany. She wrote over two dozen books in English and German.

Richard Kohn (1948–2000) was a documentary filmmaker, Tibetan Buddhist scholar, photographer, poet, and author. His best-known book and award-winning film are both entitled *Lord of the Dance: The Mani Rimdu Festival in Tibet and Nepal*.

Jack Kornfield trained as a Buddhist monk in the monasteries of Thailand, India, and Burma. He has taught meditation internationally since 1974. He is a founder of the Insight Meditation Society and Spirit Rock Meditation Center. His many books include *A Path with Heart*; *Seeking the Heart of*

Wisdom; After the Ecstasy, the Laundry; and *The Art of Forgiveness, Lovingkindness and Peace.*

Noah Levine is a Buddhist teacher, author, and counselor. He leads groups in juvenile halls and prisons. Levine has studied with many prominent teachers in both the Theravada and Mahayana traditions. He is the author of *Dharma Punx* and *Against the Stream.* He lives in Los Angeles.

Joanna Macy is a scholar of Buddhism, general systems theory, and deep ecology. She is a leading voice in movements for peace, justice, and a safe environment. Her many books include *World as Lover, World as Self; Coming Back to Life;* the memoir, *Widening Circles;* and translations of Rilke's *Book of Hours* and *In Praise of Mortality* (with Anita Barrows).

Jarvis Jay Masters is a widely published African American Buddhist writer living on San Quentin State Prison's death row. He was born in 1962 and he has been in prison since the age of nineteen. He is author of *Finding Freedom.* A growing international movement is seeking to overturn his wrongful conviction.

Michele McDonald has taught insight meditation around the world for over twenty-five years. A leader in developing meditation retreats for youth, she is also a cofounder of the Vipassana Hawai'i Sangha in Honolulu.

Lauren McIntosh. Page 131. *Alive.* 61.5" x 29.5". 2004. Gouache, mixed media on paper. Lauren McIntosh lives and paints in Berkeley, California. She attended art school at the University of California at Berkeley. She is represented by Repetti Gallery in Long Island City, New York; Anne Reed Gallery in Ketchum, Idaho; and Obsolete Inc. in Venice, California.

Patrick McMahon is a long-time Zen practitioner with the Diamond Sangha, headed by Robert Aitken Roshi.

Lucia Meijer is a prison director who introduced vipassana meditation courses into the North Rehabilitation Facility of King County Jail in Seattle, Washington. Nationally known as a specialist in the field of addictions and other hard-to-change behaviors, her risk-reduction curriculum for substance abusers is in use throughout the U.S.

Susan Moon is a writer, editor, and lay teacher in the Soto Zen tradition of Shunryu Suzuki Roshi. She is the author of *The Life and Letters of Tofu Roshi* and other books on Buddhism, and the former editor of *Turning Wheel: The Journal of Socially Engaged Buddhism*. She is currently working on a collection of essays.

Susan Murphy Roshi is an award-winning filmmaker and writer based in Sydney, Australia. She trained in Zen primarily with John Tarrant Roshi and Ross Bolleter Roshi. She is the author of *Upside-Down Zen*.

Wes Nisker is a cofounder and coeditor of *Inquiring Mind* and a meditation teacher, radio commentator, author, and performer. His books include *Essential Crazy Wisdom*; *Buddha's Nature*; and *The Big Bang, the Buddha, and the Baby Boom*. He is an affiliate teacher at the Spirit Rock Meditation Center.

Alan Novidor is the publisher of *Inquiring Mind*. In 1986, the editors asked him, as a vipassana community member and an organizational consultant, if he could help the fledgling journal develop a business model congruent with its mission. He stuck around.

Frank Ostaseski was a founder and the guiding teacher of the Zen Hospice Project for seventeen years. In 2004 he created the Metta Institute to provide innovative education on spirituality and end-of-life care. He teaches internationally. His work has been featured in Bill Moyers's award-winning documentary "On Our Own Terms," on *Oprah*, and in the PBS series "With Eyes Open."

Ma Deva Padma. Page 1. *Golden Buddha*. 28" x 38". 1997. Acrylic on cloth. Ma Deva Padma (Susan Morgan Ostapkowicz) is an artist and author. Her TAO Oracle (www.thetaooracle.com) is in its second printing, and her best-selling Osho Zen Tarot has been translated into eighteen languages. She lives with her husband, Ashika, at their Embrace of Heaven and Earth Studio (www.embraceart.com) in the mountains north of Melbourne, Australia.

Ajahn Pasanno, originally from Canada, was ordained a monk over thirty years ago in Thailand, where he served as abbot of Wat Pah Nanachat for fourteen years. He is now coabbot of Abhayagiri Monastery in Redwood Valley, California.

Steven Poe. Page 235. *Body and Soul*. 10.75" x 14". 1995. Photograph. Steven Poe is a photographer, digital artist, and educator. He enjoys time outdoors backpacking, skiing, and mountain biking. Fluent in Portuguese, he spends part of each year in Brazil. Poe looks to artists like Magritte for inspiration and enjoys Thai food and retro style.

Hari Lal Poonja (1910–1997) was born in Punjab, India (now Pakistan). Although he denied being part of any formal tradition, he is considered by many to be a yogi-saint of the Advaita Vedanta and Bhakti traditions.

Yvonne Rand is a meditation teacher and lay householder priest in the Soto Zen tradition. She began her practice with Shunryu Suzuki Roshi in 1966. Her other principal teachers and mentors have been Dainin Katagiri Roshi, Maureen Stuart Roshi, His Holiness the Dalai Lama, the Venerable Tara Tulku, and Shodo Harada Roshi. She is married and is a mother and gardener.

Caitriona Reed is a performance coach, consultant, and Buddhist teacher. She has trained with teachers in Asia, England, and the U.S. since 1970 and has led retreats since 1981. She cofounded Ordinary Dharma in Los Angeles and Manzanita Village Retreat Center in rural San Diego County.

Sharon Salzberg, a cofounder of the Insight Meditation Society and the Barre Center for Buddhist Studies, has practiced Buddhist meditation since 1971 and has been teaching worldwide since 1974. She is the author of *The Force of Kindness*, *Faith*, and *Lovingkindness*.

Santikaro was born in Chicago, "grew up" in Thailand with the Peace Corps, and was ordained as a bhikkhu in 1985. He translated *Mindfulness with Breathing* and other works by Buddhadasa Bhikkhu. He returned to the U.S. in 2000 and retired from the monk's life in 2004. He now lives at Liberation Park in southwest Wisconsin.

Miranda Shaw is a professor of religion at the University of Richmond. Her publications include *Buddhist Goddesses of India* and *Passionate Enlightenment: Women in Tantric Buddhism*.

Gary Snyder is an American poet, essayist, lecturer, and environmental activist. Winner of a Pulitzer Prize for poetry, he has frequently been described as the "laureate of deep ecology." His work reflects his immersion in both Buddhist spirituality and nature. For many years, Snyder was on the faculty of the University of California, Davis.

Robert Spellman. Page 161. *Buddha's Hand.* 21" x 18". 2000. Acrylic and charcoal on canvas. Robert Spellman is an artist and teacher living in Boulder, Colorado. He is associate professor on the visual arts and religious studies faculty of Naropa University, teaching studio classes and meditation and the vast overlap between the two. He has twice been invited to the Cill Rialaig artists' retreat in County Kerry, Ireland. Visit his website: www.robertspellman.com.

Judith Lee Stronach (1943–2002) lived in Berkeley, California. She worked as a journalist and devoted herself to numerous charitable and arts organizations. She established the Stronach Prize for Poetry and Prose at the University of California, Berkeley. *Love Is As Strong As Death* is a collection of her poems and essays.

Ajahn Sundara was born in France. She left her career in contemporary dance and in 1983 was ordained as a *siladhara* (ten-precept nun) and joined the community at Amaravati Monastery near London. She now teaches in Europe and North America.

Tenzin Palmo was born in London. In 1964 she became the second Western woman to be ordained in the Tibetan Buddhist tradition. In 1976 she retreated to a cave in the Himalayas and remained there for twelve years. She is founder of Dongyu Gatsal Ling nunnery in Himachal Pradesh, India, and the subject of the biography *Cave in the Snow.*

Davis Te Selle. Page 273. *Sycamores.* 7" x 10". Waterless lithograph. Davis Te Selle is an illustrator and printmaker with a studio in Burlington, Vermont. He enjoys teaching his field drawing classes through the environmental program at the University of Vermont—yet another way to go sit under a tree and reflect on the appearances and meanings of our world.

Robert Thurman is a professor of Indo-Tibetan Buddhist studies at Columbia University, holding the first endowed chair in this field of study in the U.S. He also is the cofounder of Tibet House in New York and is active against the Chinese occupation of Tibet. His many popular books include *Infinite Life, Inner Revolution, Circling the Mountain,* and *The Jewel Tree of Tibet.*

Marlene Tobias. Page 57. *Untitled*. 18" x 24". 2002. Charcoal pencil. Marlene Tobias has studied charcoal figure drawing for the past fifteen years under the guidance of master figurative artist Michael Markowitz in San Francisco, California, exploring the experience of drawing as a path to authenticity, informing the interconnectedness of our lives. She has also studied sculpture with Amana Bremby Johnson and the Italian master Bruno Luchessi.

Tsoknyi Rinpoche is a lama of both the Drukpa Kagyu and Nyingma lineages of Tibetan Buddhism. He was born in 1966 in Kathmandu to the family of the Tulku Urgyen Rinpoche, a special family lineage of tantric yogis. He is the abbot of Ngedon Ösel Ling in Nepal.

Terry Vandiver gardens and teaches yoga and sacred sound. She lives in Berkeley, California.

Francisco Varela (1946–2001) was a Chilean biologist, philosopher, and neuroscientist best known for introducing the concept of autopoiesis to biology. In 1986 he settled in France, where he taught at the École Polytechnique and the University of Paris. From 1988 until his death, he led a research group at the Centre National de Recherche Scientifique.

Anne Waldman is a poet and teacher, and with Allen Ginsberg cofounded the Jack Kerouac School of Disembodied Poetics at Naropa Institute in 1974. Over the years, she has worked and performed internationally with well-known musicians, composers, dancers, and visual artists. She has written more than forty books.

Kate Lila Wheeler is an award-winning fiction writer and journalist, as well as an experienced Buddhist practitioner and teacher of meditation and creative writing. She grew up in South America. She is the author of many books, including *Not Where I Started From* and *When Mountains Walked*.

Carol Wilson began meditation practice in 1971. She has studied with a variety of teachers and practiced as a Buddhist nun in Thailand. A guiding teacher at the Insight Meditation Society, she has been offering retreats around the world since 1986.

Diana Winston is director of mindfulness education at UCLA's Mindful Awareness Research Center. She is the founder of the Buddhist Peace

Fellowship's Buddhist Alliance for Social Engagement. She is a member of the Spirit Rock Meditation Center's Teachers Council and has taught meditation since 1993. Her writings include *Wide Awake: A Buddhist Guide for Teens*.

Nina Wise is an internationally acclaimed performance artist, playwright, and Dharma teacher. She is the founder of Motion Theater, a form of autobiographical improvised theater that is both an art form and a spiritual practice. She is author of *A Big New Free Happy Unusual Life*.

Publisher's Acknowledgment

The publisher gratefully acknowledges the generous help of the Hershey Family Foundation in sponsoring the production of this book.

About Wisdom Publications

Wisdom Publications, a nonprofit publisher, is dedicated to making available authentic works relating to Buddhism for the benefit of all. We publish books by ancient and modern masters in all traditions of Buddhism, translations of important texts, and original scholarship. Additionally, we offer books that explore East-West themes unfolding as traditional Buddhism encounters our modern culture in all its aspects. Our titles are published with the appreciation of Buddhism as a living philosophy, and with the special commitment to preserve and transmit important works from Buddhism's many traditions.

To learn more about Wisdom, or to browse books online, visit our website at www.wisdompubs.org.

You may request a copy of our catalog online or by writing to this address:

Wisdom Publications
199 Elm Street
Somerville, Massachusetts 02144 USA
Telephone: 617-776-7416
Fax: 617-776-7841
Email: info@wisdompubs.org
www.wisdompubs.org

The Wisdom Trust
As a nonprofit publisher, Wisdom is dedicated to the publication of Dharma books for the benefit of all sentient beings and dependent upon the kindness and generosity of sponsors in order to do so. If you would like to make a donation to Wisdom, you may do so through our website or our Somerville office. If you would like to help sponsor the publication of a book, please write or email us at the address above.

Thank you.

Wisdom is a nonprofit, charitable 501(c)(3) organization affiliated with the Foundation for the Preservation of the Mahayana Tradition (FPMT).